The Blair Revolution

The Blair Revolution

Can New Labour Deliver?

PETER MANDELSON AND
ROGER LIDDLE

faber and faber
LONDON · BOSTON

First published in 1996
by Faber and Faber Limited
3 Queen Square London WC1N 3AU

Printed in England by Mackays of Chatham PLC, Chatham, Kent

A CIP record for this book
is available from the British Library

ISBN 0-571-17818-9

2 4 6 8 10 9 7 5 3 1

Contents

Authors' Note

Bill Andrews, Steve and Jane Stephenson, Phil Jones, Eileen Cooke and Ben and Laura Hodgson and their families are imagined characters, and no relationship with any actual person is intended. They are based, however, on the experiences recounted and the opinions expressed by real people in conversation with the authors.

Preface

This is not an easy book to describe. Part political philosophy and part social commentary, part history and part policy analysis, it aims to offer the most complete picture so far of the transformation of the Labour Party. While the book reflects entirely the personal views of the authors, it draws on the hundreds of ideas and individual actions that have, together, contributed to the creation of New Labour.

The idea of writing this hybrid book came to us early in 1995. Labour was in the throes of its historic decision to rewrite the party's constitution, and both of us felt that our respective political odysseys during the previous twenty years or so offered a blend of experience and belief that would make a book interesting and readable. Its aims are to enable everyone to understand better why Labour has changed and what it has changed into, and to involve the public in discussion of the party's policies before the manifesto is written. Lazy or superficial commentators describe the party's process of change as merely 'taking Labour to the right', or painting a glossy image over old and unpleasant realities underneath. This is not and never has been what Labour's modernisers have sought. The BBC series *The Wilderness Years*, shown at the end of 1995, fell into this familiar trap. The harder task of getting to grips with New Labour depends on understanding that, in giving renewed expression to the party's founding beliefs, it is a deliberate move forward from both the postwar Labour Party of Wilson and Callaghan and the Conservative Party of Thatcher and Major – a political project requiring much greater radicalism and originality than simply 'moving right'. Such a stratagem would not, in any case, capture the public mood in Britain and would mean failing to learn all the lessons of the last seventeen years of right-wing Conservative rule. Modernisation is about more than developing a package of attractive propositions that can win Labour power. It is about working through a credible strategy for successful government that avoids the failures of the past.

In carrying out its radical shift, the Blair revolution is not creating a Labour Party without principles. On the contrary, it is rescuing the party's traditional values of cooperation and social solidarity and putting them to work to respond to the challenges facing Britain as we approach the new century. The principal challenges are to overcome Britain's continued slide in international competitiveness so as to create a successful economy based on partnership between the private and public sectors, and to create a more equal and cohesive society, less scarred by division and want, and capable of providing the opportunities every family rightly aspires to.

In seeing through the Blair revolution, one man has not acted alone. Scores of Labour MPs, trade unionists, party employees and individual members have worked ceaselessly to create New Labour over the last ten years. New Labour would not end if Tony Blair were to disappear tomorrow. He has a strong front bench team who share his convictions, and the changes are now too deeply rooted to be reversed. There is no better testimony to this than the seriousness with which Labour's political opponents view the changes that have been implemented. The Conservatives are trying every conceivable argument and trick in the book to discredit New Labour. Their propaganda will become fiercer as the election approaches. The Liberal Democrats too have experienced similar difficulty in coming to terms with the phenomenon, though many have understood it so well they have chosen to join. For New Labour is not just a different route for the left to take alone but a concept which joins the left to the centre of British politics and is all the stronger for that. Therein lies its enormous potency.

This book seeks to answer a simple question: 'Can New Labour Deliver?' Overwhelmingly, people like what they see in New Labour but wonder if this is what they will get in government. We have asked ourselves this question because of our personal experiences of the Labour Party since we were activists and friends in Vauxhall, south London, in the late 1970s. We both grew up steeped in the traditions of the Labour Party. Our political outlook was shaped by the strong ethical values of our respective parents. We remain intensely proud of Labour's historic achievements. But even then we were disturbed by the extent to which Labour was trapped by its past and a prisoner of an outdated ideology which had not been satisfactorily modernised by the Labour leadership. Peter Mandelson was employed in the economic department of the TUC, taking notes from which the minutes would be written of some of the most important meetings between the TUC and the Labour Cabinet in 1977 and 1978. This exercise in corporatist government was thoroughly well-intentioned but it became an unhappy and ultimately unsuccessful experience. Roger Liddle saw it even more intimately from the inside: he was special adviser to a Cabinet member, the Transport Secretary, Bill Rodgers. We both lived through the subsequent events which produced the SDP split from Labour in 1981. The question for so many at the time was whether to stay and reclaim Labour from the grip of its political madness (a daunting prospect at the time) or to decamp in order to build the party afresh on more fertile ground. Both of us fought for what we believed in and still do – a vigorous, democratic, principled left-of-centre force in British politics – but we chose different courses. Throughout, we have not stopped being friends, discussing and exchanging ideas about the best way forward for the British left.

The book is most easily understood in three parts. The first two chapters – 'New Labour' and 'Labour's Leader' – set out what New Labour stands for, its distinct philosophy and the differences, as we see them, between Blair's Labour Party and both the Labour Party of old and the new Right. A chapter is devoted to Tony Blair because, to understand New Labour, it is necessary to understand the beliefs of the man who is principally (but not exclusively) responsible for giving the Party its modern character. The recent revolution that has occurred in the Labour Party is most appropriately named after him.

Chapters 3 to 7 discuss New Labour's policies for national renewal – economic, social, political and in Europe. We hope that readers will find our analysis of the problems facing Britain as interesting as the specific solutions we put forward. These chapters contain some new ideas and explore policy options but, of course, the party's actual programme for government will be set out in the manifesto when the election comes.

Chapters 8 to 10 are about how Labour will deliver its policies successfully in government. To do this, the party must continue to change and strengthen so as to sustain the government in power; and Labour ministers must use the machinery and civil service available to them to implement their programme with maximum effectiveness.

Many people have helped us in the writing of this book. Where ideas have been inspired by books and articles we have read, we have acknowledged their authors in the bibliography. Others have given generously of their time in talking to us and reviewing manuscripts. In particular we would like to thank Andrew Adonis, Edward Balls, David Clark, Gavyn Davies, John Dickie, Philip Gould, Andrew Grice, Peter Hennessy, David Lipsey, Michael Montague, Matthew Oakeshott, Julian Priestley, Paul Richards, John Roper, Karl Sternberg, Mark Siegal, Nick Smith, and Tom Watson. There are others who we do not name to whom we are equally grateful.

We also need to thank those who have assisted directly in the production of the book. In Peter Mandelson's office, Benjamin Wegg-Prosser and Clive Russell together with Zoe Conway and Ilan Jacobs most carefully looked up documents, checked facts with the House of Commons library (to whom as ever thanks are due) and found references. In Roger Liddle's office, Sue Parsons with assistance from Rose Long and Nita Worall cheerfully bore the additional burden of producing and circulating successive synopses and drafts. Peter would especially like to thank Robert Harris and Gill Hornby, Holly and Charlie, together with Jon Snow, Oliver Walston, Fiona Millar and their families for the generous hospitality and support they offered during the trials of authorship. Roger would like to thank Caroline and Andrew for their forbearance, constant encouragement and bright ideas over many spoilt evenings and weekends.

Both of us owe a special debt to Derek Draper, Peter Mandelson's former assistant, who was closely involved with this project from the start and made a major contribution to the outcome at every stage. New Labour is fortunate indeed that it can boast a whole new generation with his quality of organisational energy, political commitment and realistic vision, and it is to their political success that this book is dedicated.

There are undoubted risks in committing so much to print. Politics is an unkind business, and when you put your head above the parapet you must expect to be shot at. In the words of the Book of Job: 'My desire is ... that mine adversary had written a book.' We do not expect everyone to agree with all the book's contents, but we hope that they will respect its honesty and sincerity and that it will be read and debated seriously. Needless to say, it bears no one's imprimatur but our own. So on our own heads be it.

Can New Labour deliver? We say yes – and this book explains how.

PETER MANDELSON
Hartlepool

ROGER LIDDLE
London
February 1996

New Labour

This book is not about how Labour can win the next election, but about how Labour can govern successfully. New Labour does not take success at the polls for granted, but recognises that the final barrier to victory is public uncertainty about the party's ability to meet the challenge of government.

New Labour has set itself a bold task: to modernise Britain socially, economically and politically. In doing so it aims to build on Britain's strengths. Its mission is to create, not to destroy. Its strategy is to move forward from where Margaret Thatcher left off, rather than to dismantle every single thing she did. Its priorities, as we will show, focus on those fields where New Labour is uniquely equipped to act.

Given the recent shabby record of the Conservatives, the length of time since Labour was last in office and the left-of-centre's long and painful journey to electability, it is not surprising that people have lingering doubts and uncertainties. They know that Labour itself has changed, but they are cynical about politics and politicians, and sceptical as to whether a new government would make much difference to them. They need to be convinced of what New Labour stands for, how its policies have changed, and that the party will remain united behind its new leadership.

Is New Labour a clever piece of positioning – a creation of spin doctors and public-relations men – that lacks real substance and will turn out to be little different from the past? Or does New Labour truly understand the challenges of the times and have a robust approach to meeting them that will weather the tests of office and improve the everyday lives of the British people?

Throughout society there is a feeling that Britain is in moral, social and economic decline. In previous generations parents felt certain that their children would go on to do better than them. Many of today's parents worry about whether their newly graduated son or daughter will even get a job. Middle Britain has never felt so insecure, as new ways of working take hold in the labour market and faith in the public services that families rely on is eroded. Millions less fortunate seem condemned to unemployment and poverty, served inadequately by a welfare state designed for another age. These new times offer new challenges. It is no good attempting to turn the clock back. We need to think anew.

For Labour, modernisation is about far more than red roses, seductive sound-bites and fancy packaging, however important these may be in the modern media age. It is about a fundamental reinvention of what Labour offers to the British people.

However, the business of reinvention does not involve abandonment of Labour's basic principles and convictions. It means a sharper definition of those core aims and values, and their thorough reapplication to the circumstances of the modern world.

To some, reinvention can only mean one thing – moving to the right. But this is the simplistic view propagated by New Labour's opponents. Every political party has periodically to renew itself, to enable it to bring new life and policies to the country.

Since the war the Conservatives have thoroughly reinvented themselves twice over, which perhaps explains their electoral success. After their 1945 defeat R. A. Butler led the Conservatives into acceptance of the modern welfare state and the commitment to full employment. In the late 1970s Margaret Thatcher and her supporters launched a counter-revolution that is still the dominant force in the Conservative Party.

Labour, on the other hand, has been more resistant to change. The last time Labour reinvented itself was in the 1930s. Then, in the aftermath of its 1931 electoral disaster, Labour reconstructed itself under Hugh Dalton's intellectual leadership and Herbert Morrison's strategic direction and laid the foundations for eventual victory in 1945.

Labour's current phase of reinvention was started by Neil Kinnock and continued by John Smith. But essentially they were engaged in a ground-clearing operation – first, to rid the party of the Bennite excesses that had led to the SDP split and to its worst ever postwar defeat, and then to restore its unity of purpose and to democratise its internal procedures. Tony Blair has built on that solid inheritance to lead the party in the restatement of its values and the wholesale modernisation of its policies.

Five insights make up the New Labour approach.

First, people feel increasingly insecure. This is caused by rapid economic and technological change throughout the world and a breakdown of society in Britain. The fundamental question for Britain today is whether we can compete successfully in the new global market-place and still live in a decent society. New Labour believes that we can, and that everyone should have a stake in the country's success. It rejects the view that the solution to people's anxiety is to create more insecurity in order to promote competitiveness.

Maurice Saatchi, the adman who has driven the last four Tory election campaigns, once typified the Conservative approach as 'cruel and efficient', whereas Labour's was 'incompetent and caring'. New Labour believes that cruelty is not necessary to ensure competence and that caring can march hand in hand with efficiency.

Secondly, by comparison with other countries Britain is badly equipped to meet the challenge of change. The nation has been in relative decline for a century, and it is now clear that Thatcherism has failed to reverse that long-term trend, even if it may have slowed its pace.

New Labour stands for investment, partnership and top-quality education for all – not just the privileged few. This involves building on Britain's current strengths, not harking back to the past; tackling the vested interests and class barriers that have held back new talent and ideas; releasing dynamism and entrepreneurial energy in business and the public services; root-and-branch reform of our political system to give people control of government; and Britain playing a full part in Europe.

Thirdly, New Labour understands why the New Right failed. This is not based on a knee-jerk rejection of everything the Conservatives have done – we have to be clear where they got things right – but their ideology has taken them too far and their own incompetence cost Britain dear. They have relied too much on *laissez-faire* and have ignored the potential of active government. They have put the interests of the few before the many. It is not just that for people of conscience the cost in social division has been unacceptably high: it is also that, even when reasonably well-off people reflect on their self-interest, the economic and social cost has been huge in lost human talent, national wealth foregone and gravely weakened public finances.

Fourthly, New Labour is fundamentally different from old Labour in its economic, social and political approach. It goes well beyond the battles of the past between public and private, and about the role of the unions and the relevance of public expenditure, to the achievement of a more equal society. Nevertheless, New Labour's concept of One Nation socialism still stands firmly in the social-democratic tradition – but with a new hard edge to its economic thinking.

Fifthly, New Labour has a distinctive message of its own that goes beyond the nostrums of old Labour and New Right. It does not seek to limit markets, but – crucially – it recognises that they need to operate within a fair framework of rules that upholds the public interest, and that public action needs to complement the weaknesses of the market-place. New Labour builds on the traditional Labour ideal of social cooperation and expands it into a more dynamic view of the need for a strong society and an active community to help people succeed.

This new tough concept of community, where rights and responsibilities go hand in hand, enables New Labour to reclaim ground that should never have been ceded to the right, and to develop new ideas for a changing world. And this involves a new type of politics – resting on a truly modernised and democratic Labour Party which is in touch with the people it claims to represent, and a credible vehicle for taking forward New Labour's values.

Can we be civil and prosperous too?

Paradoxically, the question whether we can compete successfully in the new global market-place and still live in a decent society – first posed in the above form by Ralf Dahrendorf, the leading academic and social commentator, in his 1995 Churchill lecture – does not arise because the world is experiencing the end of growth. Far from it. The Asian 'tigers' – economies like

Korea, Singapore and Taiwan – are expected to double their living-standards in less than a decade. The earth has not hit the ecological buffers, contrary to the Club of Rome's warnings more than two decades ago – though the worries about sustainability and long-term energy and environmental constraints remain real.

True, the competitive challenge from the emerging markets of the East and the countries newly liberated from communism may limit growth prospects in the West – particularly as, in a world of mobile capital, investment will be pulled away to the fastest-growing markets that offer the highest returns. But only a handful of doomsters would suggest that living-standards in the West are about to enter a period of absolute decline. So why is this the first generation in which, as Robert Reich, the American labor secretary has remarked, parents cannot feel confident that their children will enjoy the same living-standards as themselves? After all, their children will mature to adulthood in what are likely to remain the richest countries in the world.

The problem is that the fruits of modest growth are not likely to be as uniformly spread as they have been for most of the postwar era. There will be winners, but many more losers. The older generation have enjoyed a seemingly permanent escalator of economic progress – washing-machines and black-and-white televisions in the 1950s; fridge-freezers and motor cars in the 1960s; telephones and colour TV in the 1970s; videos and central heating in the 1980s; computers and satellite TV in the 1990s. These have been the consumer symbols of a prosperity in which all but a growing minority have shared.

Because of the great increase in job and earnings insecurity, this progress can no longer be taken for granted. A promising career may end abruptly in the mid-forties and prove impossible to rebuild. Getting a first foot on the job ladder, even after obtaining a good degree, is now a matter of luck for many. Others rely on connections or the 'old boy' network, undermining meritocracy. For the great majority, the world has become a much chancier place.

Why is this? In part it reflects the mounting competitive challenge. By the year 2000, for example, the countries of the Asian Pacific, excluding Japan and China, are forecast to account for nearly a third of world manufacturing output – significantly ahead of the European Union's quarter. Some 400-500 million people living in East Asia will enjoy living-standards as high as or higher than those in Europe.

This economic boom is not based on low wages, low public expenditure and deregulation – as the British Conservatives maintain. These countries are huge investors in what economists call public goods. Korea spends a higher proportion of its national wealth on education than Britain. India has 60 million people with the equivalent of a university degree. Despite its historic lead, Europe is now being beaten in the stakes that matter most in today's world – in the application of knowledge and brainpower to achieve economic success.

At the same time, the new international economy has greatly reduced the ability of any single government to use the traditional levers of economic policy in order to maintain high employment. The daily turnover in foreign-currency markets through digital technology already equals the US national debt of $4 trillion, transforming the speed at which capital flows round the world. The days of simple home-based Keynesianism will not return, and national economies have to recognise their interdependence.

But the potential of national economic policy is not so much reduced as narrowed in scope. Governments can still take action to enhance skills, promote investment, and enlarge our economic capacity – to strengthen the so-called supply side. On these matters, nations are still capable of making an important difference within their borders.

Traditional patterns of work are also under pressure from the information and communications revolution, which is transforming every aspect of business, leisure and home life. Technology is both creating and destroying jobs -- not just low-skill ones, but managerial and professional jobs too. This adds to labour-market insecurity. Organisational structures that once depended for performance of key functions on geographically diffuse networks with large numbers of back-office staff, all managed in extended, rigid, hierarchies – for example, in the high-street banks – are being totally transformed.

The make-up of the labour market is changing. Eighty per

cent of new jobs are going to women, creating problems for young men seeking work, especially those with low skills. Shorter employment contracts contribute to instability, and employers demand better generic and interpersonal skills, in order to maximise adaptability, rather than more narrowly drawn vocational qualifications. This requires radical changes in learning and education.

The rapidity of technological and labour-market change is not, of course, a terrifying prospect for everyone – particularly not for some younger people – because the opportunities being created in new kinds of consumerism, work and lifestyle are very exciting. But the downside of these opportunities is their denial to many people.

This turmoil in the labour market is having a wide impact on society. Will Hutton, the *Guardian*'s economics editor, has neatly typified the consequence as 40–30–30 Britain. The top 40 per cent still enjoy job security. The 30 per cent at the bottom are effectively excluded from the labour market, condemned to live in unemployment and poverty, trapped by a welfare state designed for another age. The 30 per cent in the middle hang on to jobs, but live with chronic insecurity as these new ways of working take hold in the labour market.

These issues determine what ought to be the central battle-ground of British politics today. What are we doing to prepare for inevitable change? Are we going to gain from it and create a sense of social order alongside it, as New Labour wants, or are we going to let change wash over us, with the result that we slip further backwards economically and disintegrate further socially?

The Conservatives would, of course, argue that their stress on deregulation and low labour costs is the only way to prepare Britain for a competitive future. Their instinct is to accept the situation of increasing insecurity – even welcome it and further promote it – as the price of remaining competitive in the modern world.

New Labour utterly rejects this counsel of despair. The more secure, more cohesive and, as a result, more equal our society, the better our chances of economic success.

This is not to delude ourselves that wealth is somehow created by governments or society. Wealth comes from personal effort and entrepreneurial flair, exercised through companies that have found the right formula (which differs from business to business) for bringing together individual talent in common endeavour. But, just as good companies can pull countries up, bad government policies can drag companies down.

Companies suffer if the school-leavers they want to employ are illiterate or innumerate; if their potential customers can't buy because they are unemployed; if the shops they sell to are wrecked by young hooligans; and if they and their employees have to pay higher taxes to support millions of people on benefit. There is an important role for government in encouraging responsibility and promoting enterprise: in providing first-rate education; in offering training and work to unemployed youngsters, not benefits for idleness; in reforming the social-security system to give people a hand-up, not a handout; in preventing and punishing crime effectively, and in promoting savings and long-term investment. Success in these things will bring about a more prosperous and civil society.

Can Britain escape from its past?

The story of Britain is that of a nation that launched the Industrial Revolution yet failed to modernise and keep pace with overseas competition.

Britain's initial success was based on self-taught invention, bold entrepreneurship and a ready supply of capital for new ventures. We never developed the organisational strengths of our competitors who industrialised later: good-quality management, methodical skills training, and the systematic application of scientific research to industrial purposes. These weaknesses were already evident in the late Victorian era, but, despite public concern and the findings of official reports, they were never adequately remedied.

As emerging competition squeezed the financial returns in domestic industry, the City of London developed a thriving existence of its own, as the conduit for Britain's massive investments overseas, largely separate from the concerns of the home manufacturing base. At the same time, pressure on domestic profits heightened industrial-relations conflict. Working people developed their own crude defences against the depredations of raw capitalism – trade-union restrictive practices, demarcation rules and rigid apprenticeship systems became an entrenched part of the British industrial scene. This impeded industry's necessary adjustment to change, handicapping competitiveness for much of this century.

Meanwhile British boardrooms became ossified. Instead of being the forcing-houses of enterprise, they became the bastions of privilege. As Keynes put it in his celebrated memorandum to the war cabinet in May 1945:

> The available statistics suggest that, provided we have never made the product before, we have the rest of the world licked on cost. It is when it comes to making a shirt or a steel billet that we have to admit ourselves beaten by both the dear labour of America and by the cheap labour of Asia and Europe. If by some sad geographical slip the American Air Force (it is too late now to hope for much from the enemy) were to destroy every factory on the North East coast and in Lancashire (at an hour when the directors were sitting there and no-one else) we should have nothing to fear. How else we are to regain the exuberant inexperience which it is necessary it seems for success, I cannot surmise.

British society saw little reason to grasp the seriousness of Britain's economic position. The upheavals in the rest of the world emphasised the stability of Britain's political institutions. Victory in two world wars appeared to reaffirm Britain's status as a great power. Even as this belief increasingly lacked credibility – first in the aftermath of Suez in the 1950s and then after withdrawal from east of Suez in the 1960s – British politicians clung to the tattered special relationship with the United States as somehow proof that Britain was no ordinary European nation like France or Germany. Dean Acheson famously commented that 'Britain has lost an empire but not yet found a role.' The continuing myth of Britain's world-power status, perpetuated by the Falklands War, has delayed acceptance of our destiny in Europe and reinforced resistance to the need for modernisation.

In the postwar years, economic reform has lagged behind social progress. In social policy, the postwar Labour government transformed Britain into a welfare state. Full employment and the eradication of the extreme poverty of the interwar years were the great postwar achievements. But in one sense, for the long-term good of Britain, economic recovery came too easy, as a result of pent-up demand, and the questions of industrial as opposed to social modernisation were never adequately addressed, with the exception of the nationalised industries. When, in the mid-1950s, Anthony Crosland wrote his seminal work of social-democratic revisionism, *The Future of Socialism*, he took the continuation of economic growth for granted, concentrating instead on issues of social equality. His optimism was sadly misplaced.

The failures of the 1960s and 1970s

By the 1960s it was clear that Britain's growth performance was poor by comparison with our European competitors. Harold Wilson, in 1964, began the first serious attempt at modernisation. His government had more successes than it was given credit for – particularly by the Labour Party itself – but ultimately its efforts ended in disappointment and disillusion.

The conventional explanation offered for this at the time was that Wilson had sacrificed growth on the altar of sterling by resisting devaluation until it was too late. Economic opinion is now more divided on this issue. A present-day explanation of Wilson's disappointment would emphasise four more fundamental failings:
- the failure to provide a stable macro-economic framework;
- the inadequacy of the government's industrial strategy in addressing fundamental weaknesses of competitiveness;
- the government's retreat on 'In Place of Strife' and industrial-relations modernisation, which left the trade unions powerful and unreformed;
- a failure more generally to grapple with deep-seated institutional and interest-group resistance to modernisation throughout society – from the hold of vested interests over the education system to the grip of lawyers on the legal system.

In particular, Labour based its public spending plans on optimistic forecasts of economic growth that failed to materialise. Eventually taxes had to be raised, producing a sharp squeeze on disposable incomes which both made the operation of pay restraint more difficult and led to the alienation of Labour's better-off supporters among the skilled – which contributed to Labour's 1970 defeat, when the council estates failed to turn out.

In the 1970s, the Heath, Wilson and Callaghan governments fared no better – in fact considerably worse – though Britain at last joined the European Community. The various attempts to build a Scandinavian-style social contract foundered on the rocks of Britain's unreformed industrial relations. Whereas in the 1960s Labour tried and failed to modernise Britain fundamentally, in the 1970s Labour did not have a plan to do so. True, the 1974–79 Labour government saw Britain through the worst inflationary crisis in its history without the massive rise in unemployment which Margaret Thatcher later tolerated, and at the same time protected and improved the lot of the worst off, particularly poor pensioners. Nonetheless for those involved, it was not a happy experience. The cabinet vested more and more importance in its relationship with the TUC, viewing this as the only viable basis on which the country could be governed.

The voluntary incomes policy which the government operated through the TUC eventually helped bring inflation under control. But a high price was paid. Industrial relations law was drafted largely to meet the trade unions' wishes. Ministerial intervention as a result of interest-group pressure became an increasing drag on industrial performance. Partly these decisions were taken for sentimental and emotional reasons: 'protecting our people – because isn't that what a Labour government is here to do?' Partly they reflected political horse-trades, particularly support for incomes policy at the TUC and Labour conferences in return for industrial favours.

More fundamentally, the government's dependence on the trade unions limited its scope for manoeuvre at a time when the majority of the electorate was beginning to question old assumptions about the virtues of public spending and the operation of the public sector. There were plenty of people in the 1974 government who were brimming with new ideas on social policy, and the No. 10 Policy Unit under Jim Callaghan's premiership tried to push these issues forward - for example, on council house sales and standards in schools. But too often they foundered on the rock of Labour's unwillingness to offend entrenched interests within the party.

These failures paved the way for the Thatcherite revolution – the most thoroughgoing attempt at modernisation Britain has yet experienced.

Why the New Right failed

Feeding off the public reaction to the evident failure of old Labour corporatism during the 1978/79 'Winter of Discontent', the early appeal of the New Right lay in the simplicity of its diagnosis of Britain's ills: that the state was too intrusive, inefficient and unresponsive; that the trade-union barons had grown too strong; that the welfare system was generating ever-rising levels of tax; and that overregulation of the economy was stifling enterprise and not rewarding effort. This found an echo among many traditional Labour supporters who felt things were not going right in Britain, and that some individuals and organisations were getting out of hand. As Norman Tebbit said in 1987, 'We have been identifying the things that the chap in the pub and his wife always had a feeling were going wrong and trying to deal with them.' It was, we were told, all the fault of the postwar governing philosophy, supported by former Labour and Conservative leaders alike, which seemed designed to hold 'ordinary' people back and which Margaret Thatcher set out to 'deal with'.

For a time, it appeared as though Thatcherism's harsh medicine and 'enterprise culture' had produced the great economic leap forward that Britain needed. In the 1990s Britain can boast of some notable economic strengths – for example, the resilience and high internationalisation of our top companies; our strong industries like pharmaceuticals, aerospace, retailing and media; the pre-eminence of the City of London.

The 1980s saw lasting policy achievements in some areas, which it is right for an honest opposition to acknowledge and build upon. British industrial relations has been changed for the better, and its basic legal framework which the Conservatives established will remain in place, though new problems of exploitation have emerged in the labour market which need to be tackled. The productivity gap with our continental partners has been narrowed, though not by enough. Privatisation has brought some increased productivity, and there will be no mass renationalisation under New Labour, though reform of utility regulation is urgently required. Penal income-tax rates, which once discouraged the brightest and best from embarking on industrial careers, have been cut, and they will not return, though the prevalence of tax abuses and privileges needs to be addressed.

However, notwithstanding these achievements, it is now clear that, even in its own terms, Thatcherism has failed. Put on one side, for a moment, the increased inequality and social division, which many Conservatives would argue was an unfortunate necessity – Norman Lamont, as chancellor, described unemployment as 'a price worth paying'. Judged on the ground of the Conservative's choosing – the narrowest criterion of economic performance – the much-heralded miracle has not lasted.

Much of the so-called Thatcher-Lawson boom was due to the consumption of North Sea oil. The weaknesses of capacity that have caused Britain's recurrent inflationary pressures and the devaluation of our currency have proved to be more than a temporary blip. We do not have enough world-class companies; our innovation record is poor; human capital lacks development; and savings and investment are too weak to meet the competitive challenge being posed to us. Since 1979, Britain's slide down the world prosperity league has continued: we have slipped from thirteenth to eighteenth place, overtaken by countries such as Italy and Hong Kong.

As for the other main objectives which Margaret Thatcher set herself, the failure is even more stark. The tax burden today is higher than when the Conservatives came to power. Crime has doubled.

The Conservative attempt at modernisation carried great costs, and even then it was no more than partially successful.

Margaret Thatcher was asking some of the right questions about Britain's problems when she first came to power. But, having got part of her diagnosis right, the Thatcherite prescription went too far, and in other respects was non-existent or wrong. In her first period in Downing Street Thatcher's dogmatic pursuit of monetarism led to the destruction of a third of Britain's manufacturing industry. She thought – wrongly – that, if a small number at the top were rewarded, wealth would trickle down to the rest in increased economic activity and income growth. Opportunity for all would be the benign result. Believing that by motivating the few she would benefit the many has proved a great ideological error.

Not content with simply rebalancing public and private endeavour, Mrs Thatcher set about systematically denigrating anything public and dogmatically championing everything private. In her eyes, the private sector is always efficient and the public sector is congenitally wasteful – an attitude summed up by her remark to her hosts at a lunch party of British Rail managers that 'If any of you were any good, you wouldn't be working here.'

But an ideology which regards individual pursuit of self-interest as the best guarantee of the greater good, and collective action as always inferior, cannot build the partnership between private and public, business and government, that Britain needs. An ideology which holds that good government is invariably less government cannot best use the limited but significant power that governments have. As a result, government has failed to act as an ally working alongside citizens and companies, to create the infrastructure of transport, telecommunications, research and skills necessary for a strong economy, as happens in our successful competitors.

The shift to John Major in 1990 has made little difference to this overall assessment. Having slain the dragons of the 1980s, the Conservative Party has stumbled hopelessly, like an exhausted warrior, through the 1990s. Periodically Major has tried to formulate aims different from those of his predecessor – aims which are more centrist in language and tone – but in practice he has not taken the country on from Thatcherism. Each of his numerous relaunches and initiatives has left him more directionless than before.

Major himself appears to have some genuine social concern,

but he fails to see the connection between increasing social division and his own government's policies that actively promote deregulation, opting out and the narrowing of the welfare safety net. He likes to tinker at the margins, whether it be motorway cones or generosity towards holders of the Victoria Cross. On the big issues, such as the future of Europe or of the welfare state, there is no clarity or consistency of view, notwithstanding the peace process in Northern Ireland.

The Conservative approach still stems from a pessimistic, mean-spirited view of human nature. Their moral pessimism says that people are bound to be selfish above all else. Their economic shortsightedness ignores investment and the long term – and fosters the get-rich-quick 'boom and bust' society. Their political cynicism insists that people won't respond to a new vision and relies on the hope of bribing them once again with tax cuts. The Tories mask this appalling lack of ambition and hope with a mixture of xenophobia and nostalgia. They hope that people will be fooled by talk of 'golden ages' and 'great Britains' while they themselves preside over the decline of the people and the country they purport to champion.

For many people on the left-of-centre this moral condemnation of the New Right is enough. But for the electorate as a whole the key point is that dubious morality has led to poor results. The old Tory combination of fear and greed has not at the end of the day produced the economic strength and the 'feel-good factor' which can be its only possible justification.

The challenges of modernisation that still remain

The industrial, social, cultural and institutional question still facing Britain is how we can make the leap from being a declining, post-imperial, economically second-rank nation, which is also increasingly divided and unequal, to being a nation which is rising in the economic league, socially at ease with itself, and in which every citizen feels they have a stake. The need, as Tony Blair has described it, is to make Britain a 'young' country again. 'Young' in the sense that its economic dynamism and vitality are restored. 'Young' also in the opportunities it offers, which make a reality of the One Nation promise that everyone, from whatever background, will have an equal chance to get on.

Margaret Thatcher's work was in essence destructive – taking on the unions, nationalised industries, overspending local councils. She went around searching for enemies. In tackling the problems that we identify, New Labour's approach is essentially constructive:

- How can we take the outstanding record of the best British companies and use it to raise the mediocre performance of the rest?
- How can we take the industrial sectors where we are strong and deploy government support – for example in research and development – to build out from them?
- How can we extend the excellence of our education system for the élite in order to raise the standards of education for the broad mass of our children?
- How can we can maximise the overseas advantages we have – the power of the English language, the reputation of the BBC, our educational links with other parts of the world, our strengths in culture and design?

A different set of questions concerns how we remove barriers to new talent and ideas, and release new sources of entrepreneurial energy in business and the public services. This will be uncomfortable for some. Not only must New Labour be prepared to take on monopolies, vested interests, the artificial barriers of class and the overrigid dividing lines between public and private sectors, we need also to reinvent government and the way in which public services are provided.

Modernisation also requires a new decentralised and devolved style of politics. Under the Conservatives, Britain has become more centralised and the scope for local action more constrained. Britain desperately needs to promote a flowering of voluntary initiative and civic pride. Our municipalities need the independence of action which has enabled some of the great cities of the United States to pick themselves up from the floor through strategies of private-sector partnership and urban development. Our public services need to strive constantly to bring further imagination, commitment and innovation to their work. Our regions and nations need a voice of their own, and with it the power to act.

New Labour's governing approach

The public want an alternative vision to the tired and discredited one offered by the Conservatives and they want Britain seriously prepared for the challenges ahead. But they also insist that a new government's approach should go beyond the failed solutions of both the old left and the New Right.

New Labour does not accept the classic view of the left-right divide, in which both sides are seen to be locked in permanent conflict. The polarisation of politics between left and right has for too long obscured the way forward for Britain. New Labour believes that it is possible to combine a free market economy with social justice; liberty of the individual with wider opportunities for all; One Nation security with efficiency and competitiveness; rights with responsibilities; personal self-fulfilment with strengthening the family; effective government and decisive political leadership with a new constitutional settlement and a new relationship of trust between politicians and the people; a love of Britain with a recognition that Britain's future has to lie in Europe.

New Labour is a new type of politics. It is about building a new synthesis to which all of the centre and left can subscribe:

- Whereas the left desired equality of outcome and individual freedom to do whatever they pleased, New Labour sets as its goal real equal opportunity for all and special privileges for none.
- Whereas the left appeared to argue for rights without responsibilities and that one was responsible for oneself alone, New Labour stresses the importance of mutual obligations.
- Whereas the left favoured more public consumption and investment and the right more private consumption and investment, New Labour gives immediate priority to investment – both public and private.
- Whereas some on the left wanted top-down centralised rules, administered by powerful bureaucracies, and the right wanted to privatise everything public and leave the rest to the market, New Labour advocates diversity and decentralisation, with bottom-up solutions and public goals sometimes

achieved by market means.

- Whereas the old left saw its job as to represent trade unions, pressure groups and the 'working class', and the right saw its role as to protect the rich together with powerful corporate interests, New Labour stands for the ordinary families who work hard and play by the rules.

For New Labour there is a new set of dividing lines in politics – and a new range of issues we should be determined to colonise as our own: education; technology; the modern labour market; welfare-to-work; Europe. As a nation, we face tough trade-offs if we are to reverse decline: the long-term interests of the country must take pride of place over short-term political pressures; macro-economic stability over the desire for the quick fix; consistency of policy over interest-group claims; investment over consumption; high-quality education and training over other less crucial spending claims; modernisation over privilege and out-of-date though sometimes cherished tradition.

Putting the long term first demands a new style of politics. Political leaders must lead. They must be more honest with the voters and less pettily partisan with their opponents about the limits as well as the possibilities of what they can achieve. They must welcome more open government and a more deliberative legislative style that ensures that new laws are made to last. New Labour must aim to construct in the country a broad coalition of centre and left support for radical change with a clear consistency of direction.

However, New Labour approaches these tough decisions from a bedrock of traditional left-of-centre values and instincts. It has a moral outlook that Keir Hardie and Clement Attlee would fully have shared. When we see unemployed young men hanging round the off-licences and betting-shops, when we hear of bright children who will never have a chance to succeed because their parents don't care and they are let down by failing inner-city schools, when we come across families eking out a drab and dismal existence on social security with no prospect of work and, unless their National Lottery numbers come up, the certainty of a miserable old age – we are determined that something must be done.

There is a complacency about today's Conservative Party that is anathema to our values. And it is not just the failure to tackle social deprivation that makes us angry. It is that constant feeling of missed opportunity about Britain – when we hear of brilliant scientists who have emigrated because they see no future for their research work here; when we see the fiasco of the high-speed rail link to the Channel Tunnel; when we think of all the good ideas that have been stifled because 'that's not the way we do things in this country'. New Labour's values cannot be dismissed as those of a bleeding heart: at their core there is an iron will to tackle injustice and complacency.

The key to New Labour, as John Prescott puts it, is the application of traditional values to a modern setting. The battle to revise Clause IV of Labour's constitution, which in 1918 had famously committed the party to the 'nationalisation of the means of production, distribution and exchange', was far more than a symbolic victory for Tony Blair and party modernisation – it was the essence of what New Labour and Blair's leadership is about.

New Labour's distinctive emphasis is on its concept of community. This is not a soft, romantic concept – conjuring up images of old dears attending bingo nights in draughty halls, or the world of the tightly knit mining community that now is dying away. Community is a robust and powerful idea, and is at the heart of the stakeholder economy New Labour wishes to create. It means teamwork – working and acting together in companies, in local neighbourhoods, in the country as a whole to get things done. It means mutuality – rights and responsibilities going hand in hand. It means justice – that all interests are served, not just those of the rich and powerful. New Labour decisively rejects the Thatcherite view that individuals pursuing their own best interests represent the only road to a prosperous, contented Britain – a view typified by Thatcher's remark that 'there is no such thing as society'.

This tough and active concept of community is more than an individual obligation to be kind, loving and charitable:
- First, everyone should have a stake in society and no one should be excluded from it. That is why the abolition of long-term unemployment is central to Labour policy.
- Secondly, individuals cannot reach their full potential alone,

and nor will the 'free' market ensure it either. They need the opportunities that come from being part of a strong community that acts together to back up their efforts – for example, by ensuring a high-quality education system and a health service they can rely on.

• Thirdly, rights carry with them obligations. Yes, young people have rights to a much wider range of opportunity, but with the backing of the wider community goes an obligation to the wider community. Yes, companies should enjoy the freedom to compete in a dynamic market, but along with that freedom goes responsibility to all their stakeholders – workers, shareholders, bankers, long-term subcontractors and customers.

All these relationships should involve mutual obligation. The government itself cannot ensure this everywhere, but it can show the way and set the standard.

The concept of community enables New Labour to reclaim ground that should never have been conceded to our political opponents. The principles of working together, mutuality and justice start with the family itself. Successful families are not organisations where individuals do their own thing to the exclusion and neglect of everyone else, and where people insist on their rights and never remember their responsibilities to each other. Successful families are where partners show long-term commitment to each other, children learn discipline and mutual respect, and family members help each other to cope with their personal crises and achieve their individual potential. Successful families are the foundation of successful communities.

Once we set out this concept of community, it immediately becomes clear who are New Labour's enemies. They are the unaccountable who ignore the feelings of the community. They are the vested interests who want decisions to be taken to benefit them, not the community as a whole. They are the inefficient who let the community down and impede its success. And they are the irresponsible who fall down on their obligations to their families and therefore their community.

The Labour Party is able to speak for Britain because its rapidly rising individual membership is representative of Britain. The days when Labour was dominated by tiny groups of sectarian activists will never return. Its internal procedures have been democratised and power now rests with the ordinary members who share New Labour's values and outlook. New Labour is, in Tony Blair's words, 'literally a new Party'.

In summary, New Labour understands the scale of change necessary and what is needed to meet it. Its approach is a Labour approach because the party retains at its heart a belief in a community where all citizens have a stake and where a sense of social justice and fairness govern decision-making by those in power. It is a new approach because it recognises that to present yesterday's solutions to today's problems is not just negligent but facile. New Labour dumps the ideological baggage of the past to offer new solutions based not on dogma but on a simple test: What will deliver results?

New Labour v. old Labour

It is not just from the Conservatives that New Labour must learn the lessons of the past. Voters want to know how much of a change New Labour represents from old Labour, and what that change means in practice. What has actually altered from the policy stances that were adopted in the Bennite aberration of the late 1970s and the early 1980s, which took the best part of a decade to dispose of; from the corporatist approach adopted by the Wilson and Callaghan governments from 1974 to 1979; and from the governing philosophy of the earlier Labour administrations in 1945 and 1964? We need to be clear where the differences lie.

Labour and the private sector
New Labour firmly rejects the notion that centralised planning and state control are the route to economic success.

In practice, every past Labour government has wanted to see a thriving private sector within a mixed economy. Indeed, average economic growth was higher under Labour than it has been since 1979 under the Conservatives. The perception of hostility to the private sector was allowed to take root only by Bennite fantasies of compulsory planning agreements and of the nationalisation of twenty-five of the top firms in the economy. Nevertheless, there are clear differences between past Labour governments' view of the mixed economy and New Labour's commitment to the rigour of the dynamic market.

Although old Labour wanted the private sector to succeed, it did not always understand what was necessary to secure that success. It focused too narrowly on the fortunes of large firms, forgetting that in a dynamic market economy it is the stimulus of competition and the threat posed by new growing businesses that keep the big firms on their toes. It rightly urged investment, but it tended to forget that the quality of investment matters as much as its quantity. It correctly emphasised the need for more research and development, but it neglected the fact that successful R&D has to be part of a sophisticated approach to innovation which is based on anticipating customer wants and needs. Old Labour wanted growth: New Labour is ready to back individual enterprise and flair to get it.

New Labour welcomes the rigour of competitive markets as the most efficient means of anticipating and supplying consumers' wants, offering choice and stimulating innovation. Competition is the only effective force that prevents capitalists opting for a quiet life and managers spending their afternoons on the golf-course. But, unlike the New Right, New Labour recognises that free markets do not automatically serve the public interest. Especially where large investments are required, they may fail to deliver efficient outcomes; and, left to themselves, markets tend to reinforce inequalities and may entrench privilege. Only in these circumstances should markets be regulated.

Labour and incentives

New Labour's belief in the dynamic market economy involves recognition that substantial personal incentives and rewards are necessary in order to encourage risk-taking and entrepreneurialism. Profit is not a dirty word – profits are accepted as the motor of private enterprise.

Differences in income and personal spending power are the inevitable consequence of the existence of markets. In the past, Labour only half acknowledged this truth. In a gesture towards equality, it imposed penal rates of tax on high incomes – rising to 83 per cent on earned income (though it is important to note that this rate fell only to 75 per cent under Edward Heath). The party was pleased by these public gestures towards egalitarianism without appreciating the real economic consequences: poor rewards for top salaried management – except for those who felt satisfied by their perks in chauffeurs, company flats and long lunches.

Yet Labour, along with the Conservatives at the time, simultaneously tolerated, without public fuss, relatively low taxation of capital gains, in order not to destroy the incentives for entrepreneurship altogether. So go-ahead and enterprising individuals concentrated on share speculation in the City and on buying, developing and selling property – activities that promised large capital gains and were relatively lightly taxed. It was the perfect British combination of inefficiency and hypocrisy, deterring careers in management and damaging economic growth – and New Labour will have none of it.

The real issue is not high versus low tax, as the right tries to claim, but fair rather than unfair tax. The present tax system allows the privileges of accumulated wealth to be preserved down the generations and permits a proliferation of tax shelters and avoidance loopholes that are not in practice available to the hard-working majority. New Labour should use the tax system to attack unjustified privilege, without weakening incentives for risk-taking and hard work. For New Labour there is still scope for redistribution – and later in the book we put forward ideas to spread opportunities and strengthen the family through tighter taxation of large fortunes.

Labour and public ownership

New Labour does not regard public ownership of industry as necessary in order to manage the economy and control what Aneurin Bevan famously described as the 'commanding heights'.

The all-embracing commitment to nationalisation in the infamous Clause IV of Labour's 1918 constitution gave the unfortunate impression that Labour favoured public ownership on principle. The truth is that old Labour's approach to nationalisation was always pragmatic and considered case by case. And few would argue that the postwar nationalisation decisions were wrong in the circumstances of the time. It is difficult to believe that the rationalisation of the impoverished coal industry, the modernisation of a clapped-out railway system, the strengthening of the National Grid and, much later, the creation of a modern natural-gas pipeline network would have taken place if the industries concerned had remained fragmented and in private ownership.

But times change, and we must learn from experience and live in the world as it now is. The truth is that the record of the old nationalised industries was at best patchy. They implemented huge investment programmes which gobbled up vast national resources, but too often these plans were engineering-led, not market- and consumer-led. They employed more people than could conceivably be justified on grounds of efficiency. New Labour believes that the social objectives which once led to the call for the utilities to be nationalised can in today's circumstances be met through more effective regulation. The New Labour agenda focuses on reform of regulation in order to prevent monopoly abuse and to fulfil broader social objectives.

Labour and the trade unions

From the party's earliest days, Labour's leaders were always keen to emphasise that Labour was a national party, not the representative in Parliament of trade-union sectional interests. This was seen as essential if the infant Labour Party was to broaden its electoral appeal. Even so, New Liberals like Henry Massingham, the editor of *The Nation,* who came across to Labour in the 1920s, desperately worried that they might be joining 'a mere wages and hours party with an irreconcilable Communist wing'.

In order to anticipate fears of this kind, the 1918 constitution emphasised the party's bipolar structure. The leader was leader of the parliamentary party, not of the Labour Party itself – a technical distinction intended to make clear that he was not accountable to the trade-union-dominated National Executive and conference. (And so the position remained until the late 1970s. Today, of course, the Labour leader is elected by one-member-one-vote.) While the conference and the National Executive were formally responsible for determining party policy, the content of the manifesto was subject to an effective veto by the parliamentary party under Clause V of the constitution, which stands to this day. Parliamentarians were granted sole responsibility for Labour's conduct in office. When Harold Laski, as chairman of the National Executive, attempted to suggest otherwise in 1945, he was sent away by Attlee with the famous rebuke 'a period of silence on your part would be welcome'.

The relationship between the trade unions and a Labour government did not become a dominant public concern until the late 1960s, when the tripartite incomes policy agreed between government, unions and employers had effectively broken down. The Labour government put a large part of the blame on the inability of trade-union leaders to control militant shop stewards. The broad purpose behind Barbara Castle's 'In Place of Strife' reforms was to remedy this defect. Fierce trade-union opposition to these proposals expressed through sympathetic voices in the parliamentary party and cabinet forced their withdrawal.

The failure of Edward Heath's attempts at industrial relations reform and the breakdown of his statutory incomes policy during the miners' dispute led to the social contract of the 1970s. This approach fell apart during the 1978/79 'Winter of Discontent'. Some Labour and trade-union activists gave the impression that every wage claim and every strike was justified – never mind the consequences for inflation, the economy, essential public services, and even the burial of the dead. In the eyes of the public the Labour government appeared a helpless bystander.

New Labour has shed 1970s ideas of 'corporatist government', of taking decisions with pressure groups and in alliance with certain vested interests, over the heads of the public as a whole – a process akin more to bargaining than to governing. The concept of a stakeholder economy addresses the needs and aspirations of individuals, not interest groups acting for them.

New Labour believes that in a modern economy an efficient workforce must be motivated, well-educated and treated as partners in the enterprise. There is no place for the outdated view of the relationship between employer and employee as one of master and servant, or for institutional conflict between unions and management. New Labour stands on the side of the egalitarian style of management about which Far Eastern inward investors have so much to teach Britain.

In this modern view of employer-employee relationships, the trade unions retain a vital role as a representative channel and in protecting individuals against arbitrary management behaviour – but they have to prove to their members at the workplace that they are still relevant. They cannot expect to compensate for their loss of industrial influence by being given a privileged role at the cabinet table or in ministers' offices. Their views should be listened to because of who they represent, but there should be no expectation of unjustified favours – just as there never was, before the aberrations of the 1970s.

As for the future of the trade unions' role within the Labour Party itself, the unions' entrenched constitutional position is largely an accident of history. Trade-union MPs pre-dated Labour and transferred into it when the party was created.

Most continental socialist and social-democratic parties have strong links with trade unions, but trade-unionists exercise influence as individual party members, on the same terms as anyone else, rather than through block votes at the party conference. In the last three years the dominance of the block vote at the Labour Party conference has been drastically reduced, and a priority for the modernised party in maintaining its union links is to maximise the involvement of individual trade-unionists as happens on the Continent.

Labour and public expenditure

Ever since the publication of Anthony Crosland's *The Future of Socialism*, in 1956, social democrats in his tradition have equated high levels of public spending with progress towards a more equal society. New Labour concurs with Crosland that stronger public services are essential for the good of the individual and society as a whole, but it would not agree that one can measure progress towards equality by the proportion of gross domestic product accounted for by public expenditure. An overmighty and overly high-spending state is as much a barrier to Britain's success as a slimmed-down, minimalist state always deferring to crude market forces.

Under the Conservatives, public expenditure has increased as a result of increased spending on unemployment, welfare and social decay. New Labour wants to end this waste and replace it by economically and socially productive spending. New Labour recognises that what is important is not just how much the public sector spends but how it is spent. Cutting waste and improving efficiency should be a priority, as should ensuring that public spending reaches the groups it is intended to benefit. Ways of meeting public need and organising the delivery of public services must and should change from the municipal socialism and centralised nationalisation of the past.

Labour and the role of the state

Old Labour frequently gave the impression of believing in the wisdom and power of the centralised state. It was part of a mind-set that favoured tidy solutions, uniform standards, centralised provision – the view that 'the man in Whitehall knows best'.

New Labour emphatically does not seek to provide centralised, 'statist' solutions to every social and economic problem. Rather it aims to enable people to work together to achieve things for themselves and their fellow citizens. This may well be brought about through voluntary and community-based organisation, better community participation in local services like schools and housing, and more effective local-government working in partnership with the private and voluntary sectors. It is the job of the national government to set the right framework, not to run everything itself.

Labour and Europe

Old Labour often found itself divided on Europe. Hugh Gaitskell opposed the Common Market because of his passionate sense of obligation to the Commonwealth. The left had an instinctive dislike of what was felt to be a continental cartel of capitalist-oriented Christian democrats. The Treaty of Rome was argued to be incompatible with Labour's ambitions for more nationalisation and planning.

Labour has now totally rejected those outdated attitudes.

New Labour recognises the role of the nation-state and its historic significance and responsibilities. But it does not confuse symbols with reality. It knows that in the modern world it is only through Britain's committed participation in the European Union that we can regain true sovereignty – in other words, the political ability to tackle problems in the public interest – over many issues which have slipped beyond the nation-state's individual reach, whether the question be global warming, the prevention of future wars in Europe, or international economic cooperation to provide the conditions of stability necessary to boost economic growth in Europe and restore full employment.

New Labour has the self-confidence in Britain's values not to fear loss of national identity in this process of increased European cooperation. In contrast the Conservatives can only manage a crude and empty assertion of nationhood bordering at times on xenophobia. Because they have no real appreciation of the value of people working together for the public good – from neighbourhood council to European cooperation – because for them community is essentially an empty concept, they readily revert to flag-waving nationalism as the only emotion that can bind us together.

Is New Labour nothing more than the SDP Mark II?

The founders of the Social Democratic Party wanted to create an electable left-of-centre alternative to the Conservatives which had some realistic hope of governing Britain with success at a time when it appeared to them that the Labour Party had deserted its traditional roots and values and was set on a course of self-destruction. The political programme they initially offered was familiar fare by the standards of most continental social-democratic parties and represented much of what Labour had traditionally stood for, shorn of its contemporary excesses and ambiguities.

After the 1983 election David Owen began to reposition the SDP on to less familiar social-democratic territory. This involved a reappraisal of the role of conventional demand management; a recognition that privatisation was here to stay; and a coming to terms with the new public-service agenda of competitive tendering, purchaser-provider splits, more emphasis on standards, and greater consumer choice. Much of this was a necessary recognition that times had changed.

However, Owen's concept of the social market went somewhat further and essentially put people in boxes. In their commercial lives they were to be aggressive entrepreneurs fighting to squeeze the last ounce of profit out of their business, but in their home lives they were to be concerned citizens prepared to back a stronger NHS and, if they were better off, pay higher taxes. This combination of individualism in people's economic lives with social concern outside them finds a parallel in the attitudes Kenneth Clarke and Conservatives like him would strike today.

New Labour in contrast offers a more rounded approach. Notions of partnership and community should influence all aspects of our lives. Enterprise is applauded, but it has responsibilities. Social rights – for instance to greater equality of opportunity – are properly emphasised, but at every point rights go along with matching obligations. Unlike the Owenite SDP, New Labour marries the social market with more traditional Labour values of community and responsibility.

Is this socialism?

Opponents claim that the Blair revolution is 'dumping socialism' or 'leaving the old members behind' or just 'fishing for votes'. The truth is that the New Labour agenda stands in a long line of socialist thinking.

There have always been two clearly dominant families of socialist thought: the Marxist school and the less dogmatic ethical school in which it is a body of core values that matter.

While never being Marxist, old Labour was influenced by Marxist thought. This quasi-scientific view of the world rests on economic determinism and class analysis, propounded by those who claim to speak for 'the working class'. Always out of kilter with the real world, this socialism of centralised state control of industry offers nothing to an understanding of how the modern market economy can be helped to prosper. Its blind belief in the state is unable to recognise that the public sector too can become prey to vested interests and require reform. Its narrow view of class offers no insights into today's pluralist society in which wrongs of race and gender matter just as much as those caused by social background. Always rejected by Labour, the collapse of communism finally finished off this approach as a serious option for all but the extreme left.

It is the other brand of socialism – the ethical approach – that has unsurprisingly stood the test of time. This is a socialism based on a set of beliefs and values, and is similar to the social democracy found in other European countries. It is founded on the simple notion that human beings are socially interdependent and cannot be divorced from the society they live in.

Some socialist parties, such as the SPD in Germany or the Australian Labour Party, resolved a generation ago that they were unequivocally believers in this brand of socialism. The SPD renounced Marxism at Bad Godesberg in 1959 and embraced a form of social democracy that gave it the clarity and vision to rule a rapidly modernising, and economically successful Germany. The British Labour Party used to be different. Until 1995 it had never unequivocally had to define what type of socialism it believed in. In the end its leaders mostly fudged the choice, until Tony Blair threw down the Clause IV challenge.

In the past politics of the old left, socialism was a slogan that was often shouted from the rooftops and through the street megaphones by those with least in common with the values of socialism as New Labour interprets them. Yet the general public is not at all interested in the bandying around of labels. If it is socialist to be committed to community and a strong society, to justice and fairness, to maximising the life chances of all our people and preventing the exclusion from society of any, then New Labour is socialist.

But we do not stop at that. New Labour also believes in the market and in efficiency and in the need to compete. We know that we live in the new global economy, and that there is no alternative to that. Our special claim is that the practical application of our values to present-day problems is necessary – not just a cosy extra or an optional add-on – because without it the modern world simply cannot prosper.

We stand for a strong society and an efficient economy because we need both, and each needs the other. That is the essence of our belief in One Nation policies and the principle of the stakeholder economy.

2

Labour's Leader

Shortly after Tony Blair moved into the opposition leader's suite at Westminster, a friend dropped in to see him. Blair's friends know that he is not especially interested in creature comforts and how things look, but his room seemed particularly austere. 'Don't you want to make this a bit more lived in?' his visitor inquired, looking round the room. 'No thanks,' Blair replied briskly. 'My job is to get out of these offices as quickly as possible, not to make them my home.'

For Blair, there is no job in opposition really worth having, and he has never bothered to list his opposition posts in his *Who's Who* entry. He finds it bizarre that biographies should be written about him before he sets foot in No. 10. He hates 'diddling', as he calls it – being powerless to change things and put his beliefs into practice.

Ever since he entered Parliament, Blair has worked to create the radical new agenda for the left in Britain which is now embodied in New Labour. It is what social-democratic parties throughout Europe are doing, establishing a fresh identity in the wake of their failure to present a coherent intellectual alternative to the spread of right-wing thinking. This is the key to understanding everything about Blair and his determination to transform the Labour Party. He wants Labour to rediscover its identity by building on its founding values, not on any rigid ideology or economic theory grafted on since. Extracting these values from the party's traditions and redrawing everything else around them *is* the Blair revolution.

Discovering values

Tony Blair's strength lies in his political beliefs and their consistent application to the changes he has made. They flow from the values of community, which he has put at the heart of New Labour thinking. He stands for 'cooperation, not confrontation;

for fellowship, not fear', as he declared in his maiden speech in the House of Commons back in 1983. His is an ethical socialism which draws on the ideas of Ruskin and Tawney, but it is also a modern socialism which takes account of changes in society and the economy and the experience of other governments that have tried by various different means to put the same values into practice.

An interviewer once accused Blair of holding opinions rather than convictions. 'Not true,' said Blair: 'I have core beliefs which take the form of strong left-of-centre values. With my class background [Blair's father was a modestly well-off lawyer, and he himself was educated at a private school] if all I had wanted to do was exercise power I could and would, let's be blunt about it, have joined another party.' What brought Blair into the Labour Party, unlike others who have risen to senior positions, was not a political family background or a conventional Labour apprenticeship in student activity, local government or the trade unions, but the strength of his personal convictions and his belief in what Labour stands for – fairness and social justice in society, partnership in managing economic and social problems, and greater individual opportunity for all.

These values stem from his upbringing and his acceptance of Christianity while at Oxford University. His mother was vaguely religious and his father is an atheist, but he grew up with a strong sense of religion around him first at Durham choir school and subsequently at Fettes school in Scotland, which he was able to attend on a scholarship. He was a challenger of authority and a bit of a rebel, but until he left university he was more interested in rock music and sport than party politics. It was his experience at Oxford that changed him. He befriended an Australian Anglican priest, Peter Thomson, to whom he is still close and with whom he spent a lot of time talking about how he saw the world and defining his personal faith and social philosophy.

Both Thomson and Blair were particularly influenced by the Scottish writer John MacMurray, whose philosophy centred on a blend of socialism and Christianity and who promoted the concept of community as a way of living. Thomson has described their discussions:

The idea of community wedded beautifully with our concept of religion. What we were on about was developing community in the sense of cooperation rather than a debit-and-credit ledger thing – if you do this for me, then I'll do that for you, which is the general norm of society. We were trying to develop a sense of community where people were connected to something – that is the welfare of one another – and, although that seems wishy-washy, it actually works. And it has a definite religious base.

Earliest analysis

Although Blair's family suffered money worries and insecurity when his father had a stroke (and was unable to work for several years afterwards) it was MacMurray's interpretation of the social commitment of Christianity through the idea of community, rather than personal experience of extreme poverty and hardship, that inspired Blair's political awakening.

He knew people were unequal, but previously he had simply seen this as an unwelcome fact of life, not a wrong to be righted. He had not made the connection between people's surroundings, their social environment and the life chances open to them. His intellectual conversion took place once he made the link between a fairer and better society and the ability of people to get on in life. To create opportunities of self-fulfilment for all, which was the mainspring of his Christian sense of social justice, it was necessary to change people's social conditions. In other words, Christianity was not enough by itself – you needed politics and organisation, too, to improve society.

Blair had at last found his purpose, and his desire to go into politics grew from then. His belief in the idea of individual self-fulfilment backed up by a strong society has never weakened. It led him to join the Labour Party when he moved to London in 1975, and it has been the motor of his thinking ever since.

Evidence of the development of Blair's thought lies in a lecture he gave to a university seminar when he visited Australia in 1982, shortly after he had fought a parliamentary by-election in Beaconsfield, in Buckinghamshire. Coming three years after the defeat of the Labour government and while Bennite activism was still spreading in the Labour Party, the lecture contained a detailed analysis of what Blair believed Labour should stand for and what it needed to do to recover electoral support. It was the antithesis of what Benn was arguing for. He talked of the public's dissatisfaction with both the main parties' 'rhetoric and philosophy'. Reflecting on his own modern outlook, he observed that 'growing numbers of young, often socially upward moving people are simply not prepared to accept our basic ideology just because their forefathers did'. He continued, 'There are very few of the younger age group converted to our ideology, and we rely to a dangerous degree on the loyalty vote among older citizens.'

Elaborating his theme that Labour needed to rethink its appeal, he said that both right and left in the party, 'instead of using history to explain the present and point to the future, chain themselves to the past'. What Labour had to do, he argued, was 'look for its political philosophy to something more sensitive, more visionary, in a word more modern, than Marxism', which he felt was still dominating much intellectual thought in the party – and which he totally rejected, along with every vestige of the totalitarian system in Eastern Europe. Labour needed clarity, he believed, as it 'sits uneasily, squashed between traditional Clause IV socialism and an acceptance of the mixed economy'. Little wonder, he suggested, that the SDP were then gaining support in Britain, because at least they 'offer some compromise between the overt callousness of Mrs Thatcher and the old-fashioned collectivism of Labour'.

These thoughts – radical, in the Labour Party at the time – were expressed by Blair a full twelve years before he set out the full 'modernising' agenda of his leadership bid.

He also made some very sharp remarks about the organisation of the party. Anticipating the campaign he waged later, he criticised the left for resisting the introduction of one-member-one-vote in the constituencies, and commented on their failure to 'mix sufficiently with the electorate'. 'A local party', he said, 'should grow out of a local community, the party members having roots in that community. The party will then be more sensitive to the needs and wishes of the electorate.'

It is striking that the lecture did not express any support for such fashionable left-wing totems of the time as unilateral nuclear disarmament and withdrawal from Europe.

Although the lecture contained some opinions which he would now freely admit he has developed – for example, the detail of his economic thinking – Blair has not deviated from his basic analysis then. Labour, he believes, needs middle-ground voters to defeat the Conservatives, and, to be successful, this appeal to the centre as well as the left in politics must be based on the party's values.

The extent to which Labour needed to transform its thinking became clear the year after his Australian lecture, in the 1983 general election. Blair had a lucky break. Three days before nomination day, and as a rank outsider, he was selected as Labour candidate for the safe County Durham constituency of Sedgefield, and the subsequent experience was the critical milestone in his political development. Like every other candidate, he had to fight the election on the party's nationally agreed manifesto. This was described at the time as the 'longest suicide note in history', for it contained policies that were unpopular and unworkable. Blair did not agree with these policies, but it was not dishonest to stand by them in public: as Labour's representative, he had no alternative – he, like countless other young prospective MPs, had to be loyal to a platform he had no part in formulating until such time as he could change it.

Following the election, Blair lost no time in urging the radical changes he believed were necessary. In the face of the prevailing party orthodoxy at the time, it needed some courage for a newly elected MP to speak up, but a month after the election Blair appeared on BBC TV's *Newsnight* programme and declared that 'The image of the Labour Party has got to be more dynamic, more modern. Over 50 per cent of the population are owner-occupiers – that means a change in attitude that we've got to catch up with.' Soon after, at a public meeting in Spennymoor, in his constituency, he again argued that the party had lost touch with the electorate and that it had to change, because many of the changes already taking place in society were for the better.

Underlying Blair's analysis of Labour's position was real anger about what had happened to the party in the years before the 1983 election. He had walked round his hoped-for constituency and found dyed-in-the-wool Labour supporters deserting the party in droves because they felt totally alienated from the fashionable metropolitan ideas and gesture politics of the party's ascendant left-wing activists, who did not speak the same language or appear to know anything about the lives of traditional Labour voters.

In Blair's view, the party's values, its commitment to social justice and a family-based social order, had been completely distorted by indulgent policies framed to appeal to sectarian activists and minority pressure groups. Far from Labour ministers betraying the party rank and file, as had been argued after the 1979 defeat, Labour's values and its core supporters had been betrayed by those who claimed to champion 'real' socialism, and Blair was one of a growing number of MPs prepared to stand up and say so. To them, Labour's traditional broad church seemed to have become a dumping-ground for militants of every kind who knew they could not win support if they stood under their own colours. It was time for Labour to rediscover its true values and reconnect itself to the mainstream electorate.

A modern voice

Blair rose quickly on the front bench under Neil Kinnock's leadership. In a party that had lost much talent as a result of defections to the SDP, intellectually capable people like him stood out.

Blair does not carry any animus towards those who defected to the SDP, although it never occurred to him to do so himself. He felt as little sympathy with the old right in the party, with their reliance on unattractive local-machine politics and deal-making and fixing votes with the trade unions, as he did with the old left. He was a very different sort of Labour politician, who – despite his commitment to Labour's core beliefs – felt little allegiance to the traditional structures and ways of doing things.

He used his skills as a barrister to become a noteworthy Commons performer, showing judgement and originality in his interventions. He has always prepared for parliamentary occasions very diligently, believing that these are where political reputations are made or destroyed. An early speech he made about the threat of social breakdown and the effects of the Conservatives' policies on social cohesion in the country was warmly commended in a note to him from the former Labour premier James Callaghan.

Blair had already made his mark with other leading members of the party's parliamentary leadership. John Smith had been introduced to him three years before by a close mutual friend, Alexander Irvine (now Lord Irvine of Lairg, the shadow lord chancellor, and one of Blair's closest advisers), a distinguished barrister who headed the chambers where Blair had been accepted as a pupil. It was an extraordinary encounter. Irvine had thought Blair might do some speech-writing and research for Smith, and one evening Blair arrived at the House of Commons for dinner, to offer his help. Smith was in fine form, talking, laughing, joking and drinking to excess. No research work was discussed, but they went on until dawn, emptying every bottle in sight and raiding every drinks cupboard – including Denis Healey's. It was the start of a lasting friendship between the two men.

Another of Blair's early admirers was Roy Hattersley. He had memories of speaking for the young candidate in the Beaconsfield by-election and of the note of thanks he had received for his help, which, Hattersley later recalled, 'should in itself have distinguished him from other candidates'. Hattersley claims the credit for starting Blair on his front-bench career, for, a year after being elected, Blair was appointed under Hattersley to the party's Treasury team.

It is instructive to see how he worked in this and all his subsequent front-bench roles. As a junior Treasury spokesman, Blair might have contented himself with the odd dispatch-box appearance, press release and broadcast interview. Instead, he began actively to think through new economic views for the party, bringing together a group of young university and City economists to help him.

In exploring this area, Blair worked closely with his parliamentary colleague Gordon Brown, now the shadow chancellor. The two men entered parliament together in 1983, and shortly after they shared a Commons room. Their backgrounds in the party were very different (Brown was well used to its ways and structure), but they had similar strategic minds, they respected each other's strengths, and they enjoyed each other's company. They developed a close friendship, which is rare in politics between individuals of broadly equal age and calibre. There was nothing they would not discuss and reach a common view upon. They would talk about each others' speeches, press releases and political ideas, with Blair learning a lot from Brown's political experience and tactical skills. Later on, Blair worked alongside as Brown devised his economic policies, spending hours talking, refining ideas, and swapping drafts of papers and speeches, each adding his own improvements and nuances.

Blair had had to learn a lot about economics, but he had never been a supporter of centralised economic planning and heavy-handed state intervention and he did not, therefore, need to disavow any former views when he started developing policy as a Treasury spokesman. And he was original in the way he took on the Tories' advocacy of supply-side economics.

In a way that later become a familiar practice, Blair and Brown accepted the premise of the Tories' approach – in this case, that industry needed to be more competitive – but, using a Labour argument, turned their logic back against them, pointing out that, in focusing all their efforts on privatisation, deregulation and trade-union reform, the Tories were neglecting essential investment in technology, skills and infrastructure. This economic philosophy, together with the maintenance of low inflation and macro-economic stability, was later dubbed 'supply-side socialism' by Gordon Brown, marking it out from the Keynesian thinking that emphasises management of demand as the key to economic success. It is an early example of how reapplying a traditional Labour idea made it possible to refashion the party's policies, and it is now central to New Labour economic thinking.

Blair adopted the same approach when, three years later, he was appointed as the party's spokesman on the City, and he deftly used the post to position Labour as the friend of the small investor in the wake of the collapse of the Barlow Clowes investment company. Many in the Labour Party of old would not have stood up for any sort of private investor, big or small, however burned their fingers. Blair saw the chance to redraw a dividing line between Labour, whose values meant speaking up for the underdog, and the Conservatives, who, until pressure mounted, showed no interest in protecting the Barlow Clowes investors, even though many were of only modest means and had lost much of their savings in the collapse. It was a neat and highly effective reversal of roles.

By this time Neil Kinnock had initiated the changes in policy and presentation that were the origins of New Labour, but these were not enough to save Labour from defeat in the 1987 election. It was obvious to Blair that Labour was still not connecting with the public. Wholesale change was needed, in his view, and, in terms that were far more forthright than those of others in the party, he said so in an article published in the *Guardian* newspaper in June that year.

The key statement in Blair's article was his call for Labour to rethink its attitude to society and its institutions – 'which we did most to create'. He argued that 'whether it is education, or public ownership, or housing, it is not our values that are open to doubt. The values are, in the main, shared. It is the effectiveness that is in question. The task today is to express those values through new policies in which the country will believe. To succeed,' he said 'we must have not just the appearance but the reality of being modern.'

He pointed to 1945 as a moment when the party rethought its approach to meet the needs of the time. The party had to do so again. And it had to do this not by appealing to people to put their sense of social justice before their material interests but by enabling them to satisfy both. In a foretaste of the central argument he has developed since becoming leader, he said, 'It is the Tories who say you have to choose between efficiency and social justice, that you can only have one at the expense of the other. It is Labour's historic task to show that the two, in fact, are essential partners.' Nearly a decade later, this is at the heart of the reinvention which Blair has brought about.

What is surprising about this prescient article is that it seemed to go almost unnoticed, but it reveals how clear in his mind were the tenets of New Labour even then, in 1987. He was not completely alone in his radical analysis, however, for at this time and unknown to him a secret post-mortem report on Labour's election defeat was being prepared for the shadow cabinet and the National Executive Committee, neither of which bodies had he yet joined.

This report, entitled *Labour and Britain in the 1990s*, did not pull its punches. Based on extensive social research, it concluded that Thatcherite values did not have majority support and that, in contrast, Labour's values of cooperation, partnership and social justice enjoyed strong backing. But changes in society and in the electorate were making Labour's actual policies, and the party as a whole, seem less relevant and appropriate.

Labour was seen by most people as out of date, appealing to groups who were not representative of the changing electorate. A growing number of voters were buying shares, had bought their own home, were self-employed, and were less likely to support Labour as a result. The drift of population to the suburbs was helping the Conservatives. Indeed, the population as a whole was moving southwards, leaving old associations and acquiring attitudes that were distant from traditional Labour thinking. It was not inevitable that any of these trends should favour the Conservatives, but Labour did not have enough to say that was relevant and was being shunned as a result.

Notes of the shadow-cabinet/NEC meeting taken at the time reveal that the report had a mixed reception. Tony Benn did not reject all of its findings but commented that 'many of the opinions recorded simply reflect media propaganda'. Ken Livingstone's view was that 'unattributable briefings to the media' from within the party were to blame for Labour's unpopularity – which must count as the earliest recorded attack on the so-called party spin doctors. Roy Hattersley, then the deputy leader, argued that 'intellectual strength comes from ideological convictions' and that Labour needed a 'stronger ideological dimension to its propaganda' – although the effectiveness of this would presumably depend on whether the ideology was old-fashioned Labour dogma or up-to-date and relevant thinking. Gerald Kaufman probably hit the nail on the head best of all with his observation that it was not for lack of ideological struggle that Labour had failed to tap the huge reservoir of support for its values but because Labour itself was seen as 'an incredible vehicle to deliver what we're proposing to do'.

That was also the nub of Blair's view. To make Labour electable, it was not enough to tinker with the odd policy here and there, or to polish up its famous red-rose image. Good presentation could reinforce substance, but it could not make up for its absence. The Labour Party had to have both image and substance, and its ideology, policies, membership and organisation all had to be transformed to give it the essential modern thrust it needs to be an effective governing party. This became Blair's New Labour mission.

Reforming shadow minister

In his front-bench roles after 1987, Blair continued to translate his ideas into practice. He was elected to the shadow cabinet and was appointed shadow energy secretary, rethinking the principles of energy policy and leading Labour's high-profile attack on the way the electricity industry was privatised.

Blair threw himself into this job, concentrating the opposition's attack on key clauses where the government was particularly vulnerable and where his own forensic skills and attention to detail were most useful. In doing so, he established a reputation as a formidable political operator. Cecil Parkinson, his ministerial opponent, has been quoted as saying, 'I think he's very shrewd. He had a big point he wanted to make each day and he clearly put a lot of effort into that, and that was clever. He would then let the others follow up on the point he had made, which I thought was a grown-up thing to do.'

As for the development of Labour's energy policy, Labour traditionally had tended to balance various producer interests – trading off the demands of coal miners and nuclear power workers – rather than identifying consumers' needs. Blair reversed this priority and established clearly that, in future, the country's strategic energy requirements and the consumer interest would provide the basis for Labour's policy, not the dictates and requirements of those working in different sections of the energy industry.

It was, however, as shadow employment secretary, in the two

years before the 1992 election, that Blair made a serious policy breakthrough – in the highly sensitive area of industrial relations and trade-union law.

In his first year in Parliament, Blair had served on the legislative committee considering the next stage of Conservative trade-union law, and he had loyally defended the unions against it. Blair still believes that the Tories became vindictive in their attitude towards the unions and went too far in inhibiting union organisation. It was one thing (and correct, in Blair's view) to increase the rights of members within their unions, but they also had rights in relation to their employers, and these the government refused to recognise. But, while he thought the legislation as a whole was unbalanced, he believed equally that the unions had to accept a proper legal framework for their activities. The issue, as he put it to them, was not law or no law but fair or unfair law.

As soon as he had the power to review Labour's alternative legal proposals, he proposed that, in certain key respects, the Tory legislation should stand. In particular, he backed the measures which enforced ballots before strikes and for executive elections, and he concluded that the restrictions on mass and flying pickets and on sympathy strikes were also right and should be continued.

This was difficult enough for the unions to swallow, but Blair went further. He insisted that Labour's traditional support for the trade-union closed shop, by which the unions' bargaining power was enforced at the workplace through every employee having to be a member of the recognised union, should be scrapped. Blair's motives and methods in the fight that took place on this issue provide a useful insight into his style of working. In his view, by tackling unacceptable union practices he was doing the unions a favour. It enabled them both to receive credit from the public for ending behaviour that was wrong in principle (because individuals should have the right to choose not to be a union member) and to increase their legitimacy at the workplace – ending the closed shop meant they had to organise and earn their shop-floor support, rather than rely on automatic membership.

Ending the closed shop was also in line with the much-

vaunted European Social Charter, and this strengthened Blair's
case, but the point of principle for him was not adherence to
Europe but Labour's attitude to industrial relations. This had to
be based on partnership at work, not confrontation, and on the
development of a relationship of give and take, not master and
slave. And it needed to be based on respect for the individual.
This was the root of the labour movement's outlook, in his view:
not collective organisations acquiring power at the expense of
the individual, but individuals organising collectively to
strengthen their personal rights. Labour, in his view, should
reaffirm this core belief.

Blair's endeavour to persuade the unions of the intellectual
argument in favour of his changes is characteristic of his
approach on every subject. As long as the intellectual framework
is right, and policy formation is proceeding from first principles,
he is confident that the right conclusions will be reached and
that the argument will be won. The working methods that flow
from this are that he first spends time thinking through the
issues involved for himself; he then goes around the people he
has to persuade (in this case, holding countless meetings with
trade-union leaders and officials) and gives meticulous attention
to the obstacles he has to overcome. Neil Kinnock's Chief of
Staff, Charles Clarke, saw Blair's methods at close quarters and
described his approach: 'He showed in the whole process an
ability to decide where he was going. He would set a course and
move towards the target clearly, manoeuvring round the various
obstacles, walking round the chair rather than tripping over it.
Blair both knew where he was going and how to get there by dis-
playing a mixture of intelligence and opportunism.'

The confrontation with the trade unions was difficult for
Blair, because he was fresh in the job when the argument started
and he was a relatively junior member of the shadow cabinet to
be taking on the unions in this way. In facing down the opposition he encountered, however, he set a precedent in his relations
with the union leaders which became very important after he
was elected party leader. In most cases he gained their grudging
respect (though in a few their undying resentment); but, more
importantly, he also established certain ground rules: he would
always be prepared to talk and to listen, but he would not trade

on issues where points of principle were concerned.

Undoubtedly, Blair's success in shifting Labour's policies on industrial relations helped the party gain support in the 1992 election. But this and the other changes wrought in the party's policy review were not enough for Labour to win. In Blair's view, this was because the party was still too tied to outdated ideas of what constituted left thinking – both in economics and in social policy – and, even more fundamentally, because a vote for Labour was still seen by many as voting to better others rather than yourself. In this context, he felt Labour's shadow Budget, presented at the beginning of the campaign, was a mistake. It gave the Tories their chance to land their tax bombshell campaign – hugely exaggerating John Smith's plans. Blair, as the employment spokesman, and Brown, then the shadow trade and industry secretary, had both privately warned Smith, the shadow chancellor, of the electoral dangers of his tax and National Insurance proposals the previous autumn, but, out of loyalty to their friend and senior, they had acquiesced in them. It was mistake from which Blair learned: you can get a hundred little things right, but if you fail on the big points you will lose.

On the Saturday following Labour's 1992 election defeat, Blair met Gordon Brown at his home in Sedgefield to discuss what the party should do next. They quickly agreed that Labour's future success depended on continuing the process of modernisation begun under Neil Kinnock but now in jeopardy with Kinnock's impending resignation from the leadership. Blair spoke directly to the Sunday papers. 'The issue for Labour today,' he told journalists, 'is not change or no change but what type of change. Nobody should be under any illusion that the route back to power can be achieved without fundamental reform of ideas and organisation.'

This message was targeted not only at those who would argue that the Kinnock reforms should be rolled back but also at others – including, they thought, Kinnock himself – who might now advocate an immediate commitment to reform of the electoral system. Blair and Brown's concern was that this would halt the momentum towards further change in the party. Whatever view the two politicians might subsequently take about proportional representation – and both let it be known at the time that they had open minds – they argued that you do not win elections by changing the rules. They were not opposed to a dialogue with other political opinion in the country, but it was imperative to build on Kinnock's achievements and turn Labour into a broad-based party of the left and centre, rather than watch it turn into a minority left-wing party that would have to rely on electoral reform to unseat the Tories.

Brown and Blair persuaded Smith, Kinnock's obvious successor, to embrace their modernising message. What was clear to the two modernisers was that, while they could continue the pressure for change – as they did – only the leader had the power to carry it out. This was an observation made in private by Blair on many occasions during the next two years as he continued his fervent advocacy of reform in the party.

Blair also pushed forward the frontiers of party policy in the front-bench post to which Smith appointed him: that of shadow home secretary.

Blair had asked for this job. Having established his credentials in economic policy, he wanted to add to his experience. He felt strongly that Labour had failed in home affairs, allowing the Conservatives to take on the mantle of those who cared about crime, the family, and law and order. It was, however, typical of him that, having got the job he thought was so urgent, he remained absolutely silent on the subject for a full three months thereafter. Indeed, in his speech at the Conservative Party conference, the home secretary, Kenneth Clarke, dubbed him 'the invisible man'. But this is a further illustration of how Blair works.

He knew it was possible to win in home affairs, but he did not know how best to do it. So he thought, analysed, and held meetings with every individual and organisation with something to contribute. He made extensive notes of all his discussions, which were carefully digested. He took advice from friends, trying out ideas and different approaches to the problems. Not until he had seen the big picture and identified the principles Labour should apply to home affairs did he make any move on policy. Even then he insisted on painting a broad canvas before filling in any detail.

Eventually Blair developed as the centrepiece of his approach on social order an analysis of the family and its role in society which enabled him to bring to fruition all his thinking about the moral purpose of politics and the importance of community which had begun nearly twenty years before in Oxford.

Blair's own family, and the sense of security it offers, is very important to him. His father's illness when he was young and his mother's death at the time he left university affected him deeply. When he became party leader he was worried more about the effect of it on his family's privacy and on his own young children than anything else, fearing the disruption of their lives and the adjustments they would all have to make to accommodate his different lifestyle. Early on in his leadership he took a controversial stand over his children's needs when he insisted that the choice of the best school for them would come before any political convenience for himself. 'I made a choice as a parent not as a politician, and I couldn't have looked at myself in the mirror in the mornings if I'd done it in any other way,' he said in an interview with the *Today* newspaper.

In addition to his wife, Cherie, and their three young children, Blair is close to his brother, Bill, and his sister, Sarah. They are a mutually supportive family and spend time together. Their father, Leo, recently marked his son's success in politics by converting to Labour from a lifetime's support for the Conservatives – a decision he says is 80 per cent due to personal pride and 20 per cent to rail privatisation.

When Blair is not working (and times in his diary are carefully kept clear so that he can spend time with his family at weekends and evenings), he is busy playing with his children and keeping up with their school and leisure activities. Swimming after church on Sunday mornings is a regular event. His own leisure time is spent reading (mainly literary classics and biographies) and watching thrillers, playing tennis and playing his guitar. Remarkably for a politician renowned for his use of the media, he does not obsessively watch the television news and he does not avidly read newspaper profiles of himself. He and Cherie have an enjoyable life outside politics, with a number of strong, long-standing friends who say that he talks to them of much besides politics and is an engaging, relaxed and funny companion (especially when he indulges his talent for mimicry).

When Blair talks about the importance of strong families, it is because he regards them as the foundation of a cohesive society and of strong communities. Britain cannot begin to tackle its endemic problem of crime and antisocial behaviour without rebuilding this firm foundation, in his view. He became critical of what he felt was many on the left's uninterest in social order and their confusion of liberation from prejudice with apparent disregard for moral structures.

Blair argues that the left-of-centre's commitment to racial and sexual equality was entirely right, but the appearance some gave of indifference to the family and to individual responsibility was wrong. From its first years in government earlier in the century, Labour had rightly placed heavy emphasis on responsibility, self-improvement and the family, and yet the party had allowed these important principles to be captured by the Tories during the early 1980s. These traditional Labour values and ways of thinking need to be reclaimed and made the basis of the party's policies.

It cannot be overstated just how much this view is at the heart of Blair's personal credo. This became clear to the public when, as shadow home secretary, he reacted to the horrific murder in February 1993 of two-year-old Jamie Bulger by two young boys. Those closest to Blair know of the profound impact the tragedy had on him, for it crystallised everything he hates about what is happening in Britain today. It was, he said, 'the ugly manifestation of a society that is becoming unworthy of that name'.

Ignoring the advice of some who urged him to hold back for fear that the brutality of the murder might foment an emotional public backlash, he spoke out further. In a speech in Wellingborough, Blair said 'a solution to this disintegration doesn't simply lie in legislation. It must come from the rediscovery of a sense of direction as a country, and most of all from being unafraid to start talking again about the values and principles we believe in and what they mean for us, not just as individuals but as a community. We cannot exist in a moral vacuum. If we do not learn and then teach the value of what is right and what is wrong, then the result is simply moral chaos which engulfs us all.'

This was a seminal speech for Blair. He was nervous about making it, as some said it might be misinterpreted as being redolent of the religious right in America, and he refined the text right up to the last minute. But he had found his voice, and more than any other speech this one defined the man and imprinted his character on the public's mind, resulting in a huge postbag of support and encouragement.

Four months later he took his argument further in a speech in Alloa on the subject of crime and the family. 'I have no doubt,' Blair told his audience, 'that the breakdown in law and order is intimately linked to the breakup of a strong sense of community. And the breakup of community in turn is, to a crucial degree, consequent on the breakdown in family life. If we want anything more than a superficial discussion on crime and its causes, we cannot ignore the importance of the family.' Talking about the rules of good conduct in society, he went on, 'The family is the first place we learn such rules. It is largely from family discipline that social discipline and a sense of responsibility is learned.' Public policy, he concluded, should help create 'the best circumstances for the family to prosper'.

Some people close to Blair argued that this area of social responsibility was not the right one to put at the centre of the party's philosophical thinking and that he was in danger of sounding Victorian and intolerant. More recently, Blair has been accused of social authoritarianism by those who believe that he has a nostalgic dream of society and family life that wants to turn back the clock on the position of women in society and that is based on a view of personal relationships which is out of touch with the modern age.

He takes this argument seriously but rejects it completely. Just because the family has changed does not mean to say that strong families have ceased to be important. He readily acknowledges that a two-parent family can have as many problems as a single-parent family, or more. It is just that, other things being equal, it is easier to do the difficult job of bringing up a child where there are two parents living happily together. And, conscious of the way in which, as two working parents, he and Cherie share family responsibilities (he is very supportive of Cherie's legal career as a QC), he stresses that the roles of the father and mother are changing and that a 'modern view of the family does not try to recreate the family of a generation ago –

father working and mother at home'.

Importantly, Blair is not a prude or a prig in his private life. He never tries to push religion on any one, and most people would never realise he goes to church every Sunday. He does not feel morally superior to those who choose to live their lives differently, and he is not judgemental about those friends who are not in conventional marriages or who are single parents, or who are gay.

He is not reactionary, but, unlike other politicians, he is not afraid to stand up for what he believes, even if that means being painted as a moral reformer. However, he hates being misrepresented by people who have not listened to his argument. He wants to see social justice alongside social order in Britain, and he is determined to campaign for it. This is not a mere vote-catching exercise: it is about redefining radical political thought in Britain and, in the process, enabling Labour to rediscover the best of its traditions and roots.

In his desire to shake up the party's thinking, Blair is comparable to another young, modernising Labour leader who came to office after the untimely death of his predecessor and spoke eloquently of creating a New Britain – Harold Wilson. But in crucial respects Wilson and Blair differ. Wilson saw his job as not to take on his party and confront its thinking but merely to unite it, even at the expense of clarity. Blair, although well aware of the electoral consequences of disunity, believes that clarity in the party's goals and principles is a precondition for success.

Labour's crisis in the early 1980s was caused by the sustained attempts by groups of activists to impose textbook ideological thinking on the party and then call for unity around their impractical policies and ideas. No amount of unity would, or should, have made these policies palatable. It would have been the unity of the graveyard. This is similar to what is happening to the Conservative Party today. The Tories' attempts to find unity around bad, fudged policies is not convincing to the public, because it is no substitute for clear, strong policies which are leading in one agreed direction.

An agent of change

In the two years following the 1992 election, Blair took risks with his popularity in the party by making uncompromising statements about internal democracy and Labour's links with the trade unions.

Blair had supported one-member-one-vote democracy ten years before, in his local constituency party, and had made the case for it in his Australian lecture. He was a strong supporter of Kinnock's recent attempts to shift voting power from local activists and the trade unions to the ordinary party membership, and attracted disapproval from Smith when he pursued the issue vigorously after Kinnock had stepped down.

The net effect of Blair's stand, however, was to expand his appeal. To many grass-roots members he was strong, fearless and unwilling to trim his views – qualities which raised his stature even among those who disagreed with him. He always expressed his opinions in a courteous, reasonable way, addressing the public's concerns as he did so, but taking care to use arguments that would also maximise support for his ideas in the party. He came across as an easy, approachable person, not a particularly self-centred or publicity-grabbing politician. Although he has never been a very clubbable figure in the House of Commons, Blair has always mixed happily with colleagues from very different backgrounds to his own. He is as good a listener as he is a talker, and overall he established a reputation for being a strong team player – someone who did not see himself as a one-man band and who could disagree with colleagues without making enemies of them.

This counted for a lot when Labour's popular leader John Smith tragically died in May 1994. This sad and unexpected event immediately put the media spotlight on Blair, who subsequently described it as 'a moment of bleak despair and inconsolable loss'. Within hours, and to an extent that took everyone, including him, by surprise, opinion in Westminster was talking of Blair as the most suitable successor. Tory MPs in conversation with political journalists spoke of Blair as the opponent they feared most. Some Labour MPs, following the same train of thought, said that he was the candidate most likely to win votes in the South, where Labour needs to pick up seats.

If the succession had been decided under the party's old rules, by the electoral college which gave the trade-union general secretaries huge influence, it is unlikely that Blair would have won. But, following the change in rules agreed the year before, he won the contest with strong support from the newly enfranchised individual members of the party, who wanted a modern voice to speak for them. 'He was more human, he talked about how our personal ambitions and aspirations needn't be in contradiction with our principles,' one young party member had remarked after hearing Blair talk to a group before he became leader. Blair won a convincing victory, with 57 per cent of the total vote against 24 per cent.

The party wanted to be led by someone whose views they could respect and follow, and whom they believed the public would back. They did not put Blair into the leadership because he lacked firm political beliefs and convictions but, on the contrary, because he had strong views on every aspect of policy and had expressed them with clarity and firmness.

It is, however, a reasonable question to ask whether, in voting for Blair as leader, the party was doing so because it agreed with him or was merely going along with him to win the election. The answer is that he had strong personal appeal and popularity in the party but others, at the time, did not agree with his radical modernising views; if asked to vote for his ideas rather than the man, some would not have done so. Agreement with Blair grew after he had become leader, as far-reaching debate about change in the party took place and as over 100,000 joined Labour following his election. This transformation is discussed in Chapter 9. Significantly, on every occasion that party members have had the chance to express their opinion about Blair's changes, they have chosen to back him.

The most outstanding and significant of these changes has been the decision to rewrite Clause IV of the party's constitution. More than any thing else, this change demonstrates that Labour rejects its past as a seemingly anti-private-sector, class-based, trade-union party.

In its original wording, agreed in 1918, Clause IV committed the party to 'secure for the workers by hand or by brain the full fruits of their industry . . . upon the basis of the common ownership of the means of production, distribution and exchange'. This has always been understood in the Labour Party to imply full nationalisation of the economy, and, however hard the clause's defenders tried to argue that it did not mean state ownership of everything down to the local garage and corner shop, it was difficult to see it in any other way.

The new wording agreed to replace this commitment, in stark contrast, embraces the 'enterprise of the market and the rigour of competition' in an economy in which there is 'a thriving private sector and high-quality public services'. Arguably, this is always what Labour governments have worked for, yet in the revised wording the party has stripped away the ambiguity surrounding its commitment to a market economy and has demonstrated an understanding of what is required in order for a modern economy to work both efficiently and fairly in the public interest.

Why did Blair attach such importance to changing the party's constitution when it can be argued that Labour's policies and deeds speak more eloquently than a set of words?

For Blair, Clause IV was not a harmless anachronism: it created a split identity for the party, tying it to an outdated and redundant economic doctrine which had long ceased to have any relevance to the party's thinking or policy. It prevented the party from proclaiming clearly what it did stand for, and it confused the voters about Labour's intentions and gave a huge potential propaganda weapon to the Tories. For Labour's new leader, rewriting Clause IV was indispensable to his mission to create a fresh agenda for the left and centre in British politics.

After he won the leadership, Blair lost no time in raising the issue with those closest to him. 'We've got to demonstrate that New Labour is more than a mere slogan beneath which nothing has changed,' he said to one. People were very cautious. He was warned by one intimate with a knowledge of the party that if he attempted to scrap the hallowed words he risked being defeated and worse: 'It could bring the house down around your ears.' After all, Clause IV was a totem for many on the left of the party – or so it was thought. But Blair had made up his mind. The party should no longer live with the old Clause IV, and what he wanted to know was how, not whether, to get rid of it.

This was typical of Blair's decision-making. He has an idea or vision about which he becomes firm and persistent. The suggestion that Blair's actions are dictated by media-handlers and spin doctors amuses those who are regularly on the receiving end of his instructions and strictures. He will, of course, consult – getting points and suggestions from others – but he is invariably confident of his own overall judgement.

He thinks through a strategy to be implemented, and then expects the agreed plan to be carried out to the letter by those who work for him. He believes detail is important, even though he does not feel the need to involve himself in it at every stage. At the same time, he will start to forge a consensus around his view by talking individually to key players. He sees handling the media as an essential part of doing the job, explaining to the public and party what he is doing and why. On important speeches he is likely to talk directly to influential journalists himself, and all the time he will be thinking about and reviewing his tactics.

On Clause IV, Blair knew that his leadership was on the line.

One morning in January 1995, following the autumn party conference at which Blair had announced his proposal to change the constitution, he summoned key members of his staff and others from the Labour headquarters at Walworth Road, including Tom Sawyer, the party's new general secretary. He had been alarmed by an outburst of opposition to his plans from a group of Labour Euro-MPs and by a survey (which later turned out to be bogus) in the left-wing *Tribune* publication which suggested that 90 per cent of local constituency parties were hostile to the change. The Tory vultures were circling. He felt he could not be absolutely confident of a convincing win at the special party conference called to decide the matter on 29 April, and, while he was satisfied there was no credible intellectual defence for the old constitution, he did not want to get a disappointing result through bad organisation.

He ordered a high-profile crusade for change to be mounted in every part of the country. What's more, he decided to lead it himself, and his diary for the next three months was cleared for the purpose. The Blair machine was put on action stations. Everyone was drawn into the Clause IV effort – arranging meetings, writing speech material, liaising with party staff, organising travel, and gathering information about opinion in the trade unions and the constituency parties. In addition, voluntary groups and campaigners were encouraged to organise in favour of the change, and a New Clause IV Campaign was set up in an office in Vauxhall across the Thames.

Blair's aim was simple: to make a virtue of saying the same in public as he was saying in private to the party. He wanted to win support because of Labour's beliefs, not despite them. To win the trust of the voters, he insisted, Labour had to be honest and it had to stop looking all ways, talking in double-speak, with one message for party consumption and another for the public. There was room for only one Labour Party.

Behind the scenes, some of the trade-union leaders and others on the 'soft' left who wanted to water down the constitutional change were coming to Blair with proposals to weaken its language. Blair heard them out, but he knew his own mind on the subject. A particularly contentious part of the proposed draft was the reference to the 'rigour of competition'. Blair regarded these and other words as a crucial test of New Labour's seriousness: Labour either wanted a properly functioning and successful market economy or it did not. The time for fudging was over – Blair insisted that the words go in.

On 29 April, Blair's crusade paid off. A number of the unions – led by the Transport Workers and the public-sector union Unison – refused to go along with him and voted to keep the old pro-nationalisation clause. They had hinted that if Blair met their request to set an early figure for the party's proposed national minimum wage they might be more amenable over changing Clause IV. Even though Blair was not assured of the final outcome, he said he was not interested in any sort of deal: they would agree on his terms or not at all. These unions went their way, and Blair won without them – but with the overwhelming support of the individual grass-roots members of the party. The significance of this for the long-term influence of the trade unions inside the party was not lost on anyone, and, shortly after, the unions agreed to a substantial reduction of their voting strength at future party conferences.

The final vote on Clause IV provided an important answer to the question of whether the party is at one with its leader. In the ballots of ordinary party members that were held throughout the country the margin was a massive nine to one in favour of change. Blair did not believe his staff at first when they came to him with the early returns. It was a good reward for his eloquence and party-management skills, and the best possible demonstration that there was a genuinely new Labour Party.

Nothing infuriates Blair more than London-based journalists purporting to offer insights into a Labour Party they have little contact with and claiming that the grass roots have no sympathy for his changes. Manifestly, he has always been ahead of his party, and his times. But the vote on Clause IV showed that Labour's political opponents could no longer argue that Blair was simply imposing change on a reluctant party – the individual members had made their own choice. It could not be said that Blair had got his way by forcing through the change by means of the unions' block vote – two of the largest unions had opposed him (without, it should be said, balloting their own members on the issue). And nobody could claim that Blair had failed to win by argument – he had taken his case to the party membership and had won, speaking directly to over 30,000 people: one in ten of the party membership.

After the event, Blair was asked what he had learned from the experience. 'Labour is nicer than it looks. I didn't really know it before I took over,' was his typically honest response. In his crusade, Blair had rediscovered a party of ordinary, decent men and women (in many ways the old Labour Party) who had been obscured by the more dogmatic, activist-driven culture that had taken over the party in the early 1980s.

Equally important, the Clause IV experience was instructive for the grass roots of the party. Those members who had regarded Blair as a bit of a stranger in their midst had learned to like him and respect his sincerity, and, once they had got used to his amazingly frank way of dealing with them, most accepted his analysis of what Labour needed to do. (At one meeting when a weary member asked him if they could have a rest from constant change and turmoil, Blair replied with a straight no. 'Change', he said, 'never stops.') Clare Short, Blair's close colleague on the National Executive and shadow cabinet, has observed that since the beginning of his leadership, when many party members were unsure what drove him, greater contact with Blair has revealed his substance and his humour.

Blair's deputy, John Prescott, played a key role in changing Clause IV. In a country of rather dull, grey, regimented politicians, Prescott is a welcome contrast and a popular asset to the party.

No doubt some Conservatives like Prescott because they think he puts off floating voters, and, to reinforce this, Tory-supporting newspapers like to present him as old-fashioned, heavy-handed and out of sympathy with Blair and the modernisation of the party. In reality, Prescott is very interested in policy and receptive to new ideas – as his early embrace of public-private financing of investment demonstrates – and Blair respects his intelligence and courage. Prescott has a strong instinct for public opinion, and, although he sometimes underestimates what the party will accept, he has given important backing to Blair's changes. When Blair sought advice about the handling of Clause IV in his conference speech, Prescott said if he was going to tackle it he should be blunt and honest, and the text was changed to make it clearer.

Blair was more nervous throughout the Clause IV change than in any other period of his leadership. He steels himself for big occasions such as important speeches, and has great self-discipline and control in preparing for them, carefully gathering ideas from trusted staff and advisers. But he will sometimes feel daunted at the enormity of the challenges ahead, and he can become either discouraged or irritated when he feels that colleagues are not putting their personal concerns and vanities aside in the wider interests of the party. He is not a particularly vain or egocentric politician himself, and he does not take proper account of how ego drives others in politics.

In these respects, Blair is not a typical politician. He does not really enjoy the *modus operandi*. He often forgets that the sort of relationships he had when practising as a barrister at the Bar – open and straight-dealing – are rare in politics. His style is to explain what he wants to do, to listen to others' opinions, to reach a conclusion, and then expect everyone to be faithful to it. But politics is not as simple as that. Getting your way can require a degree of intrigue and manoeuvring he would prefer was unnecessary. Sometimes in a discussion in which he feels people are not being open and direct enough he will simply lose patience and, in a swift summary, tell those present what they need to decide; he will then despatch them to get on with it.

Blair is keen to see the best in people, but he is also forthright and can be surprisingly brutal when he has to be. To one front-bencher who brought to him a voluminous policy paper packed with detail, he said it had everything in it bar the main points and the big picture and that it needed totally rewriting. But he does not enjoy such personal confrontations. In government he knows he will have to show less sentimentality, and his colleagues know that he will do so.

In opposition it is sometimes possible to get round difficult issues by skilful use of words, whereas in government you would have to say yes or no. In reading a biography of Henry Campbell-Bannerman, Blair was struck by the former premier's fearless ability to offend public opinion as well as court it. He said this offered an important model for other statesmen: having the qualities to lead a party should not be confused with the decisiveness needed to undertake leadership of the country. This is discussed further in Chapter 8.

As his career to date shows, Blair is not afraid to take controversial stands, and, together with such key colleagues as David Blunkett, Robin Cook, Harriet Harman and Jack Straw, he has reshaped Labour policy-making in ways that have brought howls from different quarters. His insistence on higher classroom standards and school performance has sparked criticism from the teachers' unions. His challenge on efficiency and value for money in the public services has been attacked by some professionals – notably in the NHS. In other sensitive areas of public opinion – for example, on race and on Europe – he has taken unequivocal positions where other politicians have been tempted to prevaricate or keep quiet.

If you asked Blair what sort of prime minister he would want to be remembered as, he would say one who, through a revitalised political system, has made a deep improvement to the education system; whose government has helped to create more British world-class companies; who has modernised the welfare system, tackling long-term unemployment; and who has given Britain a leading role in Europe.

He intends to be both a radical and a tough premier – one in the Lloyd George mould (but without the Welsh wizard's personal shortcomings). Speaking to Rupert Murdoch's News Corporation in July 1995, Blair said, 'We are ready to take on outdated attitudes that hold us back in a way that the Conservatives are not.' A short time after this, Blair encountered a friendly but sceptical journalist who challenged him on the seriousness of his anti-establishment credentials. 'If you think I'm not a radical, you're wrong,' Blair insisted. 'You can judge our success after five years in government, and that will just be the start.'

He wants to get things done, as Attlee and Thatcher also did in their different ways. Despite the enormous difference between the social goals of Thatcherism and those of the 1945 Labour government, there was one quality which these premiers had in common and which proved a decisive strength in both cases: a rock-hard determination not to revert to what were seen as the disastrous mistakes of their predecessors. Blair also has that quality. He becomes angry when critics say either that he does not want to make a real difference to people's lives – because he is not a 'real' socialist – or that he cannot make a big difference, because governments have little freedom of manoeuvre to do so in the modern world. He believes, for example, that it is possible to tackle long-term and youth unemployment, and he is determined that his government will do so. He believes Britain's educational performance can be transformed, and this too will be a landmark achievement of a Blair government.

Of course limitations exist, and Blair is the first to acknowledge the constraints of the international economy and those on any government's freedom to tax and spend. But he insists that it is still possible to make a fundamental difference within these constraints, and it is his vision of a 'young' country that can grow economically strong and of One Nation that is socially united which he believes will sustain Labour through the difficult years of government.

Making sure the mistakes of the past and of other left-of-centre governments are not repeated, ensuring that the party in the country sustains a Labour government, and changing the machinery of government to deliver its programme are the final ingredients of the Blair revolution.

To those who say that someone like him – who has never run anything bigger than his own office – could not run the country, he replies that he will do for the country what he has already done for his party: change it, make it work better, and never take no for an answer. He has carried out huge reforms to create New Labour, and he will do what ever is needed to carry out the necessary reforms to build New Britain, without accepting second-best. What this will involve is the subject of the rest of this book.

3

Economic Challenges

Taking chances

Picture a council estate in middle Britain, spaciously laid out in the 1950s, in those far-off Macmillan days when the Conservatives' proudest boast was that they had built more homes for rent than Nye Bevan had managed as housing minister in the previous Labour government. In the 1980s this estate had been transformed by Margaret Thatcher's 'right to buy' policy. The standardised green paint had disappeared. Every third house or so had made its own gesture to break the previous dull uniformity: a stuccoed front, a porch and double glazing to protect against the winter gales, or, for the more adventurous, a garage extension with an extra bedroom on top.

The council estate was in Bletchley – a Buckinghamshire concoction of old railway centre and London overspill that had once provided the electoral base for the late Robert Maxwell's brief service in Parliament, and is now part of Milton Keynes new town. It was in one of its more flamboyant driveways that Bill Andrews was explaining to a 1987 general-election canvasser why this time he was going to vote for Margaret Thatcher.

Though originally from the East End, Bill had been a lifelong trade-unionist in the local railway works at Wolverton. He had switched his vote from Labour to the SDP in 1983 because of the 'loony left', but this time there would be no halfway house. 'I've got sympathy for people who've lost their jobs. But things couldn't go on as they were. The fact is she's done all right by me – she's given us a chance to buy our own home, which we'd never have had under anybody else.'

Bill then pointed to a van parked on the road, advertising the electrical-repair services of his son, Chris. 'Because of owning the house, we were able to borrow a bit of money to help get him going.' At this moment Chris appeared, with his own version of his father's Cockney self-confidence and breezy charm. Seeing the canvasser's rosette, he smiled: 'Don't waste your time, mate. I'm a Tory. They're the ones who help people like me go out and get on.'

The Andrews were not alone in thinking that. In an area where, at the height of Harold Wilson's popularity, Labour could confidently have expected to win 80 per cent of the votes, in 1987 there was a fairly even three-way split of support. No wonder that, when you added in the more up-market districts of the constituency, the Conservatives could look forward to a large majority.

What will have happened to Bill and Chris and the thousands like them since that encounter on a June afternoon nine years ago? Bill will now be in his early sixties. He will be lucky if he is still in work, because, although according to the official statistics only 6 per cent of men aged fifty-five to sixty-four are unemployed, an extraordinary 38 per cent of the age group are 'economically inactive' – unemployed, retired, registered as long-term sick, or disabled – over a million men in all. Yet with luck Bill and his wife still have nearly a quarter-century of life to look forward to.

Will the older Andrews family be looking forward to a long retirement with enjoyment or with fear? Will there be enough money – and for how long – to keep up the touring holidays, the weekly trips to the hairdresser, the odd night out, and to buy nice presents for the grandchildren? Will they be able to leave them that little bit of money which makes all the difference to a flying start in life? And what about their own old age, when Bill, perhaps, is left on his own and is increasingly unable to look after himself? Won't he be a terrible burden on his Chris and his family? Worst of all, what happens if work forces Chris's family to move away?

People in the Andrews' position will be better off than many. They will have paid off their mortgage. They may well have some occupational pension – approaching 60 per cent of pensioners now do – but manual workers of Bill's generation are likely to have joined a pension scheme late, and the eventual benefit will therefore be small. They may have a nest egg of a few thousand pounds from a redundancy payment or some other lump sum; but they know that as long as they hang on to this money in the building society it will restrict their eligibility later in life for means-tested benefits and income support, and will bring that great new dread: the prospect of having to pay bills for long-term residential care. Others in their street claim these income-related benefits, and the Andrews know that some of them – not all, mind you – haven't worked as hard or been as careful as them. 'I don't mind the money going to those who deserve it,' Bill had said on that June afternoon, 'but too many people know how to work the system.'

And what about Chris? His infant electrical-repair business will have been lucky to survive the early 1990s. A total of 238,807 businesses went bankrupt or were liquidated between 1990 and 1994, compared with 175,163 in the whole of the previous decade. Of new businesses registered for VAT in the last half of the 1980s, only a third are still registered. Barclays have kept a record of what happened to new business accounts opened in the boom year of 1988: by 1995 fewer than a quarter were still active. The recession had taken a heavy toll.

It would be monstrously unfair to put the blame on Chris himself if he had overextended himself in the late 1980s: after all, the government was then boasting of an economic miracle and dismissing the warning signs of inflationary trouble as only a temporary blip.

Contentment or insecurity?

Five years later, in the 1992 general election, picture a similar scene in a mixed Hertfordshire constituency – a collection of former industrial towns set in a strongly Tory rural hinterland, yet where in 1964 Labour's Shirley Williams had won her first seat in Parliament. In the 1970s and 1980s rail electrification and motorways had moved the whole area up-market. Owner-occupied housing estates had mushroomed on the edge of the towns, and a new supermarket seemed to have sprung up at every major roundabout – with a damaging effect on the economy of the old, attractive town centres.

The Stephensons lived in one of the 1980s matchbox private estates – far more densely packed, inside and out, than the working-class housing for rent of the Macmillan era. Steve and Jane had two young children, then aged four and two. Steve was a salesman selling industrial detergents round the workshops of East Anglia. Many of his customers had gone bust in the recession. Some struggled on, making orders, but were reluctant to settle invoices. Getting money out of the customers was like getting blood out of a stone – but you had to be careful about stopping their supplies, otherwise you might lose them to your competitors for ever. Sadly for Steve, much of his pay packet came in the form of commission – to give an 'incentive'.

Steve had looked hard for a new job, and a possibility had come up in Basingstoke. The problem was the impossibility of moving from the home which they had bought in 1989 for what then seemed a bargain price of £69,000 but which the local estate agent had breezily assured them might now make just over £50,000 – because they'd looked after it nicely and it was well positioned at the end of the close. After all, the housing market had never been like this before and, as if a law of nature had been affronted, it was bound to pick up before long – or so the estate agent claimed. Unfortunately, these words of intended comfort were rather lost on the Stephensons; with a mortgage of £65,000, plus another £5,000 they'd taken out in loans for the furniture and carpets, they were completely stuck. 'It's negative equity, you know,' Steve explained, with the authority of someone who has mastered a technical phrase of uncertain meaning. So moving to a better life had been ruled out.

To cope with the family's reduced income caused by the recession, Jane had gone back to work. Before motherhood, she had been a midwife at the local hospital. But the only way it had made economic sense for her to return to work meant they had to avoid incurring childcare costs, which the family simply could not afford. So Jane had arranged it – using the famed flexibility that part-time work offers – so that she would work a regular four nights a week as an NHS midwife. 'It works out very convenient really, because I only go to work after Steve has returned home' – when, after his long day's travelling, he puts the children to bed.

During the week Jane had to look after the children during the day before going out to work a ten-hour shift at night: 'It's not too bad really. I manage odd snatches of sleep while the kids are watching television – and when they're at the playgroup, it's a godsend. Mind you, the money we have to pay for the play-group means we can no longer afford to pay for a babysitter to go out on a Saturday night.' As in most 'shires' that have until recently enjoyed the supposed benefits of virtually permanent Conservative administration, local-authority-provided nursery classes were very scarce and hard to get into.

One might imagine that Jane, as a midwife, would have been strongly against the Conservative government – because she was a very strong believer in the NHS. But in fact her real political anxieties were all directed at Labour. 'We just can't afford to risk Labour. Families like us just couldn't manage. Any increase in the tax we have to pay and we'll go completely under.'

Shortly after the 1992 election, Professor J. K. Galbraith, the doyen of American political economists, published *The Culture of Contentment*. This analysed the dilemma of progressives as being the problem that a contented two-thirds of the population would no longer vote for redistributive taxation to help the deprived and increasingly excluded one-third. Whatever the rel-evance of this view in the USA, when one reflects on the circum-stances of couples like the Stephensons it seems a bizarre way of describing the central questions facing the left-of-centre in Britain. The reasons why the Stephensons rejected Labour in 1992 were to do more with insecurity than with contentment.

On any statistical analysis, the Stephensons would firmly belong in Britain's 'contented' two-thirds: they were together, both in work (as 65 per cent of UK couples are), and owned or had a mortgage on their own home (as 68 per cent of UK fami-lies do). These are substantial advantages by comparison with the one in ten couples of working age where neither the man nor the woman is in work, and with those households that account for the estimate that one-third of all children are brought up in poverty.

So should the Stephensons' belief that they simply could not afford to pay more tax be condemned as the selfish attitude of people who care little for those in less fortunate positions than themselves? This is so often the knee-jerk response of those who believe, perhaps from a more comfortable vantage point, that higher taxes are the automatic answer to society's problems. The reality is that the Stephensons lived by their own version of altruism. They were prepared to make considerable personal sacrifices to keep their family together and give their children a chance in life. They were strong supporters of public services such as the NHS and nursery education, which they wanted to see improved. In those social surveys where people are asked whether they would be prepared to pay more tax in return for better health, education and social services, they would almost certainly have answered in the affirmative – because in principle that was their view. But they simply could not afford to pay more tax at that time. They did not see how they could make their money stretch any further.

The truth is that the Stephensons, like millions of others today, were the victims of insecurity. To have a job is not the same as to have a secure job with a secure income.

But insecurity also affected the Stephensons in another way. To have a mortgage is no longer the same thing as having a secure home of your own.

Mortgage arrears rose dramatically throughout the last recession and are still at historically high levels. Reputable mortgage lenders exercised great restraint on repossessions, but the fact is that unprecedented numbers of mortgagees lost their homes. Repossessions rose remorselessly, and at the end of 1992 over 350,000 families had mortgage arrears of more than six months. In June 1995, despite three years of recovery, arrears still stood at a historically high 210,000. The homes standing empty on many new estates in the early 1990s served as bleak warnings to families like the Stephensons who were struggling to keep up their mortgage payments. And negative equity made it impossible to trade down or to move to a cheaper part of the country.

Estimates vary of the continued extent of negative equity, with the argument being made that the surrender value of mortgage endowment policies offsets the loss of wealth that many households have suffered. In its August 1995 *Quarterly Bulletin*, the Bank of England estimated that 925,000 households had negative equity, valued in total at £4.3 billion – an average of about £5,000. It remains a major problem for those who took out their first mortgage as the housing market was rising towards the peak of the Lawson boom.

The Stephensons were also victims of something else: ruthlessly skilful Conservative propaganda convincing them that an incoming Labour government would load extra tax on to them. As we now know, it is the Conservatives who have targeted increased tax on ordinary families. The total impact of Tory tax increases since the 1992 election has made a typical family like the Stephensons some £17.50 a week worse off, and the 1995 Budget relieved a mere £2 per week of that extra burden.

Fit to compete?

Not far away Phil Jones still lived with his parents on a pre-war council estate. At the time of the 1992 general election he had been unemployed for eighteen months. But at one stage his prospects had looked a lot brighter.

On leaving school at sixteen he had got a labouring job at one of the local aerospace factories. Under the Tories the defence industry had done very well in the first half of the 1980s. The big expansion of defence spending, which rose by a fifth in real terms in the Conservatives' first seven years of office, was a rare example of the success of trickle-down – in this case to the local economies that were heavily dependent on defence industries (and ironically, of course, public-expenditure-led). But with the defence cutbacks of the late 1980s, confirmed by the end of the Cold War, firms like BAe had begun to shed labour. In the first rounds of redundancies they asked for volunteers – and there were plenty of eager takers at the start. But Phil had been made redundant after all the volunteers had gone. 'It was a case of last in, first out – that was how the unions ran it,' he said, without obvious complaint.

After a short break, Phil had obtained a place on a government training scheme. Initially he was enthusiastic about this, having watched all those snazzy Employment Training adverts on the television. He said sharply, 'I've no time for those professional scroungers in the JobCentre queue, and I hate being lumped together with them.'

It was about this time that he and his girlfriend would have liked a place of their own. With his parents' big family, they were all on top of each other at home, and he kept having rows with his girlfriend's father, who didn't like him staying round at their place. But private renting was too expensive, and getting a mortgage was out of the question while he didn't have a steady job. 'When we got engaged, we put our names down for the council, but God knows how long we'll have to wait.' But the question of housing was secondary to getting a job sorted out.

The government training course had not matched his expectations. He described it as useless, and when it finished all that was available was a lot of dead-end jobs in small local outfits. He took one as storekeeper in a firm that made plastic mouldings on subcontract to a major packaging manufacturer: 'But the pay was pathetic, and the gaffer treated me like dirt. It was a leading nowhere. I want a chance to prove myself – but I'm not going back on some lousy training scheme, and I'm not going to take a bum job.' So Phil was now back on the dole. It emerged in conversation that he was a keen radio ham, but no one had ever guided him as to how this interest might be put to career benefit.

Given his background and experiences, Phil seemed an obvious anti-Tory in the 1992 election. In fact, however, because he was disillusioned with all politics and politicians. Phil doubted whether he would even bother to go along to the polls.

Britain is a country full of frustrated talents like Phil Jones. There is a crisis of employment opportunity which is particularly acute for low-skilled men. Take the age group between the ages of twenty-five and fifty-five. Of low-skilled men who left school without qualifications, more than a quarter were not in employment in 1992, compared with only 5.7 per cent twenty years earlier. The comparable 1992 figure for the highly educated – those with two years' higher education or the equivalent – was less than one in ten.

Economists argue about the reasons for this collapse of job prospects for the unskilled. Is it the impact of low-wage competition from the emerging industrial nations? At present a relatively small proportion of our trade is vulnerable to this type of competition, though its impact will obviously increase as Asia struggles free from poverty and the former communist world learns how to beat free-market capitalism at its own game. Or are the dismal prospects for the unskilled the result of new technology which eliminates the need for low-skill jobs? This may be true of certain activities, and with technical advance fewer people have to work physically hard. But, in a world of continuing economic growth, new technology makes goods and services cheaper to produce and, as a result, increases consumer purchasing power – which should generate new jobs in other spheres, such as services. And given that these are general arguments that should apply equally to all Western countries, why should the unskilled in Britain have suffered to such a disproportionate extent?

For low-skilled men aged between 25 and 55, in Sweden the recorded unemployment rate in 1991 (the last year for which fully comparative figures are available) was 3.9 per cent; in Italy it was 5.4 per cent, in Germany 6.2 per cent, in France 10.6 per cent, in the United States 11 per cent, in Spain 16.7 per cent, and in the UK 17.4 per cent.

Phil's experience of the difficulty of returning to work once a job has been lost is by no means untypical, and the problem is particularly acute for the long-term unemployed. Less than a third of all new jobs that people take involve full-time permanent work; over half are part-time or temporary jobs. The proportion of the workforce in self-employment, part-time work, temporary jobs and government job schemes rose from 17 per cent in 1975 to 25 per cent in 1993. There is no obvious ladder of escape from redundancy to retraining to re-employment. Rather, once people lose a secure job, many are condemned to a half-world of unsatisfactory work, low pay and continual insecurity.

These figures would make less depressing reading if one were confident that the employment position of succeeding generations was likely to improve as a result of closing the skill gap and creating more job opportunities. But the picture here is mixed.

The proportion of each age group undergoing higher education has grown from one in eight at the end of the 1970s to nearly one in three in 1994 – a graduation rate that is double that in France and Germany but still less than in the United States and Japan, never mind the explosive appetite for learning which the emerging countries of Asia display. However there are doubts about quality in our emerging higher-education system –

the appropriateness of courses and the effectiveness of university teaching.

Staying-on rates at school and participation rates in further education have also risen, although in 1994 nearly one in three seventeen-year-olds was still not following any kind of course of study, part-time or full-time: an improvement on the situation a decade ago, but nowhere near as dramatic as the rise in the numbers studying for degrees. There is an enormous gap to be closed between ourselves and other European countries, particularly in vocational qualifications. In 1987 60 per cent of the UK manufacturing workforce – after the early 1980s shake-out – had no qualifications of any kind. The equivalent figure for Germany was 29 per cent.

For Phil Jones's younger brothers and sisters, Britain still offers fewer opportunities than elsewhere. This is largely the result of lower levels of attainment in basic education. In 1994 only a third of pupils gained a GCSE grade A–C in all three of English, maths and a science subject.

Britain's economic problems today

We have seen why ordinary people feel badly let down by the experience of the last decade or more – and rightly so. They feel bewildered about what, if anything, can be done to improve things, and are highly sceptical of most 'quack' political solutions. What should all this tell politicians?

The starting-point of any effective political programme must be to listen to ordinary people's experience. And what is the essence of the concerns that ordinary people are voicing? First, it has to be recognised that, for the majority, life is a hard struggle to keep their heads above the water. So moralistic lectures about selfishness won't wash. Don't go on about the only way to achieve a better life being by ordinary people paying out a lot more of their own scarce money in even higher taxes in order to solve their and other people's problems. Families on average earnings and below gained only a small share of the bonanza of income-tax cuts in the 1980s, offset by the extra they had to pay in National Insurance and VAT. These same families have borne the heaviest burden of the sharp tax rises in the 1990s. Of course everybody wants decent public services, and people are willing to help those who deserve help, but politicians must convince them that the benefits are real and that the money will be well spent.

Secondly, politicians must address the concerns of the broad majority: job insecurity, housing worries, lack of opportunities for education and training, the breakdown of society. Of course there are groups with special problems that need to be tackled, but don't think you can solve the problems of deprived minorities at the expense of the hardworking majority of the population. And recognise that most people – however difficult their personal circumstances objectively may be – want to think of themselves as part of the mainstream majority.

Thirdly, don't talk the about the government doing things *for* people – 'creating' employment, 'guaranteeing' jobs. The public is pretty sceptical about whether governments can in practice do any of these things, or at least do them well. Rather, politicians should concentrate on giving people the chance to do things for themselves: to gain new skills, to work on their own behalf and that of the local community, to build their own businesses, to make the most of new opportunities. Give people the power to control their own lives.

Fourthly, the experience of ordinary people who have to deal with 'the welfare state' on a daily basis is rather different from that of theorists who wax idealistic about it without having much personal contact with the way it works. The welfare state is in need of a thoroughgoing shake-up.

Fifthly, there is an all-pervasive sense of individual insecurity: Will I get a job when I've finished training or higher education? How secure is my existing job? For how long can I expect to earn a decent salary? How will I cope with a long retirement and declining health?

So what are the main economic challenges facing Britain today?

Challenge One: Stability in the economy and foundations for growth
The first challenge must be to end the excessive instability from which Britain's economy has suffered and to provide the necessary foundations for sustainable growth.

The degree of volatility in the British economy has been far greater than in the economy of any comparable country.

Boom and bust has been as disastrous for families as it has been for business. During the mid and late 1980s the unsustainable leap forward in living-standards during the Lawson boom persuaded millions of British families to take on commitments which they thought they could afford but, as it turned out, they could not. Personal hardship, mortgage arrears, negative equity and higher taxes were among the prices that had to be paid as the government let people down.

Similarly, businesses, both large and small, formulated expansion plans on the basis of a growth in demand that simply could not be sustained. This has gravely damaged business confidence and the willingness to invest for the long term. This is turn reinforces the constraints that lack of capacity places on sustainable growth and also the inflationary risks of expansion. New Labour needs to pursue a twin-track strategy – firm macro-economic policies to avoid any repetition of boom and bust, combined with imaginative micro-economic policies to promote industrial modernisation, investment and entrepreneurship

Challenge Two: Competitiveness and partnership in a stakeholding economy
The second challenge is to promote competitiveness and support good companies through building stronger partnerships between government and industry, business and all its stakeholders, managers and employees.

There has been inadequate investment of the quality that Britain needs. Too many British companies are not up to the standard of the best. And we need a new generation of entrepreneurs to fill the gap created as our world-class companies increasingly focus their attention on opportunities overseas.

The Conservatives half acknowledge these problems but are constrained in their ability to tackle them by out-of-date *laissez-faire* notions of the role of government in the economy, which are prevalent on the Tory right, and by a reluctance to embrace a modern concept of partnership between business and the wider community and between employers and employees. The road to competitiveness and higher living-standards lies through adding value, encouraging enterprise and investment and promoting modernisation and partnership, not through selling bargain-basement goods at cheap-labour prices.

Challenge Three: Using talents and opportunities

The third challenge is to use the talents of all and create opportunities that the millions who presently lack them would be prepared to work for.

This is obviously relevant to many of the unemployed, but not just to them. The two largest problems Britain faces are what to do about the crisis of unemployment among low-skilled men, and how to ensure for the next and succeeding generations that the levels of education and skill found in other countries are attained by an equal (and if possible higher) proportion of young people here.

Our education and training, while serving the needs of an academic élite, fails to equip the broad majority for a world of increasingly rapid change. Despite recent improvements, we are still way behind our competitors in this respect.

Challenge Four: Removing barriers to work

The fourth challenge is to break down the barriers to work by reforming the welfare state and tackling hard-core long-term unemployment.

Long-term unemployment destroys people's lives. Lack of opportunity blights them. Unemployment is the breeding-ground of apathy and despair. It corrodes society. It fosters drug abuse and crime. It keeps taxes high to pay the resulting costs of social security, and prevents improvements in other public services. While the Conservatives would prefer that these problems were hidden from the general public's view, New Labour is compelled to search for fresh solutions – for reasons of economic efficiency, social cohesion and moral conviction.

The present operation of the welfare state does not live up to its ideals. The complex web of means-tested benefits weakens incentives. It has created a new division between families: the work-rich, where both partners go out and earn, and the work-poor, who see no point in trying. Instead of fulfilling the original Beveridge aim of helping people through periods of temporary adversity, today's welfare state too often traps people in long-term dependency.

Challenge Five: Fairer taxation and reformed public expenditure
The fifth challenge is to make the tax system fairer and to change public-expenditure priorities, while recognising that New Labour has to work within acceptable limits of taxation and spending.

New Labour has firm priorities for action which clearly distinguish its approach from that of the Conservatives – modernisation and investment; radical change in the standards of education and training; reform of social security; and a bold attempt to tackle long-term unemployment. But it must avoid simplistic solutions which only add to the tax burden.

So, now we have explained the Conservatives' failure and listed the challenges facing the British economy today, what does New Labour have to offer?

4

Delivering Prosperity

The essential foundations of stability

Let us be clear about why New Labour emphasises macro-economic stability. It is not just to offer the electorate reassurance (though this may be necessary, given the public's lingering memories of the 1970s). It is because of principled objections to high inflation and the economic and social havoc it wreaks.

Inflation leads to recession as night leads to day. High inflation would revive excessive pay demands, engender feelings of desperation among groups left behind, and sooner or later stir up industrial conflict.

The return of inflation would also be deeply unfair to the most vulnerable, which is why no one on the left of centre should tolerate it. Inflation drives the weak to the wall, to the advantage of those who have bargaining power in the economy: entrenched monopolies as well as powerful unions. It destroys the value of small savings – the pensioner's modest, hard-earned, carefully preserved nest egg in a building society – even if the financially astute know how to protect themselves against loss.

Periodic surges in inflation have been largely responsible for the UK's poor industrial performance. They have made inevitable the roller-coaster of stop-go, which has made it difficult for companies to plan ahead, to invest and grow, without undertaking unacceptable commercial risks. Without long-term price stability there will be no sustainable investment and growth. And we have not had stability.

Avoidable errors of policy magnified the impact of the two Conservative recessions. Britain is still paying the price for the catastrophic mistakes of the early 1980s. Back in the Conservatives' first days in office, the doubling of VAT raised inflationary expectations at the same time as monetary policy was being tightened in order to depress them – with a consequent unnecessarily large cost in lost output and jobs. This was then exacer-

bated by the prime minister's determination to keep interest
rates high in order to pursue the dogmatic goal of controlling
the money supply: excessively high interest rates aggravated the
problem of a grossly overvalued pound. These errors directly
account for the collapse of virtually a quarter of Britain's manufacturing industry in the early 1980s – much of which was viable
and deserved to survive, even if some shake-out of 'lame ducks'
was inevitable after the mistakes of the 1970s.

In the case of the last recession, Nigel Lawson as chancellor
maintained too lax a fiscal stance for far too long, given the
warning signs on house prices and consumer spending. In 1988
he pressed ahead with ideologically motivated tax cuts which
fuelled the spending spree of the better-off. Directly as a result of
this fiscal irresponsibility, interest rates had to be raised very
suddenly and sharply in 1988/89 in order to apply the monetary
brakes to inflation. High interest rates squeezed the heavily
indebted consumer hard, and raised industry's borrowing costs
just at the moment when consumer demand plummeted.

These policy errors provided the worst possible backcloth for
Britain's long-delayed entry into the European Exchange Rate
Mechanism. The Lawson interest-rate hike had strengthened the
value of the pound. John Major, succeeding him as chancellor,
kept the pound strong. Then, in September 1990, he finally
joined the ERM, locking an overvalued pound into a virtually
fixed parity with the Deutschmark. Short-term political consid-
erations had outweighed medium-term economic judgement.
ERM entry was used to justify a small cut in interest rates for
which there was general Conservative clamour at the time – led,
of course, by Prime Minister Thatcher. All this was done without proper British consultation with our German partners and,
as is now known, the Bundesbank warned at the time that the
British government's chosen parity was unsustainable.

The period of ERM membership provided a shock to the
British inflation mentality the like of which it had never experienced in the postwar years, but the government's humiliating
forced withdrawal from the ERM in September 1992 led to the
collapse of a political consensus on the virtues of managed
exchange rates which had been slowly built up over the previous
decade. The Conservative Party's grass roots broke into open

revolt against John Major's European policy. To the extent that Britain is now enjoying the happy combination of export-led growth and low inflation, this is largely the fortuitous consequence of a massive policy blunder followed by an ignominious forced retreat.

This painful history of boom and bust is a powerful reason why investment in new capacity has been so weak in the present recovery. In 1994 the value of manufacturing investment was 13 per cent below the level recorded for 1979. Business is reluctant to invest, in part because of uncertainty whether present favourable exchange rates will be sustained. According to the Institute for Fiscal Studies, business investment had risen by only 5.3 per cent since the trough of the recession in the first quarter of 1992 to the third quarter of 1995. This compares with a rise of 23.7 per cent during the comparable stage of the recovery of the early 1980s.

Nor is it clear whether the government's present success with inflation will be maintained. Thatcher's true disciples have convinced themselves that it will. According to them, the labour-market reforms of the 1980s have been a staggering success in overcoming previous barriers to wage flexibility and labour mobility. They believe that the conditions have now been created where output can grow faster and unemployment be much reduced without running the risk of reigniting inflation. However, many of these arguments were made, and widely believed, in the early stages of the Lawson boom in the mid-1980s.

A plausible alternative view is that present low levels of inflation may reflect the one-off unprecedented nature of the ERM-induced shock to expectations. If this analysis is right, the British economy might eventually return to its bad old habits as memories gradually fade. If such a trend reasserts itself, the trade-off between jobs and pay restraint will remain to haunt us in the long term.

Whatever judgement one makes about likely prospects for UK wage inflation, there is no doubt that on a wider scale inflationary pressures are weaker than they have been for a generation. Some economists believe that the structural changes in the global economy which we outlined in Chapter 1 are so profound that the world is entering a new era of low inflation. Public policy in most Western countries is still, however, predicated on the assumption that we have not slain the dragons of inflation, only that they have retreated into their caves. But in New Labour thinking it is as important to guard against the risks of recession as it is to prevent the re-emergence of inflation. Economic policy throughout the European Union has rightly been focused on the need to bring down unsustainable public sector deficits, which is desirable in itself and necessary for countries to fulfill the Maastricht convergence criteria for monetary union. But as matters stand at the beginning of 1996, there may be a case for alternative action to avert the risk of renewed recession. Improved international coordination of monetary policy may well be necessary to correct the present overvaluation of the Deutschmark against the dollar and help revive European industry. Unfortunately the Conservatives fail to recognise the importance of the issues at stake.

The Conservative failure of macro-economic management is as much one of ideology as of competence. An ideology of the 'invisible hand' led the Thatcherites to search desperately for an automatic pilot by which the economy could be guided and stability be supposedly assured. But the money supply proved impossible to control. Ministers failed to take into account the consequences of financial liberalisation for the real economy. The decision on the rate at which sterling entered the ERM was taken without reference to its long-term sustainability. As a result, the actual growth rate of the British economy since 1979 has lagged behind most estimates of the increase in Britain's productive potential. Government has failed in one of its most basic tasks – to establish stable conditions for sustainable growth.

It is a failure that has cost Britain dear. The latest analysis comparing the UK's macro-economic performance with that of the rest of the OECD suggests that, if the pattern of cyclical fluctuation in the UK had matched the more even performance of the OECD average, growth rate would have been 0.57 percentage points higher. Cumulated over sixteen years of office, the Tory macro-economic failure means a loss of increment to national wealth of over £75 billion by 1996.

The consequences for the public finances of this macro-economic failure have been disastrous. There are no precise estimates of the cost of unemployment and slow growth, but since the Conservatives came to power the costs of the social-security budget has almost doubled in real terms – accounting for 31 per cent of all government expenditure in 1994/95. Some of this rise reflects demographic factors such as increasing numbers of elderly people, social factors such as the rise in single-parenthood, policy changes such as the switch away from 'bricks-and-mortar' housing subsidies to housing benefits, and discretionary increases in the real value of some benefits to enable those who depend on social security to share in the general increase in living-standards. But even when one disaggregates these factors, an enormous portion of the increased social-security budget reflects the greater costs of unemployment.

The Conservatives have exacerbated this growing structural weakness in the public finances by taking chances with the economy for electoral gain. John Major presided over a massive boost to government discretionary spending in the run-up to the 1992 election. Public spending rose by 5.7 per cent in real terms in the election year alone. This combination of government-induced recession, the long-term rise in unemployment costs, and the Conservatives' efforts to buy the 1992 election fatally weakened the public finances. The public-sector deficit rose to a peak of some 7 per cent of gross domestic product in 1993/94 – a far worse situation than the 5.5 per cent in the year the Conservatives came to power. The electorate has had to pay the price of this economic mismanagement and political cynicism in the huge increase in the tax burden since the 1992 election.

The unspoken Tory case at the next general election will essentially be an apology: 'We have learned from our own past mistakes and can now be trusted to put the goal of macro-economic stability before every other consideration.' But in all likelihood the apology will be untrue. The Conservatives will find it impossible to resist the temptation to cheat the voters once again. Pressure from Conservative back-benchers for tax reliefs is intense. It would be amazing if in these circumstances Prime Minister Major and Chancellor Clarke put the long-term national interest before their own narrow party interest. But, the public will say, could one expect that of *any* politician?

How can New Labour prove such doubters wrong? The starting-point must be realism about what any government anywhere in today's world can achieve. The trade cycle, first identified in the nineteenth century, has been strengthened in its disruptive force by the degree of globalisation and financial-market liberalisation in the modern world. Although our understanding of economics has greatly advanced in this century, and in theory enables economic fluctuations to be damped and corrected, the authorities are handicapped by two weaknesses: lack of accurate information about the present, and the weakness of existing machinery for policy coordination in a globalised economy. The scope for successful national economic management has narrowed, and when it comes to international coordination, Britain deals from an increasingly weak hand. We have already commented on the need for European action to stimulate Britain's recovery. But Britain has to recognise that the principal European currency is the Deutschmark, which is why so many of Germany's partners favour a single European currency, which they see as offering some prospect of gaining leverage over economic decisions of vital importance to them.

Whether or not a single currency proceeds and Britain is part of it, much of the UK's economic instability has been magnified by avoidable errors of domestic policy. New Labour can and should do much better.

First, New Labour has made clear that a growth objective should be set alongside an inflation target. But Labour's objectives for growth and inflation should not be seen as independent of each other, for then the government might be seen as committed to sustain expansion even if the inflation target was being breached. Rather it is arguable that they should be thought of as together constituting a single number for the growth of the value of gross domestic product at current prices – so-called nominal GDP – whether or not this is stated as a formal economic target. For government to set itself the task of actively managing demand in order to maintain growth of money (not real) incomes and expenditure on a steady path is the classic New Keynesian position, as formulated by the Nobel Prize winner, James Meade. This distinguished disciple of Keynes died aged 88 at the end of 1995 after a lifetime's intellectual endeavour to work out how governments can promote full employment and greater equality within the framework of a successful market economy. The practical implication of New Keynesianism is double-edged. If inflation is reignited, the government is required to deflate the economy to keep within its nominal GDP target. But if, as may be the risk for Europe in the present environment, inflation falls below expectations, then the authorities have a clear responsibility to stimulate expansion.

Secondly, Labour has already proposed that the accountability of the Bank of England and the transparency of its decision-making need to be strengthened. Gordon Brown has stated that the Bank's governing body will be reconstituted in order to ensure a wider representation of interests from the regions and nations of Britain, as well as from manufacturing industry and the trade unions, and that interest-rate recommendations should be made by a monetary policy committee of the Bank's executive directors, not the Governor alone. Any further steps to strengthen the Bank's independence would depend on the success of these arrangements.

Thirdly, fiscal policy should be set in the context of a clear medium-term plan. This plan should abide by the golden rule of public finance: that current income and current expenditure should be in balance over the economic cycle. While public borrowing should rise and fall in order to help offset temporary fluctuations in economic activity, as Keynes argued it should, the only purpose for which an increase in long-term government debt would be permitted should be to finance public investment.

The aim of this tight new discipline is to create the most favourable conditions for both public and private investment. Current public spending has too often taken priority over public investment. Public borrowing has too often absorbed too high a share of the country's savings. Government policy must ensure that the nation's savings are put to productive purposes, rather than immediate public or personal consumption.

Fourthly, a determination to keep the economy on a path of non-inflationary growth requires responsibility in setting pay at all levels. Centralised incomes policies are no longer appropriate, given the changes that have taken place in the structure of the economy: the shift in employment to small firms, the changed position of the trade unions, and the diminished role of collective bargaining. Nevertheless it remains the responsibility of government to show leadership on pay and help to coordinate pay settlements. Pay rises over considerable sectors of the economy – both public and private – still cluster within a narrow range. If that range is too high, it will have damaging consequences for employment. For that reason, if no other, government must take a view of the acceptable level of pay rises in the economy as a whole and ensure business and the trade unions understand the employment implications of the decisions they take.

Also, New Labour should promote increased flexibility in the setting of employee rewards that genuinely relate pay to performance, whether through profit-related bonuses, employee share ownership or share options for all.

Labour may be unlucky when it comes to power. The world economy may be at the peak of the cycle and slipping into recession of its own accord. World trade may hit the doldrums. Domestically, the Conservatives may have overheated the economy in a vain attempt to win the election, and sharp short-term deflationary action may be necessary. This may make a significant reduction in unemployment difficult to achieve for a time, despite New Labour's clear commitment to this objective. It is under these circumstances that a New Labour government would be under maximum political pressure to abandon public-spending discipline and adopt an alternative economic strategy. Such a strategy might produce temporarily satisfying results, but it would throw away the prospect of long-term sustainable growth and would set Britain once again on the cycle of boom and bust. The pressure must be resisted, whatever the short-term political pain. Stability must come first.

Economic modernisation and competitiveness

The supply-side story of the Conservative years is a curate's egg. It would be foolish of Labour not to acknowledge where there have been improvements. Only by accepting the obvious facts can Labour then legitimately attack the present shortcomings. For example, the Conservatives have set great store by their claim to have created a more entrepreneurial culture, but their success has at best been partial, even in the area which they claim as their greatest achievement.

Take privatisation. Have the Conservatives successfully boosted enterprise, or have they instead created a new class of bureaucracy and privilege?

Privatisation has brought about improvements in operating efficiency and facilitated new investment. Companies like BT and British Gas now have the opportunity to show if they are world-class on a world stage. But Labour has been right to draw attention to the all-too-prevalent excesses: lax regulation and excess profits in electricity and water where industries remain essentially monopoly activities; big salary rises for executives which are hard to justify where the nature of their job has little changed; and unjustifiable profit-taking on share options when the initial flotation price on the stock market was set artificially low.

More importantly, instead of operating under the disciplines of dynamic competition, the privatised industries now languish under ineffective but increasingly bureaucratic regulation. Price controls have failed to guarantee stability or protect the consumer interest: in some cases, prices could be lower than at present without cutting back necessary long-term investment or compromising service standards or safety. And shareholders could receive a fairer return for what ought to be a pretty low-risk investment in natural monopoly activities. Instead, existing methods of regulation have encouraged management to boost dividends by cutting costs ruthlessly – without regard to the long term in areas such as training and safety, where the old nationalised industries were conscientious and thorough. Management has played games with regulators over investment plans. The scope of regulation has tended to expand and not – as was the original promise of privatisation – wither away. Individual regulators wield enormous power over the future of whole industries. The regulatory process itself has been inconsistent and ad hoc, and lacking in transparency and any real accountability.

The government's basic mistake was to privatise industries on terms too favourable to their managements and stakeholders – in fixing give-away flotation values, in setting initial price controls that were too lax, and most of all in preserving existing monopolies. Liberalisation has come as an afterthought or in a botched, half-hearted way, in order not to hurt the Treasury's efforts to ensure a smooth privatisation.

Since then the process of introducing competition has been arbitrary and piecemeal, with no one thinking through the inevitable consequences for social obligations and industry structure. Yet sensibly introduced competition can facilitate innovation in customer services and create new opportunities for imaginative, entrepreneurial businesses.

Regulatory reform should be high on the New Labour agenda, offering fair but not excessive returns for the genuine natural monopoly; promoting a proper framework for competition wherever feasible; establishing mechanisms for fulfilment of the special social obligations of the utility sector (for example, energy conservation and help for the fuel-poor); and ensuring that regulators are properly accountable for their decisions.

Take another area of Conservative pride – the promotion of new businesses.

Venture capital – money brought into growing businesses by issuing shares – expanded dramatically in the 1980s: from £200 million invested in 1981, it reached a 1991 peak of £1.6 billion. Despite the recession, the annual figure for venture-capital investments has stayed at over £1 billion since then. Not only has this helped medium-sized businesses expand, old businesses have been broken up to regain new life through management buy-outs and buy-ins.

However, too often venture capital has turned out to be 'vulture' capital, with businesses put under tremendous pressure to boost profits in the short term, rather than develop expansion plans for the long term, and go for a public float.

What's more, growing businesses have been damaged by the absence of a coherent policy to promote competition between firms and prevent big companies dominating the market and keeping smaller rivals out. This has been an area of huge timidity, with Conservative ministers paying far too much attention to the pleadings of special interests.

Growing businesses need a policy framework for competition which aims to open up markets for expanding new entrants and

at the same time deters unfair competitive practices and predatory take-over by their bigger more established rivals who use
market and financial muscle to hide their inefficiency. And they
need competition regulators with tough powers to investigate
and act – independently, if necessary, in a way that upsets their
political masters. Since 1992, in particular, the authority of both
the Office of Fair Trading and the Monopolies and Mergers
Commission has been emasculated.

But obviously it would be foolish for competition policy to
back every self-styled David against its chosen Goliath. Not all
Davids fight fairly, and some of the largest industrial Goliaths
remain fleet of foot. Competition policy needs to focus on
abuses of dominance, not on a strong position won fairly in the
market-place.

Finally, there is the Conservatives' claim that their policies
have promoted competitiveness.

Britain has become home to much overseas inward investment
into Europe, but this is because of our attraction as an English-
speaking base with right of access to Europe's Single Market –
not due to deregulation and low social costs, as Conservative
propaganda claims. As the Conservative government becomes
more Euro-sceptic, Britain's attractions as a location for inward
investment will diminish. Indeed it is arguable that only the
prospect of a Labour election victory has so far limited the damage. There will be a substantial risk to continued inward investment if Britain refuses to join a single European currency and
insists on trying to have its cake and eat it – to be free to devalue
the pound against our continental partners, while claiming
unimpeded access to their markets.

Overall, productivity has improved in the Conservative years.
Several of Britain's top companies can now justifiably claim to
be world-class. However the benefits of global expansion by
large companies have only an indirect impact on Britain, and
there simply are not enough top-quality British companies. The
typical medium-sized British company – not in the top 100 but
in the top 500 – needs to come up to the standards of the best.
Unfortunately, many of the last decade's productivity gains have
come from cost-cutting, and these improvements have now been

largely realised. While their benefits in terms of greater adaptability will be long-lasting, what we now need is innovation-driven, investment-led growth, and the evidence to date is that we are not getting it.

Over the whole of the Conservatives' period in office, manufacturing investment has grown at a snail's pace. Levels of investment have scarcely grown since the end of the 1960s. From 1960 to 1970 manufacturing investment grew more or less steadily (there were dips in 1962/63 and 1967) from £7.5 billion to £13 billion (all figures in 1990 constant prices). In the 1980s it rose from £12.3 billion at the start of the decade to £14.2 billion at the end, with a disastrous fall to £9.4 billion at the trough of the early 1980s recession. It had fallen back to £11.1 billion by 1993.

The figures show that manufacturing investment as a proportion of manufacturing output has continued to lag France and Germany (and the gap with Japan remains enormous). If we are to rebuild our manufacturing strength on the back of more streamlined and efficient industry, as the Conservatives would have it, then investment ought for a period of years to be higher than in France and Germany.

As for business-financed research and development, the picture is equally depressing. We invest the same proportion of GDP as in France (about 1.1 per cent), but lower than the figures for Germany (1.4 per cent), the United States (1.6 per cent) and Japan (2 per cent).

Enterprise is not flourishing in Tory Britain. The Conservatives have failed to provide the steady demand conditions, stable foreign-exchange rates and dynamic markets which make firms prepared to invest and plan for the future. The new generation of entrepreneurs we need is still not forthcoming.

A critical question is whether Labour's concern to modernise industry will be fatally undermined by City short-termism – the central thesis of Will Hutton's *The State We're In*.

Hutton's argument contains some important truths about the financing of British business. While there is no shortage of finance as such, it is debatable whether it is available on terms as favourable as our competitors enjoy. British boards feel under pressure to produce short-term profits in order to satisfy the dividend requirements of their investors. Investment projects are judged by tougher criteria than in Germany or Japan and have to demonstrate that they can earn high rates of return. Relations between the banks and the small-business community are poor.

It is difficult to identify practical solutions to this problem. Because the Germans do it better does not mean we can easily become more like the Germans. For one thing, the Germans are actually becoming more like us: the old comfortable relationships between banks and company boards in the Federal Republic are under pressure. Nor can deep cultural attitudes be readily transported from one country to another. One cannot legislate for managers to take a long-term view. One can only gradually transform the underlying conditions and institutional arrangements which at present foster short-termism.

It cannot be stressed enough that many of the financing problems of British industry hark back to persistent failures of macro-economic management. Company boards want to see high returns from new investment and insist on short payback periods, in part because all past experience suggests that in Britain there is no long-term stability and no steady demand growth. Instead, we suffer cycles of boom and bust, with periodic collapses in business confidence.

The extreme volatility of the British economy has made it difficult for companies to follow the German pattern of financing expansion through medium-term borrowing at a fixed rate of interest. As a result of high inflation in the 1970s, the supply of fixed-rate, medium-term loan finance completely dried up. Companies in Britain have had to depend on short-term lending by the clearing banks for their borrowing needs, and to pay the interest rate prevailing at the time. For business, this greatly magnifies the problems of recession. Company financing costs rise as interest rates rise. But higher interest payments become a burden just at the very moment that demand for products is under pressure – facing companies with the distinctive double whammy of a British recession.

This background of demand instability and high interest liabilities has made British firms keener to secure equity finance rather than bank borrowing in order to finance their growth. As a result, far more companies than in Germany have become publicly quoted on the stock market. But the penalty of becoming a PLC is that it involves surrender of control to outside investors, shortens planning-time horizons, and opens up the possibility of take-over. That is why so-called small to medium-sized firms are so much stronger in Germany (the so-called *Mittelstand*) than in Britain: they have been able to maintain their independence, and their ability to take the long view, at the same time as securing medium-term fixed-rate loans from the banks to permit expansion.

How can we escape from these dilemmas?

By far the most important thing is to get macro-economic policy right, as has already been discussed.

Next most important is to find a better means of channelling finance for expansion to new, growing businesses – the newcomers who will take the place of failing companies at the top of the league in ten or twenty years' time. These businesses require a mixture of packages of venture capital that will offer committed long-term support to good management, together with medium-term, fixed-rate loan finance. But this venture capital should not be public money – the allocation of which is ultimately decided by ministers – even were it to be allocated by some form of National Investment Bank: that would present too great a temptation for political log-rolling and attempts to pick winners.

Labour has identified company financing as an issue that needs to be addressed and has come forward with practical ideas to assist small businesses – for example, locally based partnerships to facilitate technology transfer, and schemes to help with late payment of debt by large firms. One further idea would be to model assistance to companies on the present Investors in Industry, the forerunner of which was established by the post-war Attlee government. The purpose would be to fill the gap in financing small to medium-sized companies which are at present not adequately served by the banks and equity markets. It should be a private-sector institution, totally at arm's length from Whitehall, with decisions taken on strict commercial criteria, and enjoying a direct relationship with a more broadly based Bank of England which could raise medium-term loan finance on the keenest available terms.

Thirdly, the government must do whatever it can to promote

a stakeholder culture in industry and the City. This means tackling head-on the present Anglo-American obsession with the enhancement of shareholder value as the sole motivation of business activity, and shifting the focus of management towards organic growth and away from deal-making activity. Additional laws and bureaucracy should be avoided, but a number of institutional reforms could help here:

- tightening competition policy to limit predatory take-overs;
- putting the investment-management institutions under obligations of disclosure, so that pension funds can see how investment managers are fulfilling their responsibilities to ensure that companies are well-managed;
- making occupational pension funds more accountable to contributors and pensioners by requiring special trustees to be elected rather than appointed by companies;
- strengthening the role of non-executive directors as responsible for reviewing management performance and maintaining regular contact with large investing institutions.

However, the most radical step would be to amend the present statutory responsibilities of company directors themselves, in order to clarify their obligations.

At present there is ambiguity whether the law requires shareholder interests to be paramount. Many senior business people take the view that boards should in fact be required to take into account the full range of interests of those with a stake in a company. The danger in any such step is that it would weaken the external discipline that the threat of take-over puts on companies to be efficient and profitable. In other words, it could protect the sleepy at the expense of the thrusting and go-ahead. There are, however, alternative efficiency disciplines that could be introduced on senior management. Some have proposed that chief executives' contracts be for a fixed but renewable term of four years – in effect compelling the board and institutional investors to review corporate performance formally on a periodic basis and decide whether management changes are necessary.

The thrust of New Labour policy should be to create a new culture of long-term investment. A new government can show the way by giving a massive early boost to public-private partnership in modernising Britain's infrastructure. This enables a modest injection of public money to lever a much bigger amount of private capital into projects which in the past would have relied exclusively on taxpayer finance. The Conservatives have in theory adopted this policy, but in practice they have failed to make it work. Instead it has become an excuse for public-expenditure cuts in the public services.

Beyond that, the role of government is to create conditions in which firms will want to invest of their own accord – by guaranteeing more stable demand growth; by ensuring the availability through the private sector of finance for expansion; and by changing the nature of the relationship between the City of London and the British boardroom.

Opportunity and investment in skill

'Next time I hear the Labour Party talking about training, I'm going to scream.' This is the kind of comment the party could well do without. It reflects a common misconception among the left-wing chattering classes that somehow education and training are of secondary importance – a subject for wimps. A 'real' economic policy would be about grandiose expansion plans and full-employment targets. This is to misunderstand both the modern global economy and the reasons for the long history of British economic failure.

Robert Reich, the US labor secretary, is more responsible than anyone for stressing the primacy of investment in skills in the modern world. His thesis is a simple one, but of profound importance. We live in a world of mobile capital. Multinational companies have a vast array of choices as to where they locate new investment. As a result of the globalisation of financial markets, they can raise the money in New York, London and Paris for expansion in India, Singapore or Taiwan. But whereas capital is mobile, labour is much less so. Decisions about where new investment is made are primarily determined by the skills and attributes of the local population. Governments can best promote economic success by ensuring that their people are equipped with the skills necessary for the modern world.

'Skills' itself is a rather misleading word. Skills are not something exclusively possessed by the more intelligent school-leavers who do not quite make the grade to university – though in Britain the training and attainments of this middle group in the population have been a long-standing strategic weakness. One must avoid crude measurements of a country's skill level by counting heads – of apprenticed engineering craftsmen, for example. The usefulness of technical qualifications is limited if individuals lack people-skills and general educational attainments.

In an economy of rapid change, skill requirements change too. Adaptability is as important as the level of qualification. Concern has long been expressed about the poor level of understanding of basic mathematical concepts among UK trainees, by comparison with that in other countries, which makes skilled workpeople in Britain less adept at adjusting to technological change than their counterparts overseas.

The skill base should also be defined broadly. The country's science base is a vital part of it. But, again, it would be a mistake to try to measure the quality of this by counting the number of, say, physicists with doctorates. The critical question is the relationship between a country's academic-research base and industrial R&D. Are they addressing a common agenda? Do research priorities take account of industrial needs? Also, the success of research-based industries does not simply depend on the supply of top-level scientists: the quality of general science teaching in schools determines whether in future industry will also have an adequate supply of well-qualified laboratory technicians. There are grounds for concern on all these issues in the UK.

The weakness of Britain's skill base has been identified as a major problem for many decades. The absence of a proper structure of technical qualifications and certified training has been a particularly long-standing complaint. It was first raised in Royal Commission reports a century ago, when British industry first began to take seriously the mounting competitive challenge from Germany and the USA, and has been discussed in many official reports over the decades. But, despite innumerable government initiatives and White Papers, all the evidence suggests that fundamental weaknesses remain, and in recent years concern over general educational standards has grown.

This is not to deny that some improvements have taken place. The problem is that other countries are improving at a faster rate, so we are falling still further behind.

Why is it that these long-standing weaknesses have not been properly addressed, although they have long been recognised? The answer must lie in the strength of the vested interests who oppose fundamental reform.

Who are these vested interests?

The educational system in Britain has always given priority to the interests of an academic élite rather than to high general standards of education and the promotion of vocational qualifications for the broad majority of young people. Some teachers have seen their life's mission as providing children from deprived backgrounds with an education fitted for the limited opportunities they expect their pupils to enjoy, rather than either concentrating on the achieving of adequate standards in the basic skills of reading and writing, science and mathematics or raising expectations of what some might attain. The teacher unions have tried to focus the public debate about education on pay and resources, rather than on the curriculum and pupil attainments: on inputs rather than outputs. The educational egalitarians regard the structure of schools as far more important than the quality of what is learned, and have sometimes seemed to show a far greater concern for the social balance of a school's admissions than for the destination of a school's graduates.

There are other culprits as well. Further-education colleges have been given the incentive to attract as many students and lay on as many courses as possible, without paying too much attention to quality, drop-out rates and inspection. And then, of course, there is industry. Too often British business has regarded money spent on training as a cost rather than an investment. Large companies sacrificed training and recruitment in the spate of 1980s cost-cutting. And, because of the poaching problem, small business has never taken its responsibilities towards training seriously. As pressures on costs increase and the structure of employment changes (nearly half the workforce is now employed in firms of fewer than fifty people), the neglect of training by industry may be getting worse rather than better.

The priorities for change

The first priority is to raise general educational standards.

New Labour believes that, throughout schooling, standards are more important than structures. Each school should be made clearly responsible for its own performance and be subject to a mixture of external pressure and support in order to raise it. Performance must be regularly assessed in objective terms that parents can understand and compare with elsewhere. Heads must be up to the job. Unsatisfactory teachers – particularly teachers with low expectations of their pupils – must be retrained or removed. Bad schools should be closed – to be reopened with new management and staff. There should be zero tolerance of failure.

Where extra resources can be made available, the initial priority should be the early years – preschool and smaller primary classes, in order to address individual underachievement as soon as possible. But the logical corollary of this is that systematic testing of pupil performance should be reinforced in the early years.

For the under-fives, Britain should be progressing towards a comprehensive health and education advisory service from birth – with health visitors retrained to accept a broader responsibility for educational advice and early identification of learning problems. Similarly, to help working parents, unified packages of nursery education and day care should be put together in place of the present separate arrangements, with families who can afford it making a significant contribution to the day-care elements of the costs.

Within schools, new approaches to teaching, making wider use of new technology, should be actively encouraged: classroom educators have been slow to innovate in a world of rapid change.

To achieve the quantum leap in educational standards which Britain needs, Professor Michael Barber, a leading education expert, has made a series of radical proposals:

• Parents and teachers should accept new legal responsibilities for the education of their children. Each child should have his or her own individual learning plan devised by the teacher and reviewed with a parent at a regular six-monthly meeting, attendance at which would be a new legal requirement. Where a parent failed to meet this obligation, this would be prima-facie evidence of a child at risk of educational failure.

- A mentor should be appointed for every such child, selected by the school from industry, commerce or the local community.
- Out-of-school hour learning centres should be established – in existing school, church or youth-club premises – which can provide support for homework, catch-up classes and study visits, and opportunities for independent distance-learning. These would be staffed in part by qualified teachers but also by students, earning some part-time income, and community volunteers. As in schools, the barriers between teaching professionals and committed paraprofessionals and volunteers should be broken down.

There are two other urgent requirements: first, to recommit the middle class to state education and, secondly, to ensure that children, whatever the nature of their talent and whatever their social background, have a fair chance to achieve their full potential. These are traditional Labour objectives, championed by Labour's education spokesman David Blunkett – a united society with real equality of opportunity for all – yet it is on these issues that there is still a great gap of trust between parents with aspirations for their children and politicians who have appeared to peddle ideological solutions. New Labour can now spell out with greater clarity what its new educational policies mean in practice and how its new emphasis on standards, not structures, can in time transform state education.

The first point to be made is that there is no good reason why any school in any area should be a failure. Some people used to argue that comprehensives would never work without a properly balanced mix of social class and ability. But this belief assumed that people live in socially balanced communities, when particularly in cities they do not (and there are no serious suggestions being put forward for new policies that will change that reality). It also assumed a sameness about education: that, in the ideal world, every comprehensive should offer the same type of education – an aspiration which falls tragically short of achievement in all those inner-city comprehensives with sixth

93

forms that are unable to get a pupil a basic A-level pass in English or maths. It goes against all the evidence showing that the most successful schools are those with strong leadership from heads and a distinctive ethos of their own – whatever the balance of their intake.

New Labour wants to allow schools the maximum freedom to develop their own distinctive ethos and identity: an excellence in science, perhaps, or music, or a real specialism in some aspect of vocational studies, flowing perhaps from a successful compact with local businesses. Parents who are looking hard for something to suit their own child might then find parts of the state system increasingly attractive. Many middle-class parents are concerned that private schools are too pressured and academic, particularly if their own children do not have an academic bent. With so many conventional university graduates finding it difficult to obtain decent jobs, vocational skills should naturally gain parity of esteem. Equally, excellence in other areas such as the arts or sport might well attract parents back to the state system.

But what about parents who want the best possible academic education for their child, or the prospects of a bright working-class child from a deprived neighbourhood? Labour has rightly ruled out the return of eleven-plus-style selection. The eleven-plus pigeon-holed children as successes or failures at far too early an age, and on a single and too narrow criterion of individual achievement. However more schools should consider setting pupils according to ability in some academic subjects: where there are ideological presumptions in favour of mixed ability teaching, these should be abandoned in favour of what achieves the best results in that school. As pupils get older, a range of vocational, technological and academic options should be on offer, as well as the chance to combine them. The key issues are to ensure that young people complete their years of compulsory schooling highly motivated to learn, and to provide courses in further and higher education that best suit their particular abilities and interests. Other countries achieve this without formal systems of academic selection and there is no reason why Britain should not be able to do the same.

What about the private sector? Labour has no plans to abolish the public schools. In a free society, this is surely right: the principal educational issue is how to raise standards in the state sector, and it is difficult to justify the loss of parents' personal liberty to educate their children as they want. Rather, Labour should be seeking a new partnership between the public schools and the rest of society.

Labour has, however, proposed abolition of the assisted-places scheme. This policy is justifiable in its own terms. The scheme helps a tiny minority at the expense of the majority; that tiny minority contains many who are not the most deserving of special help; and, to the extent that the scheme helps poor children from deprived backgrounds, it does it by detaching them from contact with the rest of the state system. But the disappearance of assisted places will draw attention to the need to build new bridges and to extend new ladders of opportunity in order to overcome the undoubted divisiveness between our two systems of education.

The second education and training priority is to encourage business and education to share a sense of responsibility for the future of training. This sense of responsibility has to be developed from the bottom up, locality by locality, involving businesses of all shapes and sizes. The local organisation of training in Germany is wholly admirable, with responsibility vested in chambers of commerce and the modern-day equivalent of the craft guild. The present-day training and enterprise councils in Britain are a very poor substitute for that kind of local infrastructure.

But how can an incoming Blair government encourage more and better training?

Labour is at present studying the various options. Opposition policies have in the past tended to focus on three types of proposal. The first is a return to the old levy/grant system, with statutory training boards for each industrial sector. In the past, this proved inflexible, bureaucratic and inadequate.

The second proposal that used to be made is the introduction of some form of remittable tax or training levy on companies, such that only those that fail to spend up to a designated proportion of their payroll cost on training would pay the balance into a central training fund. This solution, however, means that companies spend money on their own training needs, rather than on an individual employee's career development, and it is also open to some problems of monitoring and potential abuse.

Thirdly it has been proposed that employers be statutorily required to release employees for approved training courses – so many days a week or weeks a year. This, however, adds to industrial costs without necessarily securing employees' motivation and commitment to the courses they pursue or guaranteeing that the programmes provided by local FE colleges will offer young people what they need.

A more fundamental objection to the above is whether training that is done 'for' people, rather than as something they want to do for themselves, engages real interest and enthusiasm. For many it may appear little more than a continuation of school, where they had already written off the curriculum as dull and irrelevant. A more interesting approach is to give individuals the power to control their own educational development, once they are launched in the world of work. That is the attraction of the *individual learning account*, the potential for which Labour is investigating.

One possibility might be for individual learning accounts to be set up with a one-off grant from government as the tax-payers' contribution to the lifetime costs of an individual's need for learning – a possible use of extra revenues raised by tighter taxation of lifetime gifts and inheritance which would spread capital, both human and monetary, more evenly through the whole community. They could grow in size as a form of tax-privileged regular monthly saving, with matching or greater contributions from employers. The funds would be available to the individual at his or her choice, to spend on approved training courses. They would facilitate the creation of a society of lifetime learning.

Individual learning accounts would be a practical expression of mutual obligations and responsibilities. The individual would gain new freedoms of career choice and development – but would need to make his or her own contribution through committed contractual saving. Society and employers would make contributions as well – but the money would be dedicated to educational purposes. The wealthy would make a practical redistributive contribution to spreading opportunities throughout society.

Full-time university education is so costly that it would still need to be funded separately. The value of the student grant has fallen to such a low level that alternative systems of student finance need to be developed. The student loan scheme introduced by the Conservatives has given loans a bad name. A more attractive replacement might be the provision of adequate state-backed loans, with interest repayments deferred and scaled down where the lifetime income of graduates does not match expectations. Under this system, those who benefit most from education would then pay back the most, while young people from poor homes would not be discouraged from undertaking the risks of higher education.

Job creation and welfare-to-work

The policies outlined above should have two broad impacts on the British economy. The promotion of economic modernisation and opportunity should raise the productive potential of the British economy – in other words, it should enable us to grow at a faster rate than we have in the past. At the same time, the rules we have proposed to guarantee macro-economic stability should both control inflation (and bring beneficial supply-side effects with this) and enable demand to expand steadily as the productive potential of the economy grows. In the right circumstances, unemployment should be firmly set on a downward path. The speed of its reduction would depend in part on the success of pay restraint.

However, this will only be part of the total answer to long-term unemployment. Increased competitiveness will not necessarily result in many more new jobs, and those created by the increased dynamism of the economy will not always be suitable for the hard core of unskilled and low-skilled men who constitute such a major element of the unemployment problem. So how do we go further and address the compelling social and economic requirement to find useful work for these idle hands?

Experts divide into two main camps on this issue: those who believe the answer lies in increasing the effectiveness of the labour market as a market, and those who think that this is either insufficient or simply won't work.

Free-marketeers argue that the labour market does not 'clear'

– providing full employment – because excess supply has not yet resulted in a sufficient fall in the price of labour – that is, wages. They want to remove obstacles to the creation of lowly paid jobs by deregulation and cuts in social benefits. Those who reject this free-market approach propose alternatives that imply higher public spending on the direct creation of publicly financed jobs in construction or the public services. Some of this additional public expenditure would be offset by reductions in the social-security cost of unemployment – the sums involved depending on the precise nature of what is proposed.

Advocates of these policies argue that society must face a political choice between somewhat higher taxes and significantly higher employment, or lower taxes and a continuation of hard-core unemployment. Are we forced to choose between these unappealing options?

Free-marketeers claim the undoubted success of the USA's record in job creation as evidence of a clear trade-off between falling wages and higher employment.

True, in the last fifteen years wage differentials have widened enormously in the USA. While a college graduate earned 56 per cent more than a high-school drop-out in 1979, the figure had risen to 104 per cent by 1993. In the 1980s in the USA the real earnings of people with low educational qualifications fell dramatically – by 27 per cent in the case of men with less than twelve years' schooling. In the USA today the pay of men at the bottom of the income distribution is as little as half the level in Germany and Italy. This decline in the wages of the lowest paid was deliberately encouraged by public policy in the Reagan/Bush years. During the 1980s the value of the US minimum wage fell from 45 per cent of the average manufacturing earnings to 35 per cent.

However, the available evidence from America does not support the crude free-market proposition that lower wages for the unskilled have been the principal motor of job creation. A massive increase in inequality has taken place, but it has not resulted in any discernible rise in employment for the group whose pay levels have fallen most.

Pay levels for low-skill teenagers have dropped like a stone, but, instead of low wages increasing the number of teenagers in work, the proportion actually fell from 48.5 per cent to 45.4 per cent. Greater inequality has not resulted in higher employment; instead it has led to more marginalisation and social exclusion of young people on the fringes of the labour market. In twenty years the US prison population has risen from 300,000 to 1.3 million, and it continues to rise at an alarming rate. Free-market deregulation has had considerable social effects, but not the ones its proponents expected.

Why, then, has the United States been more successful in creating jobs, if not as a result of the wonders of the market clearing mechanism?

Much of the explanation must relate to the dynamism of American enterprise, particularly in the service sector, and the buoyancy of labour supply as a result of immigration, illegal as well as legal. However, one pertinent lesson on wages is relevant to Europe. Restraint in US *average* earnings has been linked with a rise in employment. Over the twenty-year period 1970-1990 real average earnings in the United States fell by an average 1 per cent a year but total employment rose by 8 per cent. In Europe, average earnings rose by 1.3 per cent a year but employment *fell* by 3 per cent in total. But this is an argument for generalised pay restraint in Europe, coupled with policies to remove the advantages that labour-market insiders hold over outsiders without decent jobs: it is not a case for cutting the pay of the low-paid. As the distinguished American economist Professor Freeman concludes, 'What the evidence for different skill groups in the United States calls into question is the notion that increased inequality was needed in addition to sluggish aggregate real wage growth for the US job-creation miracle.'

What, then, of the government-led job-creation alternative? There is, of course, nothing difficult in principle about creating jobs which the least skilled could fill. For example, Parliament could legislate, or other bodies could regulate, that every public lift or petrol pump should have an attendant and every housing estate a caretaker; every urban road and pavement should be swept three times a week; and so on. But the costs of such deliberate job creation would need to be met either by consumers through higher prices or by citizens through higher taxes. If, as a result of these extra burdens, there is general pressure for higher wages, and employers agree to pay them, then costs will rise, competitiveness will suffer, and the net gain in employment in the long run may be small.

Roughly the same logic applies to schemes for compulsory work-sharing and, in particular, for reductions in working hours, which some European socialists espouse. Unless the planned fall in hours results in a compensating reduction in pay, then costs will rise and industrial competitiveness will suffer. Only if pay willingly falls in line with shorter working time can the number of jobs be increased without risk.

These approaches to the redistribution of income and work require a level of what our continental partners call 'social solidarity' which Thatcherism destroyed in British society. Even in the 1960s and 1970s, social solidarity of this kind won only partial acceptance in the UK. One of the aims of a New Labour government must be to rebuild and nourish a sense of community responsibility for the long-term unemployed. But this can only be achieved gradually, by putting forward practical solutions, being mindful of industrial competitiveness, and demonstrating the effectiveness of each new initiative along the way.

The practical difficulties should not be underestimated. How would a Labour government ensure that any extra money it allocated to public services to create new jobs was actually spent on this purpose? Would an increase in the general central-government grant to local authorities automatically result in more street-sweepers and park attendants, or would we end up with more highly paid planners and social workers? How could a Labour chancellor ensure that any extra public expenditure to create new jobs actually led to new opportunities for the long-term unemployed?

So where does all this leave New Labour's ambition to conquer unemployment?

The long-term costs of job creation must clearly be kept to the minimum. This implies that:

- Job-creation expenditure should be carefully targeted at the unemployed themselves, not given away in general public-spending largesse.
- Offsetting savings in the social-security budget must as far as possible be achieved.

- The priority should be the long-term unemployed and the young unemployed: by focusing on those presently excluded from the labour market, the government can help tip the balance in favour of the labour-market outsiders against the insiders and thereby increase the general pressure for responsibility in pay levels.
- Help to get the hard-core unemployed into jobs should be coupled with an obligation to undertake training – on the part of both the employer and the employee – in order to ensure that, once in a job, the chance of keeping it is increased.
- Policy should address the barriers in the existing social-security system which hold people back from taking low-paid work or undertaking training.
  There are five promising avenues for policy:
- Recruitment subsidies, such as Gordon Brown has already proposed, to encourage private-sector employers to take on the long-term unemployed. This financial incentive should be part of a concerted drive to encourage companies to extend their corporate social-responsibility activities so as to help the long-term unemployed back to work in their locality. Unless the leadership to back this policy comes from the top of the business community, take-up of recruitment incentives is likely to be small and patchy.
- Improving the service standards which regulated utilities are required to meet in a manner which will generate new, low-skill job opportunities. Classic examples would be energy-conservation obligations on the gas and electricity suppliers, or requirements for railway stations to be staffed at night.
- Specific grants to promote job-creation in the voluntary sector which would be made available through local authorities and other public bodies. In order to guarantee the most cost-effective use of the grant, the commissioning body would be required to invite competitive tenders from the voluntary sector for the provision of job-intensive public services (for example, community core services or gardening and decorating for old people no longer capable of carrying out these tasks themselves).
- The creation of a nationally led task force to tackle environ-

mental decay, offering young people six-month placements.
• Reform of the present social-security rules on earnings disregards, allowances for childcare costs and the transition from income support to family credit.

This range of cost-effective job-creation measures will enable Job Centres to offer the long-term unemployed a fair chance to get back into the labour market. For the more capable and ambitious, it provides access to the bottom rung of a new ladder of opportunity which could eventually lead to training, higher skills, and a much better paid job.

It is a crucial New Labour commitment that society must accept a serious obligation to find work for the young unemployed. This will end the long years of Conservative complacency and neglect. In these circumstances the young unemployed themselves have to accept obligations too.

It is not right that some people should collect the dole, live on the black economy, and then refuse to cooperate with society's efforts to reintegrate them into the labour market. It is dishonest and corrosive of our attempt to build a sense of mutual obligations in the community. In circumstances where new opportunity is being offered and refused, there should be no absolute entitlement to continued receipt of full social-security benefits. Clearly society has a responsibility to ensure that children in all circumstances are cared for, and there is no sense in applying rules to able-bodied males which force families apart, but childless young people who are of sound body and mind cannot expect to continue to receive full benefit if they decide not to take up these new opportunities – so long as the opportunities are real and of high quality. Such a tough discipline is necessary to demonstrate the seriousness of the government's efforts and break the culture of hopelessness, idleness and cynicism which a concentration of hard-core unemployment has bred in the many estates throughout Britain where a generation has been brought up on the dole. Young unemployed people, when asked, support these principles. To them it is not 'workfare'. It *is* fair, and it offers work.

Fair taxes and wise spending

No issue is more sensitive for Labour than tax. For many Conservatives, tax remains the only weapon they have left in their
attempt to avoid political oblivion, despite the extent of the tax
rises since 1992. They still believe there is power in the argument that voters can trust the Conservatives to keep tax and
public spending as low as is feasibly possible but cannot trust
Labour to do this. Conversely, for a minority on the left and the
Liberal Democrats, a willingness to put up tax has become an
index of New Labour's seriousness about reforming Britain.

This whole debate is based on a set of false premisses.

In the long run the size of the tax burden is dependent on
three main factors: the level of social provision on which the
government decides, the success of the economy, and the efficiency of the public sector. The faster the rate of growth, the
lower the tax burden for any given level of social provision. The
slower the growth rate and the higher the unavailable costs of
the unemployment which are the result of that economic failure,
the higher the tax burden will be.

When the Conservatives argue today that the tax burden is
too high, they are therefore admitting a number of extraordinary things. First, that they are sorry but their economic policies
have been a failure and they cannot control the rescue cost in
terms of public expenditure. Secondly, that after seventeen years
in power, and a cabinet policy to curb public expenditure, they
still think they can identify large cuts in discretionary spending
or value-for-money savings that have eluded them for more than
decade and a half but they are confident they can now make.
The implausibility of that assumption should have discouraged
naive Conservative back-benchers from fond illusions that large
cuts in spending and tax could have been made in the 1995 Budget. Voters will not be so easily fooled.

On the other hand, supporters of higher taxes argue that
Britain is not a particularly highly taxed country by the standards of our European partners; that there is little relationship
between the tax burden and relative economic performance, certainly in the developed world; and that if only Labour had the

courage of its convictions it could win the political argument for higher levels of spending and taxation.

It is true that the level of public spending in the UK is somewhat below that of our main European partners, but these are richer countries where the choice between public and private spending is less stark. Moreover, advocates of higher taxes cannot ignore the reality that in Britain tax as a proportion of GDP has already had to rise from 34 per cent to 38 per cent since 1992 – despite three years of relatively rapid economic growth, when one would normally expect the tax burden to be in decline.

Talk of a 'tax constraint' makes one big assumption: that a Labour government would have ambitious plans for greatly increased public spending in excess of the steady increment of national wealth available to spend on public services as a result of economic growth. No such assumption is justified.

Certainly Labour wants to increase spending on its priorities: education, training, welfare-to-work, crime prevention, infrastructure investment, and housing for the homeless. But that does not mean that every government department will be granted licence to increase its budget. In every area budgets should be thoroughly examined on zero-based principles with no presumption that existing programmes should be maintained as they are.

There may be a requirement for an injection of extra spending on some projects in order to bring about long-term public-expenditure savings. Welfare-to-work programmes are an example. Providing job opportunities for the long-term unemployed carries with it an initial cost. Once the programme is successful in reintegrating people into the labour market, the long-term social-security costs of unemployment will then fall. The great intellectual case for a one-off 'windfall' tax such as Labour has proposed for the utilities is that it provides a very necessary source of funds for catalyst spending of this kind.

Labour should adopt this same approach in other areas. Labour's aim should be to change the pattern of public spending, not to jump to the conclusion that nothing can be done without a large overall increase. The costs of social security should in time be cut sharply by Labour's attack on long-term unemployment. The introduction of income-related repayable loans in order to finance student maintenance – assuming Labour adopts this policy – should gradually enable more resources to be spent elsewhere in education. Increased priority for crime prevention and drug education should eventually cut the costs of the criminal-justice system.

The upward pressures on public spending are, however, very stubborn. Professor Nicholas Bosanquet has argued persuasively that they have been made more intense by the public-sector reforms which the Conservatives have introduced. There is also the inescapable fact that, as a society becomes more prosperous, pressure for expansion of public services such as higher education, health and community care inevitably grows. The answer to these dilemmas is not to abandon the concept of a welfare state that is universal in its reach, but to examine how private and public finance can be brought together in harness in order to pay the cost of meeting future demands, as we explain in Chapter 6.

But what about tax itself? Even many who accept the basic argument made above about the need for long-term change in the pattern of public expenditure, and greater partnership between public and private finance, will be sceptical about whether this change can be achieved without *some* increase in overall spending. And how does Labour square this reality with its opposition to the scale of the Conservative tax rises since 1992 and Gordon Brown's stated aim to lower the starting rate of income tax to 10 pence in the pound?

The dilemma is far more easily resolvable than many commentators allow. Labour is the party not of big tax rises for the hardworking majority, but of tax reform that will promote both fairness and efficiency.

The present tax system perpetuates and encourages some staggering contrasts. Take, for example, how the tax system has bolstered the new privilege of the privatised utilities. Senior managers in the water and electricity sectors have grown rich on large salary rises and share options. Their fortunate shareholders have enjoyed one of the largest returns of any sector of UK equities in recent years – when the justification for high stock-market returns ought to be that shareholders have underwritten high risks, not financed monopoly activities. At the same time, investors quick enough to spot that the electricity regulator would prove lax have been able to cash in on the huge rise in electricity-company shares, which in the autumn of 1995 had risen to a level that was more than four times greater than their 1990 flotation price.

The government's tax policies have made these abuses more pronounced. Until 1995, privileged share options awarded to highly paid managers were exempt from tax; a fair system would encourage firms to offer share options for all, in order to promote the spread of employee share ownership. In the case of the water industry, abnormally high profits have been bolstered by special tax treatment in the form of capital allowances that have cost the taxpayer over £2 billion; a fair tax system would ensure that any generosity of treatment over capital allowances was targeted on raising the general level of industrial investment in order to strengthen Britain's long-term economic capacity. As for electricity shareholders who have seen their investment quadruple in value, these lucky investors pay the same rate of capital gains tax as a businessman selling the company to whose building-up he has devoted a lifetime.

The generous treatment of the utilities contrasts starkly with that of the struggling small business. Throughout the recession there was little respite from VAT and tax bills – and tardy action on late payment of debts. When a small business's profits rise above £300,000 it faces the same corporation-tax rate as a big company – and, unlike the latter, has no chance of offsetting its liabilities by creating tax losses in other subsidiaries or by imposing management charges from an overseas holding company which artificially depress taxable profits. Equally, the growing business's access to new equity capital is highly restricted, because the pattern of tax reliefs embedded in our tax system channels savings into the hands of large institutions.

Under the British tax system, the entrepreneur has every incentive to cash in and sell his company, if possible at the peak of the next available boom, for he gets no benefit in terms of a lower CGT rate from making a long-term commitment to expand it. That is another reason why the UK has failed to develop the medium-sized-company sector which is at the heart of German economic success.

The unfairness in terms of the tax treatment of individuals is just as stark. The incentives for entrepreneurs to 'cash their holdings and run' are strengthened in the UK by the proliferation of vehicles that enable rich people to hang on to and enjoy accumulated wealth, rather than deploy it for a productive purpose: lax treatment of trusts and going offshore; an inheritance-tax regime which for large estates has become voluntary; the large number of reliefs available to the wealthy to protect their holdings against tax. All these loopholes contribute to a society where it pays to be 'undeserving rich'.

A fairer tax system ought to be about rewarding hard work whatever an individual's level of pay – not perpetuating privilege, whether it is the new privilege of privatised-utility monopoly profits and windfall gains or the old privilege of accumulated wealth which is merely inherited or passed on. This principle should stand as the New Labour approach to the taxation of income and wealth. Over 100 years ago Joseph Chamberlain attacked the aristocracy with the biblical quote 'They toil not, neither do they spin.' Winston Churchill put it even better in his defence of Lloyd George's radical 1909 Budget. In justifying 'the new attitudes of the state towards wealth', he said the chancellor was right to ask not only 'How much have you got?' but also 'How did you get it?'

For the decent hard-working majority, there are no easy tax-avoidance options. The members of a typical family save through an ordinary building-society account. They save out of taxed income, and they pay tax on the interest. They get none of the tax reliefs that are so widely available to the more sophisticated.

Those who know how to work the system can exploit the vast array of tax reliefs for PEPs, venture-capital trusts and pensions. Of course, not all these reliefs are unjustified – Labour wants to extend the opportunity for tax-free savings – but there is something profoundly wrong when such a high proportion of existing reliefs and exemptions goes to a small minority of better-off taxpayers. A classic example of abuse was the old Business Expansion Scheme which was turned by the tax avoidance industry into a means of investing in such enterprising activities as property and fine wines. Tax reform is about guaranteeing a fair deal for all types of saver and doing away with the vast array of fiscal privileges that in practice are accessible only to a minority and amount to job-creation schemes for accountants and no one else, distorting the economy and misallocating resources.

That leaves, of course, the central political issue of income tax.

The Conservatives are engaged in a cynical political manoeuvre: having raised the overall tax burden by the largest amount in postwar British history, they are attempting to open up clear blue water between themselves and Labour by now cutting income tax. So how should Labour respond?

Having campaigned so hard against the higher taxes that have been the result of Conservative failure, it would be illogical for Labour to oppose a relief in the tax burden on ordinary families. What Labour can and should argue is that it would deploy any cut in the tax burden in a fairer way.

Labour wants to see a progressive income tax, with a low starting-rate for the low paid. Not only is this fair, it will also improve incentives to work at the bottom end by reducing the very high effective marginal rates that face the lowly paid as a result of the combined impact of additional tax and benefit withdrawal on people dependent on housing benefit and/or family credit. Such a reform would promote both fairness and efficiency.

All the above measures are a serious and long-term response to Britain's economic problems. The change in economic performance from that under the Tories would not be sudden and dramatic. There is no single big idea, no clever policy wheeze which is going to transform Britain's prospects overnight, but small step-by-step changes in a consistent direction will produce gradually more impressive long-term results.

Macro-economic stability and low inflation will maintain the value of Bill Andrews's pension and building-society nest egg. They will create a climate in which Chris Andrews can operate a business with confidence, and, if he does well, there will be new instruments to enable him to borrow money at reasonable rates. They will ensure that the negative-equity problems which blighted the Stephensons' lives do not recur. Phil Jones will get the offer of a job to prevent him lapsing into the morass of long-term unemployment, putting him back on the ladder of opportunity. With the help of an individual learning account, he may then train for a more commercially valuable skill.

There is no rash promise of full employment tomorrow and ultra-high growth every year thereafter, but New Labour does offer policies to produce something much better then the despair and cynicism we see now – lasting security, and increased hope and opportunity for the future.

5
Divided Britain

Contrast the two Britains: not the classic two nations of North and South, not the widening statistical gap between rich and poor, but the respective conditions of two people in one local community and with whose everyday tribulations we can all sympathise. They live near to each other, yet their worlds are far apart. But, despite the enormous differences in their individual circumstances, and although they may not realise it, they share many concerns about the state of Britain. That fact symbolises the national purpose underlying the social agenda of the Blair revolution. Their concerns give a clue to the themes and policies needed for building a reunited kingdom.

Eileen Cooke, a widow in her late forties, lives on the third floor of a five-storey council block which dates back to Herbert Morrison's time as leader of the London County Council. It is a stone's throw from Westminster, but a world away from the sophisticated metropolitan life north of the river.

Ben Hodgson lives with his wife, Laura, and their two children in a late-Georgian house in nearby Kennington. The terrace was mostly in private rented multi-occupation until the gentrification boom of the 1960s and 1970s. It was in such a property that Charlie Chaplin was brought up, with his family occupying a single room. But it now serves as a highly convenient base, close to central London, from which a professional couple can pursue their busy careers – Ben as a successful director of a media company and Laura as a fashion journalist.

Blighted prospects

Eileen is a school dinner-lady. She lost her husband a couple of years ago. He died of heart disease in his mid-fifties. It had been terrible, but she thought the nurses and doctors at St Thomas's Hospital were wonderful. As for her GP, he is probably the only professional person in whom Eileen has trust and confidence.

The health tragedy that had hit that inner-city family is not untypical. The life expectancy of people from manual-worker backgrounds is some eight years lower than for professionals, and the gap is widening.

Eileen and her late husband had three children. The eldest son, Derek, has done well for himself. Now in his mid-twenties, he has trained as an electrician, married, and works in Harlow new town. The tragedy for Eileen is that she doesn't see nearly enough of Derek and his family. But there was no way they could have afforded a house in central London.

The economic forces and personal preferences which cause go-ahead people like Derek to leave the inner city behind also aggravate the tendency to 'sink' estates, 'failing' schools, 'hostile' ghettos and 'crime-ridden' streets, and at the same time take away the very people who can offer leadership and community support. Public policy could do more to ensure the ready availability of attractive, middle-income housing in inner cities. But it will not satisfy those, like Derek, who aspire to a safer, healthier environment for their families. According to a recent study, 45 per cent of the population would ideally like to live in a village, 21 per cent in a small town, 21 per cent in a suburb, and 3 per cent in the centre of a city. New towns, like Harlow, are special cases of their own, but they have found ways of accommodating this popular idyll and remain one of postwar Labour's most successful, if unsung, achievements.

Eileen's daughter, Tracy, hasn't been as lucky. She got pregnant in her late teens and married her boyfriend. But the relationship didn't last. The man had spent all his time out drinking with his pals – or so it seemed to Eileen – and when Tracy complained he had got violent and once or twice beat her up. After eighteen months she had arrived back on her mother's doorstep, with a one-year-old boy in tow.

Tracy's experience is not uncommon. Britain has the highest divorce rate in Western Europe – 25 per cent higher than in Sweden; 60 per cent higher than in France, Germany and Holland; and more than four times the rate in Catholic southern Europe. In Britain, one in three children is now born outside marriage – almost double the European average – and one in five children is living in a home without the natural father. There is no doubting the social consequences of family breakdown. Research has confirmed what most people instinctively feel: bad educational performance, poor life chances and a higher risk of criminality are strongly linked with family disintegration and poor parenting. This is not to put the blame on single parents like Tracy, who have suffered through no fault of their own.

There wasn't permanent room for Tracy and the baby in Eileen's flat, and, after what seemed intolerable delay, the local council accepted her and her child as 'homeless'. Eventually they were rehoused in what her mother describes as a 'pigsty' of a flat on a crime-ridden estate, three miles away. 'Our Tracy had no alternative – the council operates a one-offer policy, and if you don't take it they won't do anything for you.'

But this was not the end of Tracy's troubles. The Social Security proved really difficult about helping out when she was moving into her new flat. Under the Social Fund regulations introduced in 1986, one-off grants for the provision of essentials such as cookers and mattresses for destitute households were abolished and families in need were made dependent on the cash-limited Social Fund to deal with exceptional expenses that they have no means to meet. Grants are restricted to cases of maternity, the destitute elderly and funeral expenses. Families in Tracy's circumstances are now expected to take out 'crisis' or 'budgeting' loans, repayments of which are then deducted from their weekly girocheque.

Last year 1.6 million loans were made by the Social Fund. There are widespread complaints about the way in which the rules are applied, which varies from place to place. The whole procedure is extremely costly to administer: some £270 million was spent on administrative costs in 1993/94 alone – about £120 for every grant or loan actually awarded.

Tracy was forced to look after her child without a proper cooker and with no washing-machine. All she had for the first winter was a single electric ring. She had put together odd bits of furniture with the help of her mother and Derek, but the flat wasn't properly carpeted and it was always draughty and cold. Eileen blamed the dreadful conditions for her grandson always being at the doctor with chest infections. Also, he spent too much time indoors because Tracy feared for his physical safety outside. She was obsessed by fears of child abduction, and would never lose sight of her son for a single second on their all-too-infrequent visits to the local park.

Tracy knew that she could not break out of her situation without a job – but how could she get a job without childcare? It was difficult trying to get her child into a council day nursery, because there was an enormous waiting-list, and everybody said that the places went only to children whom the social services put on the 'at risk' register.

Eileen's solution was that Tracy should move nearby, so that she could be more help with babysitting and maybe help Tracy find a part-time job. So Tracy had applied to the local housing office for a transfer. This proved a demoralising experience. Several times when she tried to find out where she stood she was told that her housing officer was on holiday, on a training course, in court or off sick – even though a big notice on the door informs tenants when the office is supposedly open for inquiries. When she did make contact with 'the Housing', 'they' told her she was not a 'priority case' – but she might be, if only she got a letter from the doctor about her child's health, or from the social worker about the risks to her child, or from her local councillor about her need to be near her mother. Later 'they' explained that she didn't have enough 'points', or had to widen her area of choice.

Eileen felt very bitter about Tracy's treatment. 'I see lots of empty flats round here that would suit our Tracy fine, but when you ask down at the Housing they say she's got to wait her turn on the computer. It's a different story every time.' Eileen has a generally low opinion of the local housing 'service': 'It's their attitude I can't stand – they treat everybody like dirt.'

Tracy felt desperately lonely a lot of the time and missed her mother's company. She would have liked a steady boyfriend, but the local men who were good fun and she liked weren't interested in a serious relationship with a young woman with a child.

Eileen's biggest worry, however, is her youngest son, Peter. He is fourteen and attends one of the local comprehensive schools – or rather, as he is a regular truant, he is supposed to attend it. In Eileen's view Peter has got in with a 'really bad lot' and she doesn't know how to deal with him. 'He won't take a blind bit of notice of anything I say.' The truth is that she is rather frightened of her son, however difficult she finds it to admit to, and cannot cope with his thuggish insolence.

Eileen blames the school for part of the problem. 'The teachers never seem to show any interest. There's no discipline – not like when we were at school. The kids wander about, and half the time no one knows where they are or where they are supposed to be. And when they're in the classroom half the teachers haven't got a clue how to control them.'

Unfortunately, Peter is no exceptional case. Truancy is rife in inner cities in the final years of compulsory schooling. Research has shown significant differences between schools' truancy rates *after* taking account of social-class composition and the balance of pupil ability. Truancy and antisocial behaviour are strongly associated, and there is a clear link with criminality in later life. Truants suffer poorer outcomes in education, training and the labour market in the years following compulsory schooling.

Truancy is the tip of the iceberg of bad, failing schools. Many inner-city schools have an appalling track record. Nationally in England and Wales in 1993/94, 41 per cent of fifteen-year-olds achieved five or more GCSE grades A-C; for inner London the average is 27 per cent. There are many schools, of course, which manage to provide first-rate education even in the most difficult circumstances.

There are plenty of mitigating factors all too readily offered in defence of the others: disturbed homes, lack of English as a mother tongue; lack of commitment to schools by parents; inadequate resources. But inspectors' reports on failing schools tell another side to the story: poor leadership from heads; low expectations of pupils by their teachers; tolerance of poor-quality teaching; lax discipline; the absence of an ethos of achievement. Too many inner-city schools betray their pupils – and, given the pupils' frequent lack of opportunity in society to start with, it is an appalling betrayal.

Peter is also in trouble with the police. He was caught outside a local pub trying to sell a stolen car radio. Then the police picked him up when he'd gone on a joyride in a stolen car. Most crime is committed by young men of around Peter's age: 22 per cent of those found guilty by the courts or cautioned in 1993

were between fifteen and eighteen years old, though these official statistics almost certainly underestimate the amount of
crime committed by teenagers.

'Our Peter mixes with quite a lot of the local lads. But all they
do is hang around and cause trouble.' Her biggest worry is that
he will get involved with drugs. 'There's a lot of it on the estate.
You see them at night sniffing and smoking in the stairwells. It's
terrifying for people. You can see the pushers cruising round in
their big cars. The police don't seem to do anything.'

In the opinion of the many senior police officers, a high percentage of burglaries and street crime – muggings, car robberies
– are drugs-related. Some estimates suggest that of an estimated
£4 billion worth of stolen property every year, half could be
accounted for by the compulsion to fund the heroin habit. Since
1982, the number of registered heroin addicts has increased fivefold; the seizures of Class-A drugs have tripled; among under-
seventeen-year-olds there has been a fivefold increase in the
number of drug offenders. A survey on Merseyside of 800 fif-
teen-to-sixteen-year-olds suggested that almost two-thirds had
experimented with drugs of some form.

Crime and drugs have blighted Eileen's estate as they have
blighted many parts of the inner city. A high proportion of
crime is committed by people from deprived homes against people living in equally deprived circumstances. Break-ins are commonplace: vandalism is rife. As Eileen put it, 'The whole place is
out of control. The lot next door terrify me. The ghetto-blaster's
on all hours of the day and night, and as for their weekend all-
night parties I dread to think what they get up too – and I'm
broad-minded, by the way! On the other side there's a sad old
boy living on his own who gets a visit every weekday from the
meals on wheels and that's his life. I collect his pension and do
the occasional bit of shopping for him – just to check he's still
all right.

'Everybody else is too terrified to go out, unless they really
have to. You couldn't invite anyone round either. My husband
made our flat lovely inside, and I try to keep it nice, but you
couldn't expect anybody to risk life and limb coming here in the
evenings. Anyway, with all the graffiti and mess, I'd be ashamed
to invite them.'

Reluctantly opting out

Ben Hodgson has never met his near neighbour Eileen Cooke. Their paths occasionally cross on the local pavements – as he dashes past for the Tube, quietly cursing his lateness for the first meeting of the day at his West End office, and Eileen makes her regular trip to the local doctor's surgery for a prescription to cope with her backache and depression.

Ben hates the journey to work. The private domain of his working existence is a joy – the tasteful office with its comfortable sofas, designer lamps and expensive wallprints; the client entertainment; even the twice-weekly workout at the private gym. But the public domain is a misery – the litter-strewn streets which the council seems incapable of sweeping regularly, despite the astronomical level of council tax; the Northern Line, which is overcrowded and unreliable; uncomfortable taxis to and from Heathrow which sit in long jams while the high-speed rail link between one of the world's three great financial centres and the fourth-busiest airport gets postponed further and further into the future. And the short walk to the office past the most pathetic casualties of society huddled in doorways is an uncomfortable reminder of a real world which he knows exists but which he would ideally prefer not to have thrust into his consciousness.

Ben could of course drive to work. But there would be two big disadvantages to that. One is that Laura would need to walk home from the Tube on winter evenings. Ben knows from the Neighbourhood Watch newsletter that there have been several recent muggings – young men snatching handbags and then running back into the Tube station to jump on the first approaching train. Somehow this is much more terrifying then the regular break-ins which are the common gossip of his neighbours. The episode three years ago when Laura's family jewellery had been stolen had finally convinced them to invest in a burglar alarm as well as iron gates on the back windows. This at least seemed to be effective – but for how long?

One of Britain's greatest growth industries has been crime prevention – not surprisingly given that the number of notifiable offences has doubled since the two and half million recorded by the police in 1979. By 1993, over two-thirds of those whose homes had been burgled had subsequently fitted window locks and double locks, over a quarter had invested in a burglar alarm and light-timers or sensors, and 9 per cent had installed window bars or grilles. Economists, of course, measure this activity as an addition to national wealth and an improvement in living-standards. As it is privately financed, it counts as consumers' expenditure. This is somewhat perverse, as, given the choice, most people would prefer less crime and less need to spend their own money on its prevention. But convincing them that higher taxes and wise public spending would cut the crime rate is another matter.

Laura also uses the car to run the children to school, which is on the way to her South Kensington office. The children attend a private school in Battersea – not overformal and stuck up, but where there is a really happy and committed atmosphere. To pay the fees and employ a nanny is, of course, one reason why they both have to work full-time – though the truth is that they would both want to anyway.

Ben and Laura had been reluctant purchasers of private education. They are not natural 'opters-out' who regard 'going private' as a sign of having made it. Although Ben's firm pays for a subscription to a private health scheme (and they feel that that is a useful insurance), Ben and Laura are strong supporters of the National Health Service. The children were born in the maternity wards of St Thomas's, because if anything went wrong it was much safer to be in a well-equipped hospital. And the standard of care – as opposed to the peeling paint on the walls and the unappetising food – was excellent. One of Ben's student friends is an Aids victim. Ben admires the level of NHS care he receives. He also knows that his own elderly parents depend totally on the NHS.

The decision on schools had been an agonising one. Ben and Laura had visited local primary schools before deciding to opt out. At one school they hadn't liked the atmosphere: the avoidance of any competitive spirit, and learning to read through 'real books' rather than a structured reading scheme. At another they liked the teachers, but the facilities were poor and undermaintained: the classrooms were dingy; the school roof was leaking. An additional worry was the number of children from disturbed backgrounds or whose English was virtually non-existent, as there was no effective support for children with special needs. A teacher they knew warned Ben and Laura that in any class containing three or more children who required exceptional amounts of individual attention, the chances of teaching the rest properly were much reduced. In the state sector, quality largely depended on the luck of the draw.

'If one of us had been at home, it might have been worth taking the risk,' Ben often said, somewhat defensively, when, as frequently happened, the topic came up in conversation at dinner parties. 'But there would still be the problem of where the children would go after primary school.' The local neighbourhood comprehensive had a dismal reputation, and there was no certainty of entry to better state schools north of the river as other parents had arranged.

Ben was a first-generation university graduate. He had won a scholarship to Oxford from a grammar school in the North of England in the 1960s. He wanted his children to have that same opportunity, but he knew there was no guarantee of this even if his children attended the best schools in the country. There was the fearful example of a colleague's eldest son – educated at a leading London day-school with one of the finest academic records in the country, but now gone off the rails, addicted to drugs and a drop-out. That was the great middle-aged, middle-class nightmare. Somehow, because of changes in society, it seemed a greater possibility than it had been in his day.

Ben harboured doubts about private education in its own terms, not just because of its divisive social effects. He worried that it was too pressured and too socially exclusive to produce balanced young adults. But, in inner London, he saw no acceptable state alternative.

Ben and Laura's experience is not uncommon. Although the overall growth in private education has been small, our education system is becoming steadily more segmented. In 1969, as Ben was graduating from Oxford, independent schools accounted for just 38 per cent of the freshers admitted. A quarter of a century of educational opportunity later, the public schools account for over half the Oxbridge intake. The public-school grip on the best opportunities in British society has if anything strengthened in the last two decades. Of the 180 young officers passing out from Sandhurst in 1995, two-thirds were educated at public schools. Of ninety-four top Whitehall mandarins who made Grade 3 (under-secretary) before the age of fifty, just over half attended state schools; but of the twenty-six state grammar schools they attended, seven, like Manchester Grammar, have now become private day-schools.

Judged purely on academic results, the public schools sweep the board. The independent sector accounts for forty-six of the top fifty English and Welsh schools by A-level results and three-quarters of the top 200 judged by GCSEs. As the *Financial Times* journalist Andrew Adonis has written, 'What marks out Britain from other European states is the degree to which the professional classes are divorced from the state school system. It is not a question of academic élitism or selection. The leading French lycées and German Gymnasien are unashamedly élitist, yet they are integral to a single state school system whose fate indeed dominates the breakfast tables of ministers, mandarins, lawyers and businessmen.'

Parents worry so much about education because it is the key to opportunity. Ben Hodgson knows that. Without that scholarship to Oxford he would not have been able to achieve the success he has. Yet in a curious way Ben is dissatisfied with his own life. When he graduated from university he had wanted to achieve something, and in his own way he has. But getting there was distinctly more exciting than the actual arrival. Though he loves his family and is very happy with Laura, he would like a challenge – to do something more. He doesn't know what, but something for society. He feels he could make more of a contribution.

Tackling common concerns

Eileen Cooke and Ben Hodgson live worlds apart. But many of their concerns are remarkably similar:
• Whether because of the terrifying anomie of the inner-city

council estate that is Eileen's daily experience, or Ben's more general worries, they both fear that society is breaking down. Both are fearful for the future of their children and grandchildren.

- They both worry that families and communities are falling apart. The single most important symbol of social breakdown they see is crime and antisocial behaviour in its many different manifestations – in particular, too many young people just seem irresponsible and out of control.
- From very different perspectives, Eileen and Ben share a common concern about failing schools: the 1960s promise of greater equality of opportunity rings hollow in their personal experience.
- Both Eileen and Ben feel there is something badly amiss about the public domain in Britain which is most visibly expressed in lack of care for the physical environments they inhabit and the transport systems they use.
- Both Eileen and Ben are strong supporters of high-quality public services – particularly the NHS. But attitudes towards existing public services are at best mixed – even among those who are supposedly most dependent on them.
- Both Eileen and Ben have low confidence that the public sector as it now exists, whether it be council street-sweeping or the housing service, is effective in tackling their problems. They need their faith restoring in traditional collective solutions.

Eileen and Ben share these sentiments despite the contrasting experience of their families in the Conservative years.

The story of the changing pattern of income distribution is now well documented. Since 1979 there has been a massive redistribution in favour of the better off. The incomes of the top 10 per cent have risen by over 60 per cent in real terms. The bottom 30 per cent of the income distribution have seen at best a marginal improvement in living-standards. The bottom 10 per cent may actually have experienced a sharp fall of at least a tenth after taking account of housing costs. Trickle-down simply hasn't worked for the bottom third.

The traditional agenda of redistribution in response to these figures has, however, very little resonance with either Eileen or

Ben. Ben and his family would be very taken aback by the statistics and surprised that a couple on their earnings count among some of the best-off households in Britain. They would regard themselves as no more than comfortably off, hard-working professionals – not part of the rich and privileged who live off unearned income and boast vast inherited wealth. They are not natural enthusiasts for a whopping increase in their tax bills: their running expenses are high, and they know that something would have to be cut.

Eileen on the other hand, with her £100 a week take-home pay, counts as badly off by most people's standards. But she does have a job. And because her wages are low she gets housing benefit to pay part of the rent, as do two thirds of council tenants, particularly in deprived urban areas. When Eileen's pay goes up, her housing benefit is adjusted so it seems to make little difference at all. And it is all the more confusing because the rent tends to go up around the same time. People like Eileen would undoubtedly like to be better off. Many people would agree that they deserve to be better off – and in a civilised society they ought at the minimum to share in the country's growing prosperity. But they are caught in a trap where the world seems set against them.

Maybe if Labour had been elected in 1992 the party's redistributive Budget would have helped Eileen a little. Her child benefit for Peter would have risen by 30p a week (significantly more if she had had a second eligible child). She would no longer have had to pay the 2 per cent starting-rate of National Insurance on her earnings, which would have been worth £1.08p a week to her, and her income-tax bill would have been reduced by the proposed increase in the personal allowance, benefiting her by about another £1.20 a week – a net increase in income of about £2.60 a week overall.

Labour's shadow Budget would certainly have taken significant amounts of money away from Ben and Laura – together over £5,000 a year, depending on the extent to which they took advantage of pension reliefs and other legitimate ways of reducing tax liabilities. But there are many more Eileens than Bens in the world, and the net gain for the badly off would have been marginal. Eileen would of course have been pleased by the extra money, but the real issue is different: In what way would that modest measure of redistribution actually have helped solve any of the real social problems which Ben and Eileen are most concerned about?

In the past, Labour would have taken it as axiomatic that higher public spending was the solution to these social problems. But how much confidence would either Eileen or Ben have in simple 'tax and spend' solutions in today's world?

Of course better public services would make a massive difference. Better pay for teachers would help increase the quality of the profession. More money for the NHS would reduce waiting-lists in some areas. More comprehensive labour-market programmes would offer better opportunities for the unemployed. More investment would improve the Northern Line. But, this having been said, would more money for the local council actually result in housing officers who deal efficiently and politely with queries? Would it help Eileen's daughter be given the housing transfer she desperately wants? And what about all the extra bureaucracy in the NHS which hits Ben every time he reads the *Sunday Times* appointments pages and sees the numerous ads for well-paid management and administrative jobs?

Finally, how much would it actually help Eileen and her family by levelling down Ben and Laura's 'privileges'? For example, if private education were to be abolished (which is not Labour policy) the couple would move to an upper-middle-class suburb like Kew, suffer a longer 'commute' to work, but send their children to the local schools. The chances are that standards there would become even higher than they are today. Their middle-class comprehensive could end up almost as socially exclusive as the private day-school that they now pay for.

Such an inevitable outcome would do little to assist directly Eileen's difficult son, Peter, to enjoy greater educational opportunity. The weaknesses of his education need to be addressed at first hand, by tackling failing schools and finding means of remotivating disaffected adolescents. True, in the longer term the political will for action might be strengthened if all parents were committed to the state sector. But the issue here is how, by raising standards throughout the state sector, we can change the present culture of 'opting out' to 'opting in'.

So the Blair revolution should follow a different social agenda – an agenda based on the common concerns which society shares.

6

A Reunited Kingdom

A strong society can be rebuilt only on firm foundations. For New Labour this means strengthening the family, a new strategy for tackling crime, and a reformed welfare state based on revitalised public services and a switch in culture from opting out.

Strengthening the family

Strong families are the foundation of a strong community. But family breakdown is a complex issue. It is a symptom as well as a cause of a wider breakdown in society. Both lack of economic opportunity and changing social norms contribute to it. The left-of-centre cannot be passive about these trends. 'Strengthening the family' has to be a number-one social priority.

Traditionally the family has been seen as the political territory of the right. Prejudiced nonsense about the recklessness of single mothers and the alleged generosity of their treatment on welfare has constituted the stock-in-trade of the American fundamentalist Bible-bashing right, and any decent, humane and tolerant person would rightly be suspicious if a so-called 'family agenda' were drawn up on these lines. But why should we take it for granted that the family agenda should exclusively occupy this narrowly drawn territory on to which John Redwood and his like would dearly like the Conservative Party to move? And why, politically, should the left-of-centre surrender all claim to be concerned about the family to the apostles of the fundamentalist right?

It is unease about its fundamentalist associations that in the past twenty years has caused the left-of-centre to shun the language of 'the family', even though much of Labour's traditional agenda can be interpreted as being about the strengthening of the family. Labour has been concerned to make available affordable housing – an essential foundation of family life and one which the Conservatives, through their emasculation of provision for social housing, have done so much to undermine. It has shown consistent support for child benefit, which channels financial help to mothers with children. It has argued for comprehensive provision for retirement, which guarantees dignity in old age.

New Labour goes further in recognising the importance of the family unit as a social institution for the proper bringing-up of children, where the difference between right and wrong is learned, and where a sense of mutual obligation is founded and practised. And the stronger the bonds that tie the extended family together, the more it will be able to contribute to the larger responsibilities of care across the generations – whether it be grandparents assisting with day care, parents ensuring that their grown-up sons and daughters get off to a good start in life, or adults helping their aged parents to cope with the growing infirmities of an increasingly prolonged old age.

The foundations of family life

How could public policy strengthen the family?

Tax incentives are the politician's favourite gimmick, but caution would be advisable here. For example, the reintroduction of child tax allowances for married couples would channel income towards better-off families, because of the additional benefit any tax allowance provides for higher-rate tax-payers. Even if relief was restricted to the basic tax rate, that would be of no value to families with low or no earnings.

But public policy is not totally powerless to strengthen the family, and specific initiatives can give a lead about the values that government believes society ought to hold dear

A critical area for reform is the social-security system. Unemployment among male manual workers causes an acute loss of self-esteem, which conflicts with all traditional notions of how marriage should operate. In addition to that, if a married man loses his job it too often makes little economic sense for his wife to continue in work if the husband has been the higher earner: the couple are caught in a benefits trap where the earnings of one partner simply reduce the benefit entitlement of the other. The social-security system puts wives under financial pressure to sacrifice their own modest sense of independence, which women rightly value, at a time when their men's self-esteem is at a low ebb. This is bound to pose an enormous strain on relationships – additional to the practical consequences of the loss of income which unemployment causes.

The present social-security rules also make it more difficult for single mothers to find long-term partners and husbands. If the woman is ambitious to find a pathway out of poverty through childcare, training and ultimately a decent job, one thing that can throw her plans into total disarray is a serious relationship with an unemployed man. If the man moves in and the DSS gets to know about it – as under the rules it ought – then the disincentives to self-improvement become much greater, because her earnings should reduce his benefits. In this way the social-security system unintentionally encourages casual, not committed, sex. If further children result from such unstable relationships, there is a significantly higher risk of long-term social problems. For a single parent like Tracy Cooke these are very real dilemmas.

The solutions to these problems are many-sided.

In the short term, the most important step is to provide new jobs and opportunities for the long-term unemployed, as was outlined in Chapter 4. Even if the initial work on offer under New Labour's employment initiatives is relatively low-paid, its existence lifts a family out of the worst aspects of welfare dependency – and if it is combined with a genuine training element it should help restore the long-term unemployed person's self-esteem. Combined with this, Labour should examine urgent changes to the present system of earnings disregards in order to make it economic for the partner of an unemployed person to stay in work for longer than at present.

Paradoxically, one of the ways in which public policy can most successfully act to strengthen the family is by providing effective social insurance for the individual. If individuals are entitled to National Insurance benefits in their own right when they face periods of unemployment and retraining, then it is possible to avoid the means-testing of household income which at present causes real disincentives for partners to work and puts relationships under strain.

Wholesale reform of the social-security system is needed to

restore the meaningfulness of the principle of individually based, contribution-funded social insurance against the contingencies and insecurities of modern working life. Any rapid change-over to such a system is ruled out by the extremely high cost, but the direction for reform ought to be clear. One of the more attractive possibilities on which Labour should consider modelling its long-term policy is the Singapore scheme of national insurance. This involves a partnership of individual and state. The state continues to provide a minimum 'safety net', but compulsory individual contributions to a mutual fund enable a generous range of benefits to be provided in addition to the basic minimum, to cope with the vicissitudes of working life – for retraining assistance as well as replacement of lost income, for example.

However, committed relationships and marriage itself can and should be strengthened directly by public policy.

One of the greatest sources of unfairness is the different prospects of couples setting off in life with a flying financial start from their parents and grandparents and those who have no such backing. Access to a lump sum of, say, five thousand pounds would make an enormous difference at that stage of life. If parents can contribute a mortgage deposit, it avoids the horrors of high-cost, poor-quality rented accommodation. If parents can help out with the heavy costs of setting up home in terms of carpets, curtains and furniture, then a couple can escape the burden of stressful hire-purchase commitments or the disappointment of expectations that are nowadays taken for granted in our consumer society. If parents can help provide the extra comforts that make life with a new baby so much more bearable and in the good moments a great joy, it reduces the anxiety, frustration and tension at a testing moment in any relationship. Couples who are less exposed to financial stresses and strains in their early years together are more likely to stay together.

So how can public policy encourage the spreading of wealth in order to widen opportunities for a good start to family life?

One option that Labour might investigate would be the provision of medium-term, deferred-repayment, interest-free loans to young couples without access to capital of their own – in effect a form of public dowry, available just once in a lifetime. Eligibility for these soft loans would be assessed on a scale relating to the economic circumstances of the couples themselves, taking into account the net wealth of their parents. This would be rough justice for young couples with well-off parents who refuse them assistance, but this would be no different to the similar situation with student support. Marriage would be the simplest test of eligibility; it would be for consideration whether to extend the scheme to couples who affirm a long-term commitment to each other but, for reasons of their own, reject the form of marriage.

How could such an arrangement, which would be dubbed 'Getting Off to a Good Start', be administered and financed? It would be run by the building societies and mortgage lenders, who have extensive experience of assessing a couple's financial position as part of the process of awarding a mortgage. But of course there would be some net cost as a result of the deferred loan repayments. This cost would need to be met by the government, which would make non-interest-bearing deposits with the mortgage lenders in order to match the liabilities attached to the loans. These liabilities would of course amount to considerably less than the gross amount of money lent under the scheme.

The limited public-expenditure cost of this innovative scheme to spread wealth, and strengthen the family by doing so, would be financed through the proceeds of tighter inheritance taxation on the wealthiest.

Under the Conservatives, inheritance taxes have been emasculated and avoidance schemes are widespread. Lifetime gifts are now to a large extent tax-free, and only gifts made within seven years of death are in principle taxable. At the same time, lots of other highly complex exemptions have been introduced for 'heritage' assets, business transfers, farmland (whether it is actually farmed or let) and forests. This effectively makes payment of tax on wealth transfers voluntary for rich people who take specialist advice, are not unlucky enough to die unexpectedly, and like their children sufficiently to want to leave their money to them (not always the case amongst the British upper classes).

John Major now says he wants to see inheritance tax abolished in the long term. This New Labour alternative would use the revenues of reformed inheritance taxation to give more couples a better chance of a happy life together. To those who would argue that such a scheme would discriminate against the single, there is a ready response. Such a scheme would not simply be to the benefit of the couples receiving the soft loans: the reinforcement of marriage and the family that it would provide among the less well off – where these foundations of social stability are most under pressure – would be of benefit to society as a whole.

Strengthening ties between the generations

So much for strengthening the basic family unit. How can public policy boost the role of the extended family?

Some left-wing critics would argue that this emphasis on the social role of the extended family is a cop-out. The state in one form or another should accept the responsibilities involved. If children are delinquent, it is because social workers and probation officers do not have the resources to cope. If there is a crisis about long-term care for the elderly, this is because the NHS has reneged on its proper responsibilities. But this argument falls down on several counts.

For one thing, informal care by one member of a family for another is the mainstay of social support in this country. The main issue in social policy is how to help people to help each other – and give them practical support in this role – not how the state can take over their role. This is what people want. The role of the state is as provider of last resort.

The tax and spend implications for the public sector of any other strategy would be quite unsupportable. For example, when families break down and inadequate parents simply cannot cope with problem children, or are not fit to cope with them because of violence and sexual abuse, it costs a local authority £40,000 a year to purchase a place in a private or voluntary home – three times the fees of the best public schools in Britain. It is a massively high-cost policy, with a small chance of a successful pay-off. And consider the escalating costs of long-term residential care for the elderly. Even with the government's present controversial policy of making those who can afford it pay the cost of residential care, public expenditure in this area exceeded £3 billion in 1993/94.

Even if these costs were affordable, would it be sensible to rely on public provision to meet the needs involved? The public are rightly sceptical of bureaucratic, institutional, solutions to social problems. Eileen Cooke's greatest anxiety is that her daughter should be able to get a transfer to a flat nearer her own, so that she can offer more practical support. Her daughter's most urgent wish is not a social worker but a loving relationship that will give her home life security and confidence. Ben Hodgson's greatest worry about his elderly parents in the North is that, because of the considerable physical separation, he is unable to offer them the personal support to which he feels they are entitled. Not all of these issues are amenable to political action, but surely its thrust should be to strengthen the family's capacity to cope with life's strains and stresses, while recognising that government should play a vital role in underpinning the family's support where there are yawning gaps and people cannot cope.

Consider the various ways in which the tax system might be reformed in order to reinforce the extended family and facilitate mutual support:

- Contractual payments by working parents to grandparents and other relatives who undertake family childcare responsibilities could be allowed against the parents' tax – up to a set limit. This would help the re-emergence of a traditional pattern of childcare which operated at nil cost to public expenditure in towns where there was a large female workforce – in the Lancashire cotton district, for example.
- The present pension tax reliefs, which are restricted to an individual making payments into a pension scheme for his or her own benefit, could be extended to cover insurance provision for long-term care for a more widely drawn extended family, although there would be strict safeguards against abuse.
- Individuals wishing to give up work for a couple of years to care for a chronically sick or dying relative could be allowed favourable tax treatment so that, say, their previous two years of income would be taxed on the basis that it was spread over four.

Of course tax reliefs have a revenue cost which will need to be offset by revenue-raising adjustments to the system as part of Labour's reform plans discussed in Chapter 4. Also, tax reliefs for seemingly good purposes can easily become tax loopholes that are exploited by the accountants of the rich and privileged. But the ideas are worthwhile, and the Revenue should crack down on any abuse.

Similarly a new partnership needs to be developed between the family, the financial institutions and the state to help people cope flexibly with the demands modern life puts on the extended family. Many empty-nesters in their fifties and sixties not only enjoy reasonable incomes with low commitments, but are sitting on significant equity capital tied up in bricks and mortar. That capital should at least in part be mobilised to spread wealth between a family's generations – to pay for long-term care for the very elderly, to invest in their children's or grandchildren's education and training, to give young people a better start to married life.

In theory, banks and building societies ought to meet this demand by supplying innovative partial equity-release, insurance and savings products. Perhaps a new form of two-sided savings contract may be needed between the generations – parents promising to help young adults today in return for contractual saving by their children to help with their parents' old age. The regulatory regime needs reform in order to facilitate such financial innovation, as well as to provide consumers with cast-iron guarantees against rogue companies and unscrupulous salespeople.

All these measures would facilitate mutual financial support within the extended family. But what about people like Eileen Cooke in her council flat, whose fervent wish is to give more *practical* help to her daughter – which requires that she lives close by? In her case the barrier is the difficulty of a housing transfer for her daughter.

Local authorities vary a great deal in the flexibility of their housing-allocation policies. In the past thirty years most councils have given too low a priority to the objective of keeping extended families housed near together. 'Sons and daughters' allocation schemes fell out of fashion because of concern that in racially mixed areas they were discriminatory in their effects. Other pressures have predominated: to move the homeless out of bed-and-breakfast accommodation, for example, and to deal with the growing number of management transfers where neighbour problems or violence and sexual abuse within families make moves imperative.

At the same time the supply of decent housing to rent needs to be increased. This can be achieved through the phased release of local-authority capital receipts from council-house sales in order to finance new building and to renovate decaying estates, as Labour has proposed. Pension funds and banks need fresh incentives to invest in an extended third tier of social housing, managed by housing associations and the voluntary sector.

This set of proposals to strengthen the family should be among the flagship social policies of an incoming Blair administration.

Rebuilding communities and fighting crime

For many people, crime is now the number-one social and political issue. This represents a significant change during the past thirty years. When Harold Wilson first won office, in 1964, crime hardly featured as an electoral issue. According to the Nuffield study of that General Election, not a single major party candidate made it a topic in an election address. Only with the abolition of hanging in 1965 did some Conservatives begin to fasten on to crime as a political issue that might potentially favour them.

In no area of public policy is there a greater conflict between expert views and ordinary people's instincts. For many years talk of a crime wave was dismissed as exaggerated tabloid scaremongering. A rise in the crime figures, it was said, did not conclusively prove a rise in crime itself, but instead a rise in people's fear of crime, for which media reporting was largely responsible. Indeed, plausible arguments can be put forward to suggest that the number of reported crimes may have risen faster than crime itself – higher public awareness of crime, the need to report crime for the purposes of insurance claims, and increased police attention to crime statistics in order to win extra resources may all have led to offences being reported that would previously have been overlooked. However, the figures do record in particular that there has been a marked rise in stealing property by one means or another. This always causes great emotional distress, and sometimes, such as in mugging in the street, it can involve terrifying violence.

There are plenty of senior police officers who will acknowledge that avoidable social ills have driven individuals to break the law almost as an act of desperation. Yet for most of the public, who do not come from comfortable backgrounds, and for whom life may have been, or is, a hard struggle, this is a dangerous argument. They regard crime as the individual responsibility of the wrong-doer, not as a sickness of society. After all, for every unemployed young person under twenty-five years who has been convicted of a criminal offence, there are many many more who stay on the right side of the law.

Believers in individual responsibility argue that people face a simple choice between right and wrong. The choice is theirs to make, but if they choose wrong they deserve to be punished. They have little time for those who regard crime as a symptom of society's sickness and offer plenty of ready excuses and explanations.

This is why in popular debate about crime there has been an enormous and unbridgeable gulf between left-of-centre intellectuals and the general public – including the mass of Labour supporters. Too often in the past the left-of-centre's natural sympathy for those affected by social ills has sounded like being soft on the criminal. Too often the man and woman in the street's uncomplicated notions of justice have been set aside out of fear that punishment will constitute mindless retribution and vicious revenge. That is why Tony Blair's simple statement that Labour should be tough on crime and tough on the causes of crime was such a breath of fresh air and commonsense.

Labour's approach to crime

New Labour will only gain the public's trust on the issue of crime if it is open and clear in its view that crime is wrong and that criminals deserve to be punished. More than that, New Labour should be clear that it stands on the side of justice, which has become a tattered concept in modern society at all social levels – from the minority who cheat the social-security system by working for cash on the side to the wealthy fraudsters who appear to walk away from our courts scot-free.

New Labour needs to be tough and clear about where it stands on issues of right and wrong. Given such an approach, the public will be ready to listen to politicians who explain the complexity of the issues. This is the way to deal with the shallow law-and-order populism of the right, which has little credibility with the voters given the Tories' record.

There are four main elements in a comprehensive policy to tackle crime:

- To improve the effectiveness of the police, so that they catch more criminals: the likelihood of being caught is the key to deterrence. The issue is not just the need for more bobbies on the beat but how the police best organise themselves to exploit technological advance – from genetic identification techniques, to the use of video recorders, to data-matching systems.
- To increase the likelihood of conviction in the courts and, through reform of our criminal-justice procedures, reduce the number of technical acquittals.
- To punish wrong-doing effectively and develop new alternatives to prison through non-custodial sentences that are sufficiently tough to deter people from reoffending yet avoid the present risk that a spell in prison turns weak characters into hardened criminals.
- To emphasize crime prevention whenever possible – for example, in considering planning consent for the design of housing estates and public places; in standards of street-lighting; in the staffing of railway stations and trains; in the provision of two-way radios on buses; in the medical treatment of drug addicts and in providing proper drug education in schools; and most of all in setting the responsibilities of schools and the careers/employment services.

There is, however, a central issue that needs to be acknowledged and tackled. The problem of crime is to a large extent the problem of disaffected teenagers – like Eileen Cooke's son Peter – who are out of the control of their parents and alienated if not truant from school, or perhaps excluded from it as a result of disciplinary action. How do we end such disaffection? How do we prevent it expressing itself first in antisocial behaviour and ultimately in crime? How do we motivate Peter and his type for something better?

A *new contract between society and young people*

Britain urgently needs to put in place a new contract between society and young people – a contract that applies first to the final years of compulsory schooling and then beyond – to help young people find a sure footing in the adult world, but with tough penalties for those who refuse opportunity and fail to fulfil their side of the bargain.

First, all schools must accept new responsibilities for the welfare of all their pupils, however difficult and disruptive. It is no good teachers expressing a sigh of relief that troublemakers play truant, thereby allowing the more motivated to get on with their work.

Exclusion of disruptive children may be a solution for the school, but it is ultimately no solution for society. School attendance needs to be made the legal requirement that formally it is. Teachers should make out-of-school visits to the homes of problem pupils and their parents and monitor closely the commitments to improved behaviour and more regular attendance which parents and pupils make. Where truancy persists, prompt legal action should be taken against parents.

How can schools cope with unwilling attendees? Teaching in some schools can be a gruelling and dangerous experience, and teachers need proper protection against threatening behaviour and physical violence. Schools require a new, much tougher, set of disciplinary sanctions to deal with unruly and uncooperative pupils – such as compulsory homework on school premises, weekend and Saturday-night detention, and the banning of favourite leisure pursuits such as attendance at football matches.

This greater emphasis on school discipline should be matched in the local community. The police, schools and local-authority services must work more closely together in order to crack down on vandalism and other antisocial behaviour. It is excessive tolerance of this low-level subcriminal behaviour by unruly young people which undermines general respect for the rule of law, ruins the environment, and makes a misery of the lives of many innocent people – and provides the breeding-ground for more serious crime. The thugs and vandals must not be allowed to get away with it. Councils should make it a priority to mend broken glass and repair other damage as speedily as possible, in order to prevent the morale of local neighbourhoods plunging into a downward spiral. And the culprits must be punished. Punishment should be directed at righting the wrongs that have been committed (repairing vandalised street furniture, for example) and, under tight supervision, making recompense to the victims themselves.

In most instances of petty crime, local people know who the bad individuals are. The problem for the police at present is the difficulty of catching people red-handed and the pointlessness of pursuing charges through the courts. The situation requires a radical change in the present criminal-justice system for young people. This must become speedier and more effective, with closer cooperation between all the agencies responsible for dealing with delinquents and young offenders. Not only should there be a range of community-based penalties – in and out of school – to deal with young miscreants, parents should also be called to account for their children's unacceptable behaviour, with the possibility of fines, and requirements to attend parenting classes.

But the primary emphasis in dealing with young truants and troublemakers should be remedial. A key role needs to be played by the adult mentor proposed in Chapter 6 – in practice, a surrogate parent to substitute for the one who either doesn't exist or isn't up to the job – whom the school should appoint for each problem teenager. The job of the mentor would be to maintain weekly contact with the teenager, to act as a mixture of counsellor and wise elder brother or sister, and to report to the school regularly on problems. The aim would be to keep his charge attending school, achieving his or her potential, and out of trouble with the police – not to act as the police.

Mentors would be selected from a list which the school would maintain. In the main they would be ex-pupils in their twenties, living in the local neighbourhood, who had made something of life, with an ability to relate to their younger peers and be good role models for them to follow. In some cases, however, they might be older people from different backgrounds, like perhaps Ben Hodgson, who would have to show that they can establish rapport with problem teenagers. Mentors would be trained by the school. In this way links between schools and the local communities that they serve would be strengthened in a very practical way. Where, despite these efforts, young teenagers still get into trouble with the law, the mentor would work with the probation service to help ensure that commitments are met.

The schools themselves should aim far higher to motivate disaffected young people in the twelve-plus age group. The British public schools have long operated on the principle that every child must be good at something and it is the school's responsibility to identify what that something is and to make that child feel a success and thereby gain some sense of his or her own worth. State schools – particularly in deprived neighbourhoods – have a much more difficult task, but they need to adopt a similar approach and take on wider responsibilities for the social and emotional as well as educational development of their most troublesome pupils. There should be more emphasis on spotting and developing sporting talent. The vocational element in the curriculum should enjoy parity of esteem with academic studies and be combined with real work experience. Schools should take more responsibility for out-of-school activities, ensuring a wide choice of clubs and extracurricular opportunities at evenings and weekends: schools must have the resources to ensure that lack of money in the home is no barrier to participation.

These ideas will have a chance of success only if schools receive much greater support from the community outside. Apart from individuals recruited as mentors, a big role needs to be played by churches and local businesses. Every secondary school should have a business forum and establish long-term links with a variety of businesses and workplaces. Pupils would gain regular opportunities for workplace experience. Business people would be encouraged to support extracurricular activities at the school. Secondary schools in the worst areas of social deprivation would also provide a focus for endeavour under a new scheme of National Community Service, which would enable young adults from different backgrounds to work directly with – and learn from – each other.

Private schools should be encouraged to twin with state

schools in some of the most deprived neighbourhoods in Britain. The purpose would be to encourage a two-way traffic between the two systems. The state school might initially make use of some private-school facilities – for games, music or drama, for example. The private school could use its association with the school and the local neighbourhood to give its pupils much-needed contact with the real world, to develop leadership skills, and to create opportunities for community service (for example, as helpers in out-of-school clubs). There might be exchanges of pupils for blocks of time. This would be a modern-day extension of the charitable purposes for which most public schools were originally founded.

But the new contract between society and young people must not come to an abrupt end as the compulsory school-leaving age is reached. This is of critical importance for young people who leave school at the first opportunity but neither get a job nor follow any recognised path of training. Society has a responsibility to ensure that these young people do not disappear into the unknown – a murky underclass world of drug abuse and crime.

Practical responsibility for this must rest with a much enhanced careers and employment service. In the first instance, liaison with schools must be improved. But the whole task would be assisted by an information-technology revolution so that all the separate authorities dealing with 'problem' young people – the different arms of the criminal-justice system (the police, probation service and courts); schools and social services; and, under these proposals, a much enhanced employment service – are able to pool information and keep effective track of individual cases. We must end a situation where young men slip into a void until they re-emerge in prison.

The basic elements of the post-school contract – which should cover the period to the age of twenty-five – are a mixture of carrot and stick. The carrot is work and opportunity for those who commit themselves to it – Chapter 4 described a vision of the opportunities for work and training which a New Labour government should provide for the young unemployed. The stick is a denial of full benefits to those who refuse to participate or who drop out. Without benefits being conditional, it is too easy for a minority of young people to get into the habit of drawing dole and supplementing their income in the cash economy – cheating the social-security system and their fellow citizens.

But what about post-sixteen-year-olds who get into trouble with the police? Wouldn't they be the first to drop out of the work and training schemes – and wouldn't the resulting benefit penalties only increase their incentive to commit even more crime? This is where there has to be a convergence of labour-market programmes and criminal-justice procedures. A standard condition of probation should be compulsory participation in one of the new work or training schemes. Any breach of probation terms should be met with the penalty of compulsory weekend working for a set period, in addition to work obligations during the ordinary week – this would deprive young offenders of their leisure at the time they would most miss it.

Surely supervised labour in the community – and it would need to be supervised very closely – is better than institutional remedies such as prison or short, sharp shocks which for young people in trouble often have an undesirable 'macho' appeal.

No one is suggesting these remedies would be easy. The responsibility for management of work and training schemes for the young and the long-term unemployed will prove a demanding task for a totally revamped employment service. On top of this, the organisation of supervised labour in the community for young criminals will be even more testing.

There will be initial public-expenditure costs in getting these plans going, but we should recognise the existing huge costs of crime and the criminal-justice system. Under present policies the total costs of the police, the prisons and the criminal-justice system amount to over £15 billion a year; as a proportion of government expenditure, this total has risen from under 4 per cent to 6 per cent in a decade. But within that total the costs of the law courts have leapt from a sixth to a quarter, while far too little public money is spent in what ought to be key areas such as drug education in schools, crime prevention, and rehabilitation of young offenders. If we can change the profile of expenditure and keep young people out of crime, there are enormous potential savings.

This proposal for a comprehensive new contract between

young people and society is not the be-all and end-all of tackling crime, but it could be the centrepiece of New Labour's approach.

To make this concept of a new contract effective will require a concerted effort by all society's institutions that deal with young people, focused on the areas of greatest deprivation which are the breeding-grounds for alienation and crime. There will be no place for organisations ploughing their own furrow and responding only to their own vested interests. And the plans will work only if outsiders play a full part in their implementation, through establishing successful mentor relationships and through business involvement at the level of the individual school. This is nothing less than a mass mobilisation of every local community to counter social breakdown and crime.

A reformed welfare state

For many people on the left-of-centre, the principle of a universal welfare state has long been at the core of their political beliefs. The creation of a universal entitlement to medical care without charge at the point of use, comprehensive social insurance, and free education from school to university are for many the central achievements of the postwar Labour government. In simple historical terms, Attlee and Bevan completed the work that Lloyd George and Churchill had begun a generation before.

However, despite its magnificence, the 1945 achievement was never as universal as its present-day defenders sometimes imagine. Nye Bevan compromised with the doctors in order to establish the National Health Service: GPs remained in effect self-employed independent partnerships and did not become salaried employees of the state, while hospital consultants kept their freedom to treat private patients. Although the Attlee government dramatically raised pensions from 10s to 27s 6d a week, this was less than the 35 shillings which Beveridge had recommended and barely adequate for the pensioner without other means or extended-family support. The new family allowances which again Beveridge had recommended were originally denied to the first child and were not set high enough for an unemployed man with a large family in receipt of insurance benefits not to have to depend on means-tested national assistance.

As for education, the centrepiece of Labour's achievement was to open the door for all children, whatever their parents' means, to have access to free education at grammar and direct-grant schools. No one seriously suggested abolition of the public schools. Indeed the old Haileyburian Attlee would have been horrified by the thought.

In terms of welfare benefits, the fabric of universality was never tightly woven and, as the decades passed, the means-tested holes have become gradually wider. The Beveridge insurance principle was always dependent on the Keynesian assumption that the government could manage the economy so as to ensure that periods of cyclical unemployment were temporary. The return of mass long-term unemployment has completely undermined that assumption. In addition, the scope of other means-tested benefits has greatly expanded. Housing benefit, which was first introduced in the early 1970s, is now claimed by millions of tenants as public-sector rents have rocketed due to cutbacks in so-called 'bricks-and-mortar' subsidies. Family credit, originally conceived as an income supplement for low-paid workers in full-time jobs, has grown enormously as a means-tested lifeline, particularly for single parents undertaking low-paid part-time work.

In terms of universal access to health and education, the theory of the 1945 settlement was always that top-quality provision would be available free, at the point of use, regardless of means – but, if you could afford it, there was always the option to buy something which was arguably even better. From the 1970s onwards, those who could afford it began to opt out of the health and education services in large numbers. As NHS waiting-lists grew, private health insurance expanded – often under the auspices of employers, who in some cases incorporated private healthcare coverage in trade-union collective agreements – and, as a result, over 7 million people are now covered privately in some way or other (which is, of course, a very different thing from comprehensive coverage). The figure was much lower – just over 2 million – when Labour lost power, but private health received a massive boost as a result of the disruption in the NHS during the 1978/79 'Winter of Discontent'. Between 1979 and 1992 the number of beds in private nursing homes, hospitals and clinics quintupled to around 150,000.

In the same period the widespread loss of middle-class confidence in the quality of the education system, which occurred at the same time as the abolition of direct-grant places in 1970s and the teachers' strikes of the 1980s, led to a 25,000 growth in private day-school places – offset by the declining popularity of boarding schools, particularly for younger children. (Since the early 1980s the number of boarding places at independent schools has fallen by 37,000, to 94,000.) Overall more than 600,000 children are educated privately, and with the fall in the total pupil numbers by over a million to 10.5 million in the last ten years the private sector's share has maintained a gradual rise.

A new model of the welfare state has therefore emerged during the past half century. Instead of a universal system, with minor opt-outs and means tests around the edges, we increasingly have a welfare state that offers a rather holey safety net, with people on average incomes and above having little alternative but to make increasing provision for themselves, while those millions on below-average incomes are caught in a complicated web of means-tested benefits and poor-quality provision.

The New Right are absolutely clear about their long-term intentions. They would like to take this process further. They would like to offer tax incentives to the better off in order to encourage people who can afford it to opt out of state entitlements and provision altogether and rely on their own savings and capital. The aim of this policy would be to reduce public expenditure dramatically and enable taxes to be cut, while at the same time continuing to provide basic means-tested minimum provisions for those who cannot afford to make provision for themselves.

The risks attached to this process are well known. Large sections of society would lose any stake at all in the future of the welfare state: unless their attitudes were entirely altruistic, it would become a burden and a drain. Political pressure for improvement in state provision would diminish. Social divisions would increase between those trapped on means tests and the rest of the population who for their welfare, health and education would choose what they could afford from a series of multi-tiered packages.

From a New Labour perspective, this outlook is deeply unattractive. It divides rather than reunites society. It loosens rather than strengthens the ties of obligation we feel towards each other. It weakens the common bonds that tie the country together. It is wrong. But it not practicable to return to some 1945 'New Jerusalem' that never really was. Society has changed too much – not just in terms of patterns of family and employment, but also demographically as a result of people living far longer.

New Labour should have different aims:
- to uphold the goal of a welfare state which is universal in its reach but no longer uniform in what it offers;
- to guarantee access for all to a decent minimum quality of life and fair life chances, while permitting greater individual freedom of choice;
- to marry public and private finance and provision, rather then seek to drive them apart;
- to promote individual responsibility, not dependency;
- to ensure effective provision of services that offer people a hand-up, not just cash payments that give them a hand-out.

In other words, New Labour would turn its back on the present trends to social apartheid and would promote opting in, not opting out.

Opting in, not opting out

A new framework for pensions

It is in pensions that the growth of private provision has been most staggering. The spread of occupational pensions has lifted whole sections of the current generation of pensioners out of poverty. According to the Joseph Rowntree Inquiry into Income and Wealth, in the 1980s the proportion of pensioners with an occupational pension of their own has risen from 44 per cent to 55 per cent in the last decade. Unfortunately there has been no consistency of policy for those without adequate provision of their own. With the erosion of 'jobs for life', this is an increasingly important issue for future generations. It is a classic example of how the British system of politics has failed to tackle a long-term issue of crucial importance to people's lives and provide a settled framework of policy.

In the 1970s, in a rare display of political consensus, Barbara Castle established the State Earnings Related Pension Scheme – 'SERPS' – a pay-as-you-go scheme where payments to pensioners are financed by today's working population. This scheme promised earnings-related pensions up to a modestly generous earnings limit. The conditions of eligibility were favourable to individuals who had an interrupted or chequered employment history. As with all pay-as-you-go pension arrangements, the start-up costs of these promises for the future were not very high and would not become significant until age groups with the full earnings-related entitlement reached retirement. In the mid-1980s, when the Fowler Reviews looked at the potential future cost and expenditure implications, SERPS was drastically modified, and opting out became the far more attractive option for under-45s. In other words, the government of the day cheated on its predecessors' promises.

The government introduced National Insurance rebates to encourage the spread of private portable pensions, and these have led to dramatic growth in the private-pensions industry. Unfortunately this policy was implemented without adequate regulatory safeguards. The administrative and marketing costs of many schemes are excessive, and, even worse, millions have been innocent victims of pension misselling. Also, the take-up of private pensions is far from universal or adequate. A recent survey by the Abbey National discovered that 43 per cent of the adult population have made no provision for their retirement – 8.4 million women and 5.6 million men. Among those who have made private pension provision, more than half of those who opted to contract out of SERPS are paying no more than the minimum – the SERPS rebate – into their private scheme. For a forty-year-old earning £15,000 a year this will produce a total pension, including the state pension, of less than a third of that salary – in present money values.

In addition, since the early 1980s the value of the state pension has been frozen in real terms as a result of the government's withdrawal of the automatic link with the rate of increase in earnings. The effect has been a dramatic lowering of the floor of universal state provision for old age. In the last twenty-five years it has already fallen in value from 20 to 15 per cent of average earnings. This trend is set to continue, and it is forecast that the state pension will amount to only 9 per cent of average earnings by 2020 – assuming that growth in average earnings continues at an annual 2 per cent in real terms.

What should be New Labour's principles of pensions provision for the long term? Chris Smith, Labour's new social security spokesman, is working on these in preparation for the election, but there are some options worth considering.

At the moment every employed person pays a minimum of 3.5 per cent of their salary into a pensions scheme – either into SERPS (the state-run scheme) or, if they choose, into a personal or occupational pension. One option is to reform SERPS so that instead of being a pay-as-you-go scheme it evolves into a funded system. This would give individuals their own personal fund, just as they would have with a personal pension.

Pension contributions could be channelled not through the state but through mutually owned funds established by law to receive them. These mutual funds would not be subject to political interference: the governing bodies of the funds would contain an elected element and would be fully independent of the government. The new mutual funds would give individuals a choice of personal pension into which their savings would be paid. This would give individuals freedom to choose when to retire and what type of provision they wish to make for the rest of their family.

The role of the mutual funds would be to use their purchasing power to select a choice of pension schemes for their individual members, to negotiate the best available package of terms with the pension providers, and to lay down guidelines for investment policy. The mutuals would compete with each other to offer their members the best deal.

The role of government would be a limited one: to regulate the arrangements, as it already regulates the financial-services industry, and to pay into the scheme contribution credits for people with low incomes or who are unable to make contributions of their own because they are dependent on state benefits. (Clearly the generosity of these credits would depend on how the government of the day makes the political choices between public expenditure and taxation.)

The present state pension should be maintained and indexed in line with price increases as a firm base, on which the adequate provision of several pensions can be built.

This is a plan for the long-term. It needs to be started immediately if it is to meet the full pension needs of people who retire in a quarter-century or more's time. At that point in the distant future, when the adjustment to funded pensions is complete, reform of the universal state pension will become feasible – enabling resources to be targeted more effectively towards people with a life history of low earnings. But in the long transitional period, of course, there will be many people whose contributions to the mutual funds will not have been sufficient to fund an adequate pension. And of course there are pensioners today who still live in unacceptable poverty – not as many as there once were, but still one million dependent on income support and an estimated half a million or more who would be eligible but do not claim.

The independent Social Justice Commission, set up by the former Labour leader John Smith, proposed that a minimum-pension guarantee is the best way to deal with this problem of transition. The tax and benefits system should be integrated for elderly people, and a supplementary pension should be paid to people whose total income from all sources (including occupational pensions, annuities, dividends and interest) falls short of a defined decency threshold. The level of this threshold might rise in extreme old age as household essentials purchased long before wear out, costs such as heating and care rise, and savings are run down. Tax/benefit integration would deal with the unacceptable aspects of means-testing and would guarantee very high take-up. Such arrangements will inevitably disadvantage those among the less well off who have been able to save something for their retirement and have built up some private or occupational pension of their own, but any short-term damage to the incentive to save will be overcome by the clear transitional nature of what is proposed.

In the present circumstances, this strategy for pensions is much more effective than the traditional Labour approach of advocating a large increase in the universal state pension. This might have been the right approach in the 1970s, when the great majority of pensioners were totally dependent on state support. The big pension rises in that period, of which Jack Jones was the leading champion, helped lift millions of pensioners out of penury, and Labour can and should be proud of that historic achievement. But a similar approach today would simply increase living-standards for the better-off pensioner while doing little to help those in poverty. Most poor pensioners would lose in income support what they would gain on the state pension – except for the minority too proud or too confused to claim, and tax/benefits integration can largely solve that problem. New times require new policies.

Maintaining the basic principles of the NHS
Almost fifty years after its creation, the National Health Service is still an incredible success story. Given that we spend less than most European countries on health, we have a quality and level of patient care that most countries envy. And nowhere is a sense of duty and public service more apparent than among NHS staff.

New Labour believes that the principles of the NHS – unified and national coverage, availability to all regardless of the ability to pay, and free provision at the point of use – are values that should be supported and strengthened where now they are being undermined.

The NHS will always be short of resources, in that the amount of money that could in theory be consumed in promoting good health and keeping people alive is almost infinite. As technological advance expands the boundaries of what medical science can achieve, this problem will grow – though perhaps not as much as the doomsters imagine, because advances in pharmaceuticals will greatly reduce hospitalisation costs. But before we accept the argument that the NHS is at breaking-point – an argument used by many who have an interest in seeing new opportunities for the private sector in the NHS – there are some immediate changes that would make better use of NHS resources.

First, there are clear savings that can be made by reducing some of the £1 billion a year increase in bureaucracy that has resulted from the internal market. The NHS needs managing – any large organisation does – but the internal market has created whole tiers of new bureaucracy, accountancy and form-filling that could easily be cut out.

Secondly, we know that some treatments given to patients do no good or, worse, actually cause harm. The estimate of one House of Commons report is that up to 10 per cent of treatments are ineffective. That is why best practice and proper clinical audit should over time be linked to the funding that hospitals receive, to ensure that resources are spent on things that are judged by the best clinicians in the field to produce the best results. The cost of different medical procedures and how they can vary widely from one hospital to another should be identified. And there is still an enormous deficit of comparative information that needs to be collected about the therapeutic effectiveness of different procedures.

But however much New Labour improves the effectiveness of the NHS, private provision is going to continue to exist. People who can afford it will want better hotel facilities than the basic service that the NHS provides when they are hospitalised. This must never involve a fast track to preferential treatment. However, many who originally believed that private finance could be used to good effect in the NHS, to provide much-needed new facilities, have now rightly become deeply worried about the direction of present government policy. Private finance is being used as a way of cutting the NHS capital building programme and giving private companies the chance to move into the provision of clinical services.

The future agenda for the NHS is to move beyond arguments about structure to questions about how patients are treated. In short, how we can ensure that more people get a better service more quickly?

Our vision is of an NHS that uses the new technology of the information superhighway to deliver quality health care of the highest possible standard as close as possible to where people live.

That means there should be more regional centres of excelence which provide the very best care and expertise in, for example, cancer or heart-disease treatment, linked to cottage hospitals or family doctor surgeries by new technology. This will enable a patient to get the best surgeon in the field to help with diagnosis and treatment. This is already beginning to happen in some areas: there are district hospitals which link up operating theatres to the local teaching hospitals via new technology, so that regional expertise can be tapped.

This vision involves a new culture of cooperation between consultants and family doctors to improve choice and quality for patients. Put crudely, before the government reforms consultants appeared to hold sway in the NHS; through fundholding, the reforms aimed to shift the balance to GPs. The problem with fundholding is not that it gave GPs the chance to be innovative and responsive to patients – that is a good thing, and should be spread more widely. The danger is that a two-tier system emerged which meant that money followed contracts and not patients, with some patients seeming to jump the queue not because they were most in need but because their doctor was a fundholder. We need to encourage and promote innovation from family doctors but ensure that the commissioning of health care includes all doctors and not just fundholders. In the future primary care centres should include consultants doing more out-patient surgery, if that is better for the patient.

High-quality public services

Eileen Cooke and Ben Hodgson are both strong believers in high-quality public services.

Eileen depends on the health service. She is critical of her son's secondary school, and she has total contempt for her inner-city council's housing department. Ben equally admires the health service, is affronted that he feels it is necessary to pay twice for his children's education, regards London's public transport as a national disgrace, and would like to see the public environment of the local streets and parks improved.

For both Eileen and Ben there is a gap between their expectations of public services and the quality of service they perceive in practice. But neither would be easily persuaded that the only sure way to close that gap is through higher public expenditure and higher taxation. Again there is an irony. There is the greatest consensus that, of all services, the NHS is 'underfunded', yet it is the NHS that enjoys the highest esteem.

Under New Labour economic policies there will be no public-expenditure bonanza which permits greatly increased resources for public services. Available resources will initially need to be focused in the clear priority areas – on the young and long-term unemployed, education and investment. Available tax revenues will be constrained by the scale of the existing tax burden on the low-paid and on ordinary families.

So if there will be limited new money with which to tackle social problems – at least until the economy moves on to a higher trajectory of growth (and policies such as improved education and training will take a considerable time to have much discernible impact) – what can New Labour's policies be for public services?

A new vision of public service

The quality of public services is largely dependent on what individual public servants do in their time at work – how much preparation the teacher has put in; how conscientious the social worker is in keeping in contact with families of children at risk; whether GPs take time at surgery to get to the bottom of people's problems. Policies for the public services must be founded on an understanding of what motivates individual public servants to do a good job. They have to be in tune with the ethos of why people want to work in the public service.

Over 70 per cent of the cost of providing most public services goes on wages and salaries. Because earnings in the whole economy rise by more than prices, and because public servants are as entitled as any other section of the population to share in rising living-standards, the underlying cost of any given level of public services will therefore always rise faster than inflation. Pressure for efficiency improvements is therefore constant. Public-service management has to run hard in order to enable services to stand still.

But it is no good hoping to squeeze efficiencies out of the system by methods which run counter to the values of the individuals who choose to be public servants – this will serve only to damage their commitment and morale. The problem with the Conservatives' public-service 'reforms' is that in many areas they have done precisely this – particularly through the NHS 'internal market'.

So New Labour's task is to articulate a vision for the public services which motivates dedicated staff and at the same time spurs the whole system to greater consumer-responsiveness, efficiency and 'value for money'. How is this to be done? The tension between these objectives is not as great as at first sight it may appear.

Revulsion at waste – whether private excess or irresponsibility with public money – is a core New Labour instinct. New Labour is right to condemn the explosion in the costs of NHS bureaucracy which followed the introduction of the internal market, as well as unjustifiable staff absenteeism in some local councils. In the early 1990s, despite the unprecedented increases in NHS resources in real terms, NHS facilities were closed (and beds cut even in sectors for which there is growing demand, such as geriatrics) at a faster pace than ever before. The NHS experience is a classic example of how to drive apart the values of public service and efficiency, when in New Labour's vision of the future they ought to be as one.

New Labour needs to provide a framework of greater stability for the public services: one in which efficiency and good management can be pursued by committed professionals, which allows more financial and management freedom than the old bureaucracies of the past, but avoids the insecurity, waste and lack of trust which are generated by insensitive application of market models to public services.

Good management and investment in modern systems are crucial – and in the public services they have have been woefully neglected. Contrast, on the one hand, the ease of booking a British Airways ticket to anywhere in the world and then ringing up to change the flight with, on the other, the hassle involved in some local authorities in sorting matters out if your bank has overpaid a standing order for the council tax. Or try offering the local social services some surplus baby clothing and equipment that your family has grown out of, which is still in good condition and would be greatly welcomed by the Tracy Cookes of this world. The difficulty Tracy had in obtaining a housing transfer nearer to her mother is a classic example of these problems. Public authorities aim high for fairness and equal opportunity, but insensitive bureaucracy, incompetent management, and lack of modern systems have led to disenchantment on the part of the people they serve.

A new contract with the professions

The first requirement is to seek to establish a new contract with the public-service professions, defining new values of public service for the modern age. The elements of this contract are clear:

- A radical renegotiation of the employment relationship so as to strengthen commitment and build a new partnership between professionals and their employing authorities. Also, voluntarily negotiated employment contracts might involve restrictions on the freedom to undertake industrial action in the emergency services, as long as these were balanced by fair-pay mechanisms and proper provision of arbitration in disputes.
- Respect for professional judgement in areas of professional competence – but combined with genuine openness to legitimate outside opinion (such as the views of industry on the school curriculum).
- Proper recognition of exceptional performance, but no job protection for professionals who consistently fail to deliver.
- Acceptance of independent outside inspection and tough, decisive action to remedy areas of service failure.

It is just as important to concentrate effort on raising the quality of teachers, doctors and other professionals – who should be decently rewarded – as it is to measure services by the numbers employed. Local authorities have begun to introduce competency testing of staff in many different white-collar functions. This has had strong Labour support in councils with a bad record, such as Lambeth. The principle of competency testing could be extended more widely in the public services, particularly where standards of performance were perceived to be inadequate. Where there are problems, staff should be offered retraining before redundancy is contemplated.

Local councils as enabling authorities

The second requirement is to recognise that there are circumstances in which local councils are much better at planning, financing and regulating public services than they generally are at owning, managing and directly providing them. There may be clear exceptions to this, but, in general, good management requires flexibility and freedom of action which rule-bound local authorities are not always good at providing. This has been recognised by Labour in its policy that not every local service has to be carried out by the local council, and that councils should be allowed to choose how best to get the job done – directly, through formal contracts with private operators, or through partnership with voluntary bodies and other organisations. The important thing is to ensure the highest quality, the most responsive service and the best value for money.

The direction of change, therefore, that is emerging for democratically elected local councils is that their role should be to commission services that their area needs, not to assume in every case that they must deliver them themselves.

The principle of market testing is in principle a sound one. If any group is doing its job badly, others should have an opportunity to do it better, or at lower cost – as long as an unfair competitive advantage is not obtained by organisations who offer 'poverty' wages, and as long as the outcome of the tendering process is not prejudged. But Labour is right to propose modification of the present government's insistence on compulsory competitive tendering – the existing rules are neither transparent nor fair, and impose undesirable inflexibility. Instead of building a relationship of trust between purchasers and providers, compulsory competitive testing leads to a new form of inefficiency – sticking to the letter of the contract: so-called 'working to contract'.

New Labour's objective should be efficiency, diversity and innovation in the provision of public services – not privatisation for its own sake. Service providers will not necessarily be conventional private companies. They might be employee-owned or they might be cooperatives. Many will be in the voluntary sector. They might also be arm's-length, wholly owned subsidiaries of the local council – as long as it is clear that they are operating with others on a level playing-field. However, what is most desirable is the emergence of a new generation of 'social entrepreneurs' – individuals motivated by the desire to serve the public, but keen to have the freedom to run their own show. That is one way for the public service to draw on the frustrated talents of highly capable people like Ben Hodgson.

Innovation – and, where it is successful, its fastest possible spread – is the key to better public services and greater value for money. An approach that 'allows a thousand flowers to bloom' – particularly in the voluntary sector – is more likely to be successful than top-down service provision. But a key role for the public sector is to disseminate successful innovation quickly.

This commission-delivery model has many other attractions. Because the providers are separate from the democratically accountable commissioning authority, there is not the same level of defensiveness when specific services come under criticism. Instead of hiding problems and protecting failure, local councillors in particular will become much readier to attack them and root it out. They will find it easier to set benchmarks for performance, as many Labour authorities have begun to do.

It will also be easier for service innovation to cross the traditional departmental boundaries of education, social services, housing and health. This will facilitate area-based solutions to pressing social needs.

Poverty and social deprivation are increasingly concentrated in particular neighbourhoods. Research for the independent and highly acclaimed Joseph Rowntree Inquiry into Income and Wealth showed that whereas in the 1960s and 1970s fewer than half of those in council housing were in the poorest 40 per cent, by the 1980s the proportion was 57 per cent and by the early 1990s three-quarters. The needs of deprived council estates have to be thought through as a whole. What can do most to turn an area round is the provision of jobs for the long-term unemployed. Local councils need to develop commissioning strategies for public services which take account of people's economic as well as social needs. They should judge proposals by the extent to which the total amount of money available for a deprived estate will actually be spent on generating useful economic activity and jobs for the unemployed within it – not providing jobs for professionals who live miles away, or starting construction schemes for big contractors. One of the greatest needs, of course, is the provision of services which provide jobs and training for the long-term unemployed in these areas. That is the approach that deprived estates like Eileen Cooke's desperately need.

However, this new enabling model will work successfully only if three further conditions are met.

Firstly, service delivery managers should have the incentive to get maximum value out of the money they have bid for, and use the efficiency savings they achieve for the benefit of their own organisation – not in profits for their own private consumption, but in making available extra resources to strengthen their own long-term capabilities.

Secondly, as far as possible the consumer should be involved in the setting of quality standards – in other words, ask the people of Eileen's estate what they actually want, before deciding what to provide. Such efforts at consultation are often derided as form rather than substance, but this should not be the attitude. Top-down planners are not good at taking local needs and circumstances into account. Bottom-up involvement, however painfully tedious and time-consuming, has a much better chance of delivering effective results.

Thirdly, public services need proper external regulation. Specialist inspectorates are the key to quality. They should be independent of commissioning authorities but under a legal requirement to provide these authorities and the public with regular reports on performance. But there may also be a need for a new economic regulator for the public services – to ensure fair play in the commissioning and tendering processes and to deal with any abuses of a dominant position by large private companies who have already amassed considerable market power in the provision of some contracted-out services.

The measures described in this chapter would begin to rebuild the strong sense of community that so many people in Britain are crying out for. The concerns of Eileen and Ben would be addressed, their faith in public services restored, their sense of belonging improved, their commitment to the family vindicated. There would be no overnight revolution for society perhaps, but a real difference for countless millions throughout the land.

7

People's Europe

Early one morning during a parliamentary recess in 1995, Tony Blair drove out to Heathrow to catch the first flight to Bonn. It was to be a packed day. He was making two keynote speeches on Europe and was holding his first private meeting with a senior European head of government, Chancellor Helmut Kohl. It might have been a difficult encounter, as Kohl is not one of Labour's ideological allies. But, as in Blair's meeting with President Chirac of France six months later, the discussion was relaxed and open, and went on for longer than scheduled. Chancellor Kohl's conversation flowed so freely that Blair nearly missed the last plane home.

Throughout its construction, modern Europe has been built on such intimate contacts between its leaders. Jean Monnet, the father-figure of European integration, deliberately worked through Europe's national élites rather than its public, generating enthusiasm for European unity within these inner circles rather than beyond. In retrospect, it might have been better to establish the principle of doing both.

In travelling to Bonn, Blair's aim was to reinforce his own European credentials. Like his predecessors, Neil Kinnock and John Smith, he strongly believes that nations need to work closely together not only to ensure the avoidance of war (although there is no more important prize than that) but to organise more widely on a European scale what nation-states cannot achieve alone. He believes that it is in Britain's interests to be fully engaged in this activity, and that Britain should exercise influence and leadership in Europe to shape its future development.

Unlike those many British Conservatives whose commitment to Europe is now based on the single, narrow, principle of an enlarged free-trade area, New Labour believes that the European Union has a broader vision: of deeper economic integration among nation-states bound together by common rules and united by a clear social purpose. Competitiveness is the essential precondition of a successful social market, not a goal to be achieved simply for its own sake.

However, this restatement of New Labour's European commitment was not all Blair had to say to his German audience in Bonn. He had a warning to add. Although Labour will be more constructive than the Conservatives in its approach to Europe, no one should expect his government to fall in with every new idea and integrationist move proposed by Europe's enthusiasts. Europe – and, notably, its public opinion – has moved on in recent years, and it can no longer be assumed that electorates will go along with every step of European development agreed by their governments. Prime Minister Blair will want to join Chancellor Kohl and President Chirac in offering strong leadership to Europe, but he will not be a soft touch for whatever they may propose.

Kohl's response was interesting and more measured than might have been expected. He is more closely identified with moves towards federal government in Europe than any other European leader. He wants to reduce decision-making between governments in favour of arrangements which transcend national limits, with a consequent reduction in the power of the national veto – so enabling national governments to be overruled by a European body – and he believes that a single currency is essential to the onward march of European integration. He wants to keep alive a strong, positive vision of Europe's future development – which is why he is so frustrated by the British government's negative attitude. But Kohl is also a realist. He knows that Europe can proceed only by consensus and that, given the doubts among the German public, for example about relinquishing the successful Deutschmark for a single currency, proposals to integrate further cannot run ahead of public opinion.

Jacques Chirac, the newcomer to the Élysée Palace, might be Kohl's political junior but he is likely to be in power for longer, and his view of Europe will be crucial. Chirac, unlike British Conservatives, is a confirmed European and is committed to European nations working together more effectively, but he is much less of an instinctive federalist than Kohl. His preference is to maintain the present balance of intergovernmental and supranational working and, unlike Kohl, he emphasises decision-making in the European Council of Ministers with accountability through national parliaments rather than through the European Parliament in Strasbourg.

The big question about Chirac is his attitude to the proposed European single currency: in principle he is committed, but in practice he may become more concerned about the obstacles that will have to be overcome in order to realise it within the planned time-scale.

These are the leaders with whom Blair would work after the election, and there is potential for their agreeing common objectives and interests in Europe. But the idea that there is a united federalising 'juggernaut' gearing up to impose centralised European political structures on Britain is far from the truth, notwithstanding the new impetus that has been given to the creation of a single currency in recent months. Germany and France have, in the past, provided a powerful motor for political and economic union, and both countries are trying to forge a united view again. But, following the departure of Jacques Delors from his post in the European Commission and of the late François Mitterand from the French presidency, Europe's drive towards federalism has weakened.

Those in Britain who portray continental politics as a hotbed of federalism are therefore behind the times. There is no appetite to create a giant federal superstate, as some in Britain fear. As the president of the European Parliament, Klaus Hansch, said recently in a speech at Bruges, 'The old federalist dream of a United States of Europe is a thing of the past. We are doing a disservice to European integration if we carry on talking about the construction of Europe which does not, will not and cannot exist.'

The European agenda has moved on to focus on the enlargement of the EU, its internal functioning, and the need to meet the competitive challenge from Asia. This is a sensible agenda for the EU to pursue, and the one that New Labour is addressing.

The public and Europe

More and more people think of Britain as a European nation, having travelled, worked or studied in Europe at some time in their lives. The overwhelming majority of Britons are committed to strong cooperation within the EU, and, in answer to the straight question whether we should stay in or get out, the vote in Britain would be to stay in. However, there is substantial hostility towards certain aspects of the EU among large sections of the public.

In the past, Europe has been seen by most people as an important engine of economic growth, because of the massive marketplace it has created, its success in opening up markets and opportunities for trade across the world, and its stimulus to inward investment. Recently, however, the high economic expectations in these areas have not been fulfilled, and public disenchantment has spread. Recurrent recession and the impact of worldwide competition, particularly from Asia and the USA, have hit Europe's economies hard. High unemployment has persisted through the recent recovery. From the public's point of view, Europe has become associated more with unsettling economic change than with the solutions to the problems created by this change.

This has coincided with a period in which Europe has irritated the public by the harmonising steps needed to create the Single Market and, even more, by the dramatic steps taken in the Maastricht Treaty. This represented a sudden step on the accelerator of integration without agreement on the precise destination being pursued or clarity about which road to take to get there.

Establishing the Single Market, between 1986 and 1992, required an enormous amount of highly interventionist European legislation to provide an agreed framework for national laws and to level the playing-field on which companies could compete with one another in a market of over 370 million people. This extensive programme of legislation has now virtually dried up, but it involved nearly 300 different laws and made the Commission seem intrusive and domineering, causing a lot of public irritation, tension between governments, and media criticism throughout the member states.

Maastricht challenged attitudes to Europe even more directly than the Single Market. The whole nature of EU cooperation seemed to be changed by the treaty. For instance, the introduction of a single currency which was agreed at Maastricht is unarguably a logical extension of the Single Market, but no one can doubt how big a step this would be in the eyes of the public. And a similar leap forward was envisaged in the creation of a common foreign and security policy and, in time, common defence arrangements.

These and other steps taken at Maastricht (concerning the free movement of people between states, for example) sparked public alarm – and not just in Britain. In Denmark a national referendum went against the treaty, and in France a similar referendum was only narrowly won. This was a great shock, and it fomented a rebellion against the treaty by Tories already excited by the collapse of Britain's membership of the European Exchange Rate Mechanism. This rebellion was backed by some Tory-supporting newspaper editors, who made unthinking hostility to Europe respectable among Conservatives.

The impact made by the British Euro-rebels, however, lay not simply in their opposition to the treaty but in their use of it to campaign against all the premises on which European cooperation had been built.

The economic case for European cooperation was, and still is, attacked by them on the grounds that, by integrating strongly within Europe, Britain is shutting itself off from trade opportunities with the rest of the world. This is nonsense, and overlooks the fact that by being part of the European market British firms are better able to grow large enough to compete internationally.

The case for monetary union is attacked on the grounds that it is impossible to introduce a single currency without sacrificing national control over our economy, ignoring the fact that Britain long ago began to lose independent control of its monetary policy in the increasingly globalised international economy.

As for the attack on deeper defence cooperation, on the grounds that it would never work and would weaken America's commitment to NATO and Europe, this ignores the history of successful cooperation in NATO and the case for stronger European collaboration as America's European commitment weakens following the end of the Cold War.

But, however misconceived, the argument mounted by the Euro-rebels has struck a chord with a section of the public because it is routinely presented as a defence of Britain's independence and sovereignty.

In every European country there is a strong sense of national identity, but in Britain there is a powerful, traditional belief in the superiority of our way of doing things and of our political institutions. To many, Britain is still the 'cradle of democracy', Westminster is the 'mother of parliaments', and any European-tinged system of government seems neither necessary nor attractive. These emotional instincts do not sit well, however, with any realistic appraisal of Britain's true interests in the world and how our national influence can be enhanced through closer European ties.

Being part of Europe gives us more and not less control over economic and environmental forces which do not respect national borders and are beyond the reach of national government. This does not mean subordinating Britain's national interest to Brussels, let alone dissolving our national institutions into European ones (which, in any case, is not being proposed). It does mean recognising that in an increasingly interdependent world it pays for European nations to coordinate their economic and foreign policies so that their combined weight makes them harder to ignore by the rest of the world. It also means Europe doing more in areas where this serves the public interest – for example, in protecting the environment, standing up for consumers' rights, and combating crime.

If the British Parliament runs its full term, a new Labour administration will come to power just as Europe's forthcoming intergovernmental conference (the IGC), called to discuss Europe's next steps following Maastricht, comes to a conclusion.

The IGC will need to grapple with a number of thorny practical issues like the future of European defence cooperation and the operation of a common foreign and security policy. It will review the EU's activities in relation to justice and home affairs. Overhanging all these, and other issues, is the progress of EU enlargement and the complex changes that are inevitable if more members are to be taken in.

There are substantial questions for the IGC to address:

• Is the EU's remit broad enough to reflect the public's economic concerns? For example, in Sweden there is pressure to add employment to the EU's responsibilities, and this will find an echo in many other countries.

• Are the EU's decision-making procedures adequate for its tasks and, as its membership grows, will these have to be made simpler and quicker through the extension of qualified majority voting in areas which are not fundamental to national sovereignty?

• Does the EU strike the right balance between efficiency and representativeness? All member states need to be represented in the EU's institutions, but is the balance between the influence of large and small member states in need of change in the light of enlargement?

• How, in the EU context, should democratic accountability be strengthened: through the EU's own directly controlled institutions like its Parliament or through national ministers and national parliaments?

In the background, but not part of the IGC itself, is the issue of economic and monetary union (EMU) and the implementation of the timetable agreed at Maastricht for the creation of the single currency. In the meantime, the EU has to take further measures to complete the Single Market and must also take the lead in liberalising global markets. For Britain, financial services, telecommunications and energy are important areas in which our businesses stand to gain from vigorous European Commission action to promote competition and access to markets, in Europe and beyond.

In considering all these issues, the EU's priorities need to be geared to those of the public. Its operation needs to be less cumbersome and bureaucratic. Waste and fraud need to be tackled with vigour. Overprescriptive regulations should be made more flexible. The Common Agricultural Policy must be reformed. And the EU needs to be more outgoing towards the rest of the world.

These changes must be part of a clear-sighted plan for the EU's future and, above all, they must be capable of restoring the public's respect and faith in the EU.

There are great prizes in European cooperation which the

public understands a reformed Europe could win. For example, there is tremendous concern, particularly among young people, about the environmental challenges facing the globe, but many of the issues can be addressed only on a continental scale – a purely national approach would be damaging for competitiveness and jobs.

There is also great concern about world poverty and the problems of sustainable economic development. Britain can and should make its own contribution through bilateral aid and other policies, but the scale of this pales into insignificance by comparison with the influence a united Europe can wield, for example, in trade negotiations and through the new World Trade Organisation.

And our future depends on European cooperation on potentially the biggest issue of all – maintaining peace and security, and avoiding another European war. Following the end of the Cold War and the collapse of communism, a united Europe is the only way to prevent the re-emergence of the balance of power politics which triggered past conflicts.

But Europe can address these big issues only if it reforms itself and develops institutions that command the confidence of the public.

A new, practical vision for Europe

There is a positive European agenda, but it is up to politicians to shape it and articulate it against the sceptical European climate which has developed since Maastricht. Moving on from those days of intense integrationist activity, Europe needs to prepare for a new phase in its development. The goals which it is now important for Europe to advance and which it should be possible for all the EU's member states to agree on are threefold:

- to extend the EU's membership in central and eastern Europe so as to stabilise Europe, strengthen security, entrench democracy, and ensure economic and social progress across the whole of the continent;
- to deepen cooperation in economic and social areas and to pool sovereignty wherever this brings real advantages without threatening the identity of Europe's nation-states;

- to strengthen the EU's legitimacy in the eyes of the people of Europe by ensuring that its institutions work more openly and efficiently, with less waste and unnecessary intrusion.

Enlarging the Union

Underlying the above goals is the need for Europe to address what has occurred on the Continent since the dismantling of the Iron Curtain and the re-emergence of nationalist, ethnic and religious tensions to the east.

Fully reintegrating the newly liberated former Soviet satellite countries into the European fold, so that their economic prosperity and social stability are assured, is both an historic obligation and a massive challenge. It requires the sort of combined response that was mounted by the Allies in 1945, with the same strength of vision provided then by such politicians as Labour's postwar foreign secretary, Ernest Bevin. As a priority, and as a minimum, it is important to associate these countries with the EU's political infrastructure by involving them progressively in decisions on foreign policy and security.

The process of enlargement could in time embrace Poland, the Czech Republic, Slovakia and Hungary, then Romania, Bulgaria and Slovenia, Malta, Cyprus and finally the Baltic States. Although each country is in a different state of preparedness, their desire to join both the EU and NATO – however long it takes – is uniformly strong and raises important issues for both organisations.

In the case of NATO, no new countries can be admitted unless the existing members are prepared to extend to them the copper-bottomed security guarantees contained in the NATO charter. Also to be considered is the need to consult and reassure Russia about this extension of the West's sphere of influence without giving it an effective veto.

In the case of the EU, the implications of enlargement are immense – both for its decision-making processes and for its budget (particularly agricultural subsidies). If the way the EU works now is complex and overloaded, and if the public feels uninvolved in a Europe of fifteen members, imagine what it could be like with twenty or even thirty countries in membership, with a radical alteration to the balance between big and small states.

Some prominent current members – Spain is an example – fear that widening the EU will be achieved at the expense of deepening its integration. This need not be the case – in fact every previous enlargement has been accompanied by closer working between the member states. But a larger EU will need more give and take in the way it decides its policies, and the argument will grow for more majority voting to prevent decision-making being paralysed by the application of vetoes. If, therefore, the EU is to be expanded to the east, greater flexibility will be required in the way that its institutions evolve and in how sovereignty is shared by its members.

Some European sceptics in Britain believe – and, indeed, hope – this flexibility means a loosening of existing ties, with Europe doing less and individual countries opting out of any European initiative they do not like. But flexibility must not become disintegration. Rather, the purpose of flexibility is to permit a diversity of approach, a necessary protection of vital national interests in some spheres, and variable speeds towards common goals in others.

In practice, three principles are important:

- First, cooperation need not conform to a single institutional pattern. The Single Market requires binding rules and the machinery to enforce them (through the European Commission and the European Court), because they would simply break down if left to loose intergovernmental agreement. However, in the case of the EU's Common Foreign and Security Policy and in the fields of justice and home affairs (the second and third pillars of the Maastricht Treaty), key national interests are involved that call for more pragmatic intergovernmental working.
- Secondly, the leadership role of big states needs to be buttressed within any enlarged union.

When the original European Community was created it consisted of three big, populous states (West Germany, France and Italy) and the Benelux countries (Belgium, The Netherlands and Luxembourg). The balance of power was unmistakable, but there was no question that Europe's direction would be shaped by the three countries representing the bulk of the population.

Now there are fifteen member states, of which only five (including Britain and Spain) are large. The smaller nations are now overrepresented in EU decision-making, and this situation will worsen with enlargement unless fundamental change is introduced – changing the rules of representation and voting to weight these in favour of the larger members without disenfranchising the smaller and newer members.

• Thirdly, a pick-and-choose attitude to Europe should be opposed, although inevitably some member states will integrate more quickly and further than others. This is already recognised in the agreed introduction of economic and monetary union, which all member states can converge to in time, and will also apply to defence.

This last principle raises what is probably the biggest question facing the EU in the medium term: What should happen if differences become entrenched such that there emerges an inner core of countries proceeding with rapid political and economic integration while others form a second tier?

For Britain, under the present government, this is a particularly relevant issue, for, while it is Labour's strong aim that Britain should be seated at Europe's top table, many Conservatives are happy for Britain to dawdle *en route* in Europe's slow lane – or, in the case of some of them, not to start the journey at all. Nowhere is this attitude more dramatically illustrated than in relation to the creation of the single European currency.

Economic and monetary union

There are those in all parties who believe that creating a single currency in Europe will be too big a step for any country to agree to so we might as well stop worrying about it because it will never happen.

Doubts about a single currency are certainly growing in a number of countries – including Germany and France as well as Britain – but to dismiss the prospect of economic and monetary union is unwise. At the EU's summit of government heads in Madrid in December 1995 the decision to press ahead with monetary union was reaffirmed, on the original Maastricht timetable. Eight member states – including Britain – are likely to fulfil the Maastricht Treaty's economic-convergence criteria by

1998, which is the date specified in order to form a monetary union by the end of the century.

The single currency is the natural complement to a single market, and Britain would benefit from lower transaction and exchange costs for businesses and holidaymakers if we joined. A single currency would reduce the uncertainty of exporting to or investing in the rest of Europe, as exchange-rate risks would be eliminated. And a new monetary system could bring lower interest rates and lower inflation, consolidating the conditions of stability which Labour's new economics regards as fundamental for sustained non-inflationary growth.

The determination of many European governments and central banks to go ahead with a single currency – with or without Britain's involvement – should not be underestimated, if the economic conditions are right and if public opinion can be persuaded in its favour. The political momentum behind the move will be continued if German and French leaders maintain their determination to deepen Europe's integration in this way. If a group of European countries around Germany and France decides to join them, the pressure in the British business and financial sectors for the UK also to participate is likely to be immense, because of the trade and investment penalties for Britain of staying out.

Naturally, however, an important issue in Britain is the political one: Would monetary union result in such a loss of control over policy that it would mean Britain relinquishing its economic independence?

We should be clear about this. Sovereignty would be pooled in order to bring about the benefits that eliminating exchange costs and creating exchange-rate stability would bring for business and the economy as a whole. This would mean sharing responsibility for monetary policy with our European partners, and the European Central Bank (in which we would actively participate) would be in the driving-seat of monetary policy. This would take place within an agreed policy framework and to economic guidelines drawn up by Europe's finance ministers, who would be accountable to their respective national parliaments for their actions. The charge that this would mean that Britain would cease to be an independent nation-state is simply nonsense: if there were any possibility of its being true, neither the Conservatives nor Labour would entertain the idea of a single currency for a minute.

In fact the loss of national sovereignty in these arrangements would be more theoretical than real. At present, because of the scale of international capital flows and currency transactions, markets are more sovereign than ministers. True, the markets cannot prevent governments making foolish decisions, but they make them pay a heavy price for their folly.

The question about a single currency, therefore, is not primarily political or constitutional but economic: Would it work?

The experience of the Exchange Rate Mechanism, when European currencies were locked together in only narrowly variable exchange rates, demonstrates that there are advantages of such a system but that fixed parities will not last in the face of large and persistent differences in economic performance – particularly inflation – between member states. It is inconceivable, therefore, for EMU to go ahead unless there is adequate convergence in the performances of the national economies involved.

Such convergence would not be the end of the story, however, because high regional unemployment could still be generated even if inflation rates converged. This would lead to political pressure for ever-greater subsidies from the centre to the poorer areas, so as to even out the differences between the regions. But the budgetary implications of this could be huge, and the relatively well-off nations like Germany – and Britain – would be reluctant to contribute more to meet the costs of both EMU and enlargement of the EU during roughly the same period of time. Without such subsidies, however, monetary union could soon set up intolerable social and political strains that might undermine the legitimacy of both the single currency and the EU as a whole, and put in jeopardy the achievements of the Single Market.

Also, for public confidence to be maintained in a single currency, the European Central Bank itself would need to enjoy a degree of authority and public legitimacy in each member state which it is a long way from achieving at present.

Undoubtedly, economic and monetary union requires a considerable leap of faith – but there will be a big economic prize if it is successful. For this reason it is right to keep open the option of joining a single currency if the economic conditions exist to make it a success, even if the timetable slips (as seems possible).

It would be wrong to rule out joining in the course of the next Parliament, as Tory Euro-sceptics are pressing the government to do. The decision whether to join should be a pragmatic one. We should weigh the costs of staying out against the risks of participation, and decide in accordance with our long-term economic interest and our commitment to Britain playing a leading role in Europe and shaping its future development.

The Social Chapter

The relevance of a single currency is the contribution it can make to economic growth and creating employment in Europe. In Britain, however, our relatively poor economic performance requires concerted macro-economic and supply-side action, independent of progress towards EMU, if competitiveness is to be restored. It is in this context that arguments about the Social Chapter are frequently made, and they need to be answered.

Unemployment has risen through every business cycle in Europe in the last twenty years, and it is accepted that this is not simply the result of world depression. In both domestic and world markets, European-based business is losing ground to non-European (and, in particular, Asian) competitors across the whole range of industrial and commercial activity. As a result, Europe's economy has not generated the same numbers of jobs as have our industrial rivals.

Economic recovery by itself will not solve this problem. It is a structural problem, and the chief cause is that the proportion of Europe's GDP spent on investment has fallen by about a fifth during the past two decades, while real wages have continued to rise. Europe's investment gap has directly affected its trade performance: Europeans have got better at exporting to each other through the Single Market, but we have got a lot worse at exporting to the rest of the world.

The competitive challenge to Europe is intensifying as our competitors spend more on research and development and stretch their technological lead further, forcing Europe to compete more on price. While our economies have been driven by wages and consumption, Asia's economies have been led by savings and investment. Cheap labour costs in Asia have been balanced in the past by Europe's higher productivity, but in many sectors this is now threatened by the rapid spread of higher skills among Europe's new challengers.

The implications of this have been described in Chapters 1 and 3. They mean that every European company must raise quality, lower costs, stimulate innovation, strengthen research and development, develop new products, and break into new markets – that is, change in almost every respect – to regain a competitive edge. But this has to be complemented by government action: in education, in reskilling the labour force, and in facilitating necessary infrastructure investment – specifically in transport and telecommunications.

There is considerable scope for the EU's members states to coordinate their economic policies and investment plans so as to foster competitiveness and growth. Britain, because of the government's prejudices, has discouraged Europe-wide initiatives to promote investment, and ending this obstruction would be welcomed by many in business.

But companies are also concerned about the costs that EU governments choose to place on them to secure social objectives. This is an issue frequently raised in relation to the Social Chapter, which has made a range of rights and conditions at work commonplace throughout the EU, though not, because of the government's opt-out, in Britain.

No one is in favour of introducing rigid costly rules and importing to Britain inefficient practices which will harm our competitiveness and deter inward investment. But that is why Britain needs to sign up and be present at the negotiating table when proposals for legislation to implement the Social Chapter are being made. An empty-chair policy, as we have at present, simply allows others to make the rules – which, in all likelihood, Britain will be obliged to implement eventually by one means or another.

There needs to be a strong social dimension to the EU if it is to bring real benefits to ordinary people. The question is, on what terms? Britain gains nothing by refusing to influence these by opting out.

The notion of a basic framework of employment rights ought

to be unobjectionable. The labour mobility which such a framework facilitates both enhances individual freedom and promotes economic efficiency. But it would not be sensible to standardise social costs across a whole range of policy areas when economic conditions in member states vary as they do. Britain under New Labour would not be alone in taking this view.

Foreign policy and defence cooperation

Western-European countries have been cooperating in collective defence arrangements since the last war, and there are clear advantages in continuing to do so. No change in underlying principle is being suggested, therefore, in the proposal to integrate further. This is necessary in view of the inevitable reassessment of NATO's future following the ending of the Cold War and the resulting pressure in the United States to cut back its international commitments.

Bosnia has shown Europe's continued dependence on US military power to force warring parties to a peace agreement, but we cannot necessarily rely on this power for ever. European countries need to work out a new basis for defence and security partnership with America, to face the new challenges of the post-Cold War world. This will include deciding whether the Western European Union (WEU) should evolve into a stronger organisation for European military cooperation.

The end of the Cold War prompts the need for a new vision governing relationships among nations no longer dominated by the East-West rivalry of the last fifty years. A great deal of thought has been devoted to this new vision, not least by experienced American thinkers. One such is Robert McNamara, the former US defense secretary and president of the World Bank, who has argued that a new international framework should be directed towards five goals: to provide all states with guarantees against external aggression; to codify the rights of minorities and ethnic groups within starte; to establish a mechanism for resolving regional conflicts and conflicts within nations; to increase the flow of technical and financial assistance to developing nations; and to ensure preservation of the global environment.

The conflict prevention and conflict resolution tasks and the peacekeeping functions necessary to accomplish these functions would, in Robert McNamara's view, be performed by multinational organisations: national security would be supported by a system of collective securiry.

In keeping with these principles, Europe has to find new ways of keeping its immediate neighbourhood secure in the face of fresh challenges to its peace and stability in central and eastern Europe and in North Africa. The task of the forthcoming intergovernmental conference, therefore, is to strengthen the EU's Common Foreign and Security Policy (CFSP) and to develop defence cooperation in sensible ways which are compatible with NATO.

Britain will always want to retain an effective independent diplomatic and military capacity to pursue its own international interests. Britain's historic links with America, and the benefits these bring in shared intelligence and nuclear capacity, are also very important. From outside Europe, however – and especially from America's viewpoint – the EU is increasingly seen as a single entity with a common interest. This means that Britain should also add its weight to ensuring a more decisive and united European voice in the world, with a strengthening of the machinery of the CFSP to make this possible.

To maximise cooperation and the chance of any necessary action being taken jointly, a stronger secretariat, separate from the Commission, is required to manage the CFSP. There are strong arguments for appointing a single individual to head this and provide a focus for the EU's wider diplomatic role.

For policy to be pursued vigorously, however, the situation cannot persist whereby every member state, big or small, has the same weight in decision-making and can exercise a veto over any initiative. This does not mean extending the system of qualified majority voting to foreign-policy decisions, but the principle needs to be established that nothing goes ahead without the unanimity of the big five states, reflecting their true weight in the world, and that if these nations want to act they should not be frustrated by other states casting a veto. (If these other states do not want to participate in the proposed action, of course, they can choose not to.)

What teeth will any policy have unless it can be backed up by military force? Few in Britain would suggest that the EU should become a fighting organisation along with its other responsibilities, and so a clearer link needs to be established between the CFSP, NATO and the WEU. The aim should be to enable the European members of NATO to act separately from the USA, when America does not wish to take the lead, but not independently of NATO's structure.

This points to the development of the WEU as the European pillar of NATO, and real effect should be given to the decision of the NATO summit in January 1994 to make 'the collective assets of the Alliance available for WEU operations undertaken by the European Allies in pursuit of their Common Foreign and Security Policy'. In other words, there should be separable but not separate capabilities for the WEU and NATO.

The European countries at present rely on American intelligence and logistics, but the assumption is (or should be) that in time the Europeans will provide more for themselves – an assumption the Americans themselves share. Britain and France are already demonstrating how their respective military capabilities can be enhanced through close cooperation. It would be desirable for Germany to play its full part by engaging in military operations outside its borders.

While, of course, there can be closer cooperation between the WEU and the EU – for example, through 'back-to-back' meetings of their ministerial councils – the time has not come to tidy up their institutional arrangements by merging the WEU into the EU. The memberships of these organisations differ, and it would be unacceptable for some EU members to decide on defence matters without bearing any defence commitments under the WEU/NATO treaties. It should be possible, however, to devise new collective approaches to defence resourcing.

Britain currently bears an unfair share of the burden of Europe's defence. Many EU states at present make little financial commitment to Europe's collective security and peace-keeping operations, and is about time that they pulled their weight. One suggestion is for every country to commit, say, 2 per cent of GDP to fulfil common defence objectives agreed within the WEU as a European contribution to NATO. It would be possible for each country to spend above this level in accordance with its national requirement.

Another idea is to strengthen arrangements for common

defence procurement for the WEU countries, for which agreement on common staff targets and requirements would be needed among member states. To rationalise costs and get best value for money, two or three major national research centres in Europe would specialise in the development of weapons systems and equipment, but production tenders would be invited for just one company to be the prime contractor for the aircraft, tank or vessel in question for all WEU members. There would be plenty of opportunities for subcontracting to other firms, but the principle would be to concentrate production to a standard specification for the benefit of all. Britain's world-class defence manufacturing firms would be particularly well placed to benefit from such an approach – especially when, as should happen in time, countries in central and eastern Europe become full members of the WEU/NATO.

Institutional and organisational change
The development of foreign-policy and defence cooperation illustrates the need for institutional change which enables the EU to operate flexibly, giving greater weight to the larger nations, which carry the bulk of responsibility, and permitting different speeds of integration among member states. How should this be achieved?

If the EU is not to stagnate but to change in ways that better meet the public's needs, its decision-making system must prevent individual members or groups of relatively small member states from holding up progress indefinitely in key areas for the EU's future success. This is an important issue now, but it will become even more significant as enlargement takes place and the possibility is created of larger and more long-standing member states being frequently outvoted in the EU's institutions.

Change in this respect is necessary in the two crucial decision-making institutions of the EU: the Council of Ministers (which consists of representatives of the member-state governments and agrees the EU's legislation) and the European Commission (which initiates and administers the legislation).

In the Council of Ministers, the necessary change could be brought about by insisting either that two or more large countries always have to figure in the majority for decisions to carry, or that, unlike the smaller nations, such countries have the right to cast a veto where the system of majority voting is operating. Alternatively, a new system of double majority voting could be introduced, whereby states representing, say, 70 per cent of the population permanently enjoy the same percentage of the votes. There are variations of this, but the principle of qualified majority voting is important, and other issues, like the composition and functioning of the Commission, will become easier to resolve once it has been established.

With twenty members, the Commission is already unwieldy. As the EU grows, it might be desirable to limit the larger member states to one full commissioner, while smaller nations and microstates (like Cyprus and Malta, if they are admitted) might only have the right to nominate deputies or not have commissioners at all.

An alternative, and preferable, approach would be to fix the size of the Commission at, say, twelve members and then allow the president of the Commission to choose his team from a list of nominees supplied by all the member states. This would encourage countries to nominate potential commissioners of stature. The president would then have to use discretion (and political sense) to ensure that representation properly reflected the big and small member nations. The large states would be allowed to dominate, while the smaller nations could be compensated with appropriate positions and representation in other EU institutions and spheres of activity. Such a flexible and politically sensitive approach is far preferable to the application of arithmetic national quotas, but it would involve a lot of trust and considerable give and take on the part of all member states.

The other big issue to be resolved in the context of enlargement goes to the heart of what has been termed Europe's 'democracy deficit': What should be the balance of powers between the EU's different institutions – the Council of Ministers, the Commission and also the Parliament?

It is easy to make the jump from recognising the problem – that the public feels insufficiently in control of what the EU is doing – to concluding that the solution would be to boost the powers of Europe's only directly elected body, the European Parliament. But the EU is an organisation of freely associating, independent nation-states, and its democratic centre lies not with a Europe-wide parliament linked to the Commission and assuming the status of a federal executive but with its member states' elected national governments and national parliaments whose representatives are on the Council of Ministers, exerting control over the Commission.

However, there is scope for extending the European Parliament's role in scrutinising what the Commission does (for example in the use of EU resources and eliminating waste). Also, if decisions taken at the IGC result in qualified majority voting being extended to routine EU legislation, there will be a case for extending co-decision with the Parliament. When the Council decides matters by a majority, the ability of national parliaments to hold their ministers to account is undermined. If important legislation is to get on to the statute-book through a majority of member states, its legitimacy would be strengthened if it also had majority support in the European Parliament.

The European Council (of heads of state and government) and the regular meetings of the Council of Ministers will remain the EU's legislative motor, and they need vastly to improve their working methods. By and large, the Council of Ministers works by consensus – with much late-night haggling on the way – but votes are taken periodically and, in a range of policies, by qualified majority voting. To stop obstruction of essential decisions, there is a case for extending this system to social, environmental, industrial and regional policy – on condition that there is a reweighting of the votes in favour of the bigger countries – but not to areas like taxation, foreign policy and revision of the basic European treaties.

There has to be more rigour, more continuity and greater preparation in the Council's decision-making – starting with an improvement in its presidency. This key post in Europe's political system is held by each country in turn, but at present it rotates too frequently (every six months) and there are sometimes not the resources or people to manage the job effectively when it is in the hands of small and poorer states. To overcome this, the troika system, in which successive presidencies cooperate, should be strengthened.

To improve its overall running, the Council of Ministers must be more open in conducting its legislative business, doing more to show the public what it is deciding in their interest and why. The whole decision-making and legislative process throughout the EU machine should also become simpler and more transparent, assigning clear roles to each institution.

National parliaments also have to play a more committed role in European affairs if public accountability is to be increased. Two proposals have been put forward to achieve this:

- the creation of a senate or council of national parliamentarians which would in effect become an upper house of the European Parliament;
- a system of joint committees between the European Parliament and national parliaments which would introduce a collective parliamentarians' view to the functions of the EU, adding legitimacy to the process of parliamentary oversight.

In principle both ideas are attractive – the second more than the first – but the expense would be hard to justify to the public, and it could be argued that national parliamentarians would find it hard to keep pace with EU business as well as their national work. However, the opportunity to inquire into EU actions and expenditure in greater depth must be created in Britain, so that Westminster (along with other national parliaments) has more leverage in the EU political system. The important point here is to ensure that national parliaments are fully involved in debating and influencing EU directives before they are issued and when the Council of Ministers is at an early stage in considering them.

The EU budget and the Common Agricultural Policy

All these democratic and institutional reforms in the EU's system are valid whatever progress is made in enlargement. However, their implementation – and, indeed, any consensus about enlargement, and the long transitional periods that will be needed – assumes a degree of solidarity among the EU states which is already being tested. This will be aggravated when, towards the end of the decade, the EU budget comes under review.

At the moment the EU budget is capped, and net contributors (like Germany, France and Britain) will, understandably, resist any increase. This position will be challenged by the net beneficiaries of the budget, who could become so alarmed at the prospect of losing income if resources are redirected to help pay for the transitional arrangements of the applicant EU members that they might decide to veto enlargement all together. This would be a grave set-back for any positive vision of Europe's future.

Opening EU markets to goods produced in eastern Europe will require complex negotiation, and the preparation of east-ern-European economies for integration into the Single Market will involve a huge amount of work on legal structures, state subsidies and competition policies, as well as cooperation on transport and information networks. The thorniest question of all will be agriculture. The Common Agricultural Policy is already intolerably expensive and wasteful (it consumes 60 per cent of the EU budget), and if it were applied in with present structure and price levels to a community extended to the east the cost would be prohibitive and the policy would collapse.

The CAP provides a good illustration of the immense prob-lems the EU encounters in carrying out internal change, although there can hardly be a more powerful case for reform. Designed to ensure steady supplies of food, it has encouraged farmers to overproduce at excessive economic and environmen-tal cost, and it is estimated that the CAP adds £20 to the weekly food and tax bill of the average family of four in Britain.

Some reform of the CAP has recently taken place, shifting the emphasis from subsidising production to supplementing farm-ers' incomes, but change must go further. Agriculture justifies support, but this should be entirely uncoupled from production and should instead go directly to those farms which need and deserve assistance. Support should be put alongside wider investment in rural areas, to stimulate new jobs and investment which will benefit the whole rural economy, and the CAP should offer new incentives to farmers to manage land in ways which are socially and environmentally acceptable.

A new London-Paris-Bonn axis

No change, whether in the CAP or any other aspect of the EU's working or its enlargement, will be easy or even possible without fresh agreement emerging between Germany, France and Britain. The relationship remains strongest between France and Germany, despite the political changes in France, and these two are likely to submit joint proposals to the forthcoming intergovernmental conference.

Wider agreement is being frustrated by the paralysis inside the British government due to the Conservatives' internal divisions. Under the conservatives, Britain's record in Europe is one of such persistent ambivalence that it is edging close to national humiliation. Faced with the choice of fighting for change in the EU – setting a new national strategy that engages us in Europe and recognises the need for us to offer leadership – or quitting the EU (as many in the Conservative Party would secretly like to do), Tory ministers simply fudge with more opt-outs, more caveats. A realistic view is needed of what more the EU can do and how it can do it better in its next stage of development. It needs to take account of the fact that Europe has passed through its intense integrationist phase and must now concentrate on pragmatic moves towards greater economic, social, foreign-policy and defence cooperation where this is justified and practical to achieve.

Britain, France and Germany do not have the power to impose a new European settlement on everyone else – Spain and Italy, for example, have substantial influence of their own – but, more than others, they can guide the member states if they can agree on what they want. Such agreement is unlikely at the moment.

France wants to share Germany's positive vision of Europe's future and wants progress in Europe's integration, while sympathising with the sort of flexible British view of the EU's institutional development described in this chapter. The tragedy is that Britain, under its present government, is incapable of embracing any sort of European vision and is thereby managing both to alienate Germany and to lose France's support.

The British Conservative Party has increasingly set itself apart from any sort of European consensus. In contrast to Tory *laissez-faire* beliefs, European governments of left and right share Labour's belief in partnership and social action – not just on the domestic plain but internationally – and want to build sensible

European cooperation on that basis. The concept of a stake-holder economy, whether applied to firms and companies or more widely, is firmly established on the Continent. But perhaps the EU's commitment to a strong social agenda and a social-market approach make it inevitable that the Conservatives should be cool towards Europe. Both the Social Chapter and a single currency involve an emphasis on cohesion and taming crude market forces which is unexceptional in Europe but heretical to them.

In Labour's view, Britain cannot duck Europe's choices any longer. Britain cannot be a half-member of the European Union. The challenge of enlargement makes it imperative for Britain to cooperate with Germany and France in finding solutions to the issues involved, for Britain gains nothing by watching others shaping Europe's future in ways that are unacceptable to us – unless, of course, the government imagines that Britain can simply ignore the views of others and veto everything it dislikes at the end of the day, leaving the IGC – and Europe's future – in a shambles.

The danger is that, within an enlarged number of loosely tied member states, a core of European nations will finally agree to cement their own military and monetary cooperation – with Britain, unable to make up its mind, excluded. This would do nothing for our world role, and nothing to boost our influence; and we would ultimately find the benefits of Europe's Single Market denied to us too, as the core group, increasingly, would make its own rules from which Britain would have to opt out, with a resulting catastrophic loss of jobs, trade and investment.

It is a Labour government's task to make sure that, as European cooperation deepens, Britain is among the core group of leading nations.

As long as we are confident that our economy and security would be strengthened by further integration, and no constitutional threat to Britain's nationhood is involved, a Labour government should support closer cooperation in Europe in the practical ways described above. It must, however, be a Europe that is reformed within the sort of flexible institutional frame-work which the public wants, and which is affordable. It must advance step by step and not hurry if, by a slower pace, success is more assured. It will need strong political leadership, a spirit of give and take, and a determination to agree. It is a big diplomatic test which Britain must pass as much as every other European state.

Europe will be one of the battlegrounds in the next election. With Conservatives' minds set only on what will keep their party together and what they think will offer the best tactical advantage against Labour, the government will attempt to rally British opinion against Europe rather than behind what is the best deal for Britain in Europe. As the former Tory deputy premier Geoffrey Howe has commented, it will be 'the equivalent of wrapping ourselves in the Union Jack in preparation for burial at sea'. Labour, in contrast, will fight the election on a settled and positive view of Europe – a view which is being reinforced by the new generation of younger members coming into the party.

The sort of realistic settlement in Europe outlined in this chapter has the potential for strong backing among other EU members. It would command wide public support at home and would be the basis for defining Britain's interests and international role on a constructive, lasting basis. The relationship between Britain and Europe does not have to be an unhappy and doubtful one, but it does have to be changed and clear.

To recall the words of a former premier in another context, there is a wind of change blowing across the European continent, and Britain should be poised to take advantage of it. If we do not, the likelihood is that others will go forward while Britain is left behind – isolated economically and politically in a way that is as unnecessary as it is undesirable.

8

A New Politics

A parliamentary time warp

If a professional man from the beginning of this century were to find himself transported, by dint of a time machine, to his place of work today, one might think that he would be completely mystified by the changes that had taken place in the intervening decades. He certainly would be at a loss if he was an industrialist beamed to a robotised factory, or a banker appearing on the high-tech trading-floor of his City office. It would be the same story in almost any walk of life.

But what if our Edwardian gentleman was a member of Parliament? He might find his present-day colleagues' dress bizarre (though he might find his top hat in demand for some procedural point or other), and the presence of the women MPs would bemuse him. But if he turned a blind eye to these innovations, would he instinctively feel at home?

Decidedly so. He'd soon find his usual perch in the chamber, painstakingly rebuilt after its destruction by German bombers in 1941. The elaborate rules of debate, with members trying to catch the Speakers' eye, 'intervening' and 'giving way', the circumlocutory courtesies with members not referring to each other by name but as honourable and right honourable members and friends would all be very familiar. The parliamentary manual of precedent, Erskine May, would guide him, as ever, through the procedure, and when the time came to vote he'd consult his party whip and queue up to go into the 'aye' or 'no' lobby. After the traditional ten o'clock vote he'd saunter off to the smoking-room or one of the other bars and eventually find his way to the Members' Entrance to take a cab elsewhere. If he went to the other end of the Palace of Westminster he would find the House of Lords intact, with the great-grandsons of many Edwardian peers adorning its red benches.

But our Edwardian member would notice some differences.

He might be taken aback by the astonished faces at his well-meaning offer of late supper and a game of cards at his Pall Mall club, and surprised by the number of his new colleagues who protested about the burden of urgent constituency business to which they had to attend early the following morning. He would have consoled himself with the thought that, as was his habit as a Radical member for an East Midlands industrial town, he had just paid his annual visit to his constituency. Also, the debate he had just witnessed did appear rather full of superficial name-calling by the standards to which he was accustomed. In his day it had been rather different. One of the more memorable occasions on which he had been present in the House was to hear Mr David Lloyd George launch his People's Budget, which he had expounded in a speech of four and a half hours' length, broken by a thirty-minute adjournment to enable the chancellor of the Exchequer to restore his fading voice with a cup of beef tea (proffered, apparently, by Arthur Balfour, the Conservative leader – a gesture of cross-party friendship which it would be difficult to imagine today).

Since those days politics has become professionalised, with far more members intent on making it their career. The days of disinterested public service by gentlemen of independent means and stalwart trade unionists have largely disappeared. MPs are now paid to do their job full-time, though many still pursue the centuries-old outside interests of the bar or journalism to supplement their earnings, and others engage in more modern and sometimes controversial business. The role of committees has expanded, though it was only recently (in 1979) that select committees were established to monitor each government department, and their record has been mixed. In 1989, more than thirty years after they filmed the coronation, TV cameras were finally allowed a permanent presence in the Commons. Yet, to all outward appearances, the way Parliament works has changed little.

What has changed is the standing of Parliament in the country. Think back to our Edwardian Radical MP. It may never have occurred to him to issue floods of press releases to his local newspaper, but he would nevertheless have felt confident that Parliament was being intently followed in his constituency. His leading local supporters, gathered in their Nonconformist chapels, working men's institutes or public reading-rooms, would have read avidly the extensive reports of parliamentary debates in the columns of the regional and national press. To follow the gladiatorial contests on the Commons floor was something of a national pastime – one that lasted through to the debating jousts between the two Harolds – Macmillan and Wilson.

Today, the normal business of Parliament makes little public impact, apart from Prime Minister's Questions. (The televising of the Commons has intensified attention on this twice-weekly circus, which only became fixed in its present, absurdly formalised, ritual in the 1960s.) Set-piece debates still make some impression, particularly on the political fortunes of the individuals for whom they turn out a triumph or an endurance, but newspapers no longer recast their late editions to catch the cut and thrust of the once crucial ten o'clock wind-up – except for rare government defeats – with the result that the old drama and sense of occasion have largely drained away. The tradition of gallery reporting is virtually dead, apart from the occasional high-quality sketch.

Leading politicians still get plenty of public exposure, of course. The last decade has seen an explosion of new media outlets, but politicians' ability to make a persuasive case or illustrate a point in language of poetry and colour is much diminished because of the limitations of the thirty-second sound-bite, repeated by a dozen or more different channels and news bulletins in a single day. Their ability to develop a sustained argument before a wide public audience is confined to opportunities such as the *Today* programme or *Channel 4 News*. Too often the mass media's treatment of politics leaves the general public with an impression of partisan shrillness and shallowness which is steadily devaluing the currency of politics.

But it is not just the media which is at fault. Politicians haven't helped themselves. The polarisation of politics which became acute under Margaret Thatcher has, it seems, permanently changed the terms of political discourse for the worse. In an earlier era the normal tactic of political debate was to identify as much common ground as possible with your opponent in order to bring out the narrower but real points of difference. In the last twenty years it has almost become *de rigueur* never to agree with the other side about anything.

To the general public, politicians talk in a language of absurd exaggeration and tit-for-tat point-scoring, blaming their political opponents for all the country's problems. From Conservative spokesmen one gains the impression that all the problems of the country are due to the past record of Labour governments – despite the fact that Labour has been out of office for seventeen years. No cabinet minister would even acknowledge, never mind apologise for, such patently obvious mistakes as the poll tax or the ERM débâcle. Labour meanwhile has been slow to admit in public where the Conservatives have introduced changes which are right. Politicians too often sound as though they are addressing their remarks to small bands of faithful fanatics, rather than to the country as a whole. This is not to argue that the only legitimate style of politics is that of soggy consensus – politics should not be about seeking the lowest common denominator – but national debate should focus on real issues where hard choices have to be made.

The respect in which politicians are held has been further damaged by the widespread impression that 'they're only in it for themselves'. Our Edwardian MP, well versed in every twist and turn of the notorious Marconi scandal before the First World War, would be surprised at the suggestion that 'sleaze' was a new phenomenon of the 1990s. The history of politics is littered with individual lapses of judgement and occasional sordid episodes: politicians are no more perfect than the rest of humanity. However, the past decade has seen the growth of a more widespread culture of sleaze, which the modern brand of Conservatism has nurtured.

From the Thatcherite point of view it is axiomatic that the public good is best advanced by individuals and businesses pursuing their own profit. But too often the easy step has been made from that principle to the less acceptable notion that anything anyone in public life can do to assist a private interest in making profit is somehow in the public interest as long as people keep on the right side of the law. And it is made worse when those who are elected to serve the public interest see nothing wrong in helping themselves to their own share of the consequent commercial rewards in directorships and consultancies. The idea that there is nothing objectionable about a public figure pursuing a dubious private commercial interest as long as it is declared is one of the most corrupting principles in public life today. As far as the electorate is concerned, many think we have a government that consists of business back-scratchers and a Parliament made up of politicians on the make. Prime Minister Major felt compelled to establish the Nolan Committee because of the damage which successive scandals had inflicted on the Conservative Party and parliament itself. It remains to be seen how far the new rules which Nolan recommended, and which were forced on the reluctant government by the House of Commons, succeed in curbing abuses and restoring respect for politicians and parliament.

But the decline of politics and the loss of standing of the Commons are about more than this. Not only does Parliament look corrupt, it appears weak and powerless.

Our Edwardian time-traveller would be astounded by the centralisation of government in Britain since his day. In the proud East Midlands borough he represented, the Edwardian age was a high point of municipal endeavour and civic pride. Responsibility for the rudimentary public services that then existed rested with elected members of the borough council, school boards and Poor Law guardians. The borough council enterprisingly ran the newly established gas, electricity and tram undertakings. The magnificent public buildings in the centre of the town were the result of the munificence of local manufacturing families who wanted to leave a permanent memorial to their locally made fortunes. And, at a different social level, the working men who gave our Edwardian Radical political backing were strong believers in self-help: in the town, trade-union friendly societies and cooperative societies would have flourished.

The centralisation of decision-making in Britain today is absurd. Take the national roads programme as an example. A new junior minister in the Department of Transport in Westminster's Marsham Street will soon find himself or herself deluged with two or three inch-thick buff folders submitted by eager officials wanting quick decisions. These might cover such questions as the route of a Hertfordshire bypass or whether a pedestrian bridge can be built across a busy trunk road in Hartlepool. The chances are that the minister will never have visited the site. He or she will have no feel for the particular circumstances of the locality. Nor will the minister have any sense of the strength of local feeling on either side of an argument. The minister's only guidance will be contained in the dry and technical brief from a civil servant, and maybe an inspector's report from a local inquiry and the accompanying case file of letters and submissions – which even the most conscientious minister will have time only to flick through. This is supposed to be part of the excitement of British government: the thrill of power in opening the red box and burning the midnight oil over the various delights it contains. But many of the decisions concerned should never be taken by ministers in the first place.

Defenders of this system argue that ministers alone are in a position to examine the issues objectively, free of local bias, and that NIMBY pressures would be all too prevalent if decisions were left in the hands of locally elected representatives. But the assumption that local politicians would inevitably lack wisdom or objectivity on what is in the best interests of their locality smacks of bureaucratic arrogance.

What makes the degree of centralisation worse is that there is little or no genuine accountability to Parliament for ministers' actions. Ministers exercise wide powers by administrative fiat. Even in the case of new legislation, existing procedures take Parliament for granted. Bills are often so badly drafted and ill-thought through when they first reach the legislature that reams of important new amendments can be produced by government departments as a bill reaches its final stages of supposedly deliberative consideration.

Another cause of concern is Europe. European legislation has an increasingly important influence on our daily lives, but parliamentary scrutiny of it is farcical, with matters coming before the House well after British ministers have signed up for new legislation in the Council of Ministers. And the fault is Britain's, not Europe's, and the remedy lies in British hands. The problem is the reluctance of the executive to contemplate prior discussion in Parliament – on the grounds that this might 'tie ministers' hands'. A more acceptable balance can be struck.

The executive's increasing power, combined with the lack of parliamentary accountability in the exercise of it, must be one reason why the judges are now much more ready to interfere in what they would have once regarded as political decisions and the exclusive preserve of ministers. For example, the number of successful applications for judicial review (claims before the courts that ministers have not followed reasonable procedures) rose from 160 in 1974 to 2,886 in 1993. This is another indicator of the fall in Parliament's standing. The once-famed balance of the British constitution has been eroded.

The new politics proposed to deal with these challenges is not – or rather should not be – a question of high theory or fancy schemes of constitutional reform. What is at stake is the vitality of British democracy. Is it healthy? Is it strong? Can we put our hands on our hearts and honestly proclaim that the millions who gave their lives defending our country's democracy this century died for something of which we can still feel justly proud?

In part, the issue boils down to whether one is impressed more by outward form or by the reality behind it. Does the seemingly effortless ability of the great British ship of state to sail calmly on through the centuries engender respect and relief, or does it inspire incredulity and anger at the forces that allow such complacency in the light of Parliament's increasing ineffectiveness?

The argument for constitutional reform

Most Conservatives refuse to consider the case for political reform on its merits. Instead they find it comforting to wrap their critical faculties in tradition and nostalgia. Of course, it is right to be thankful for the historical stability that our political system has achieved. Since the Glorious Revolution of 1688 the British constitution has adapted to the emasculation of the powers of the Crown, the political emancipation of Catholics and Jews, the Great Reform Bill and the piecemeal enfranchisement of first the new industrial classes and then the masses, the resolution of the Irish Question and reform of the House of Lords, the coming of votes for women, and the gradual establishment of a modern, industrial society with universal education. These are real achievements. But a good track record is not a sufficient test today.

Admirers of the British constitution tend to write about it in an almost mythical way. In the nineteenth century Walter Bagehot famously pleaded on behalf of parliamentary procedures, 'We must not let daylight in upon magic.' Well, perhaps it now is time to open up the shutters and let in some light – and fresh air!

The British constitution – or rather the lack of it – has long been a passionate cause for a select band of enthusiasts. Liberals have consistently argued the case for a formal constitution, but mainstream politicians have been more sceptical – especially when in a position to do something about it.

The most famous example of a constitutional reform package being dumped when opposition turns to government is that of Lord Hailsham. In his 1976 Dimbleby Lecture and his later book *The Dilemma of Democracy* (1978), Hailsham ranted and railed against the terrible 'elective dictatorship' befalling the British people under the extremist (*sic*) Callaghan government. Could this be the same man who served so happily in Mrs Thatcher's cabinet only a few months later, all worries of elective dictatorships banished from his mind? By 1991 his volteface was complete and he was claiming that 'We are probably the most successful political society that has ever existed.' Clearly elective dictatorship is in the eye of the holder. The eminent political scientist Dennis Kavanagh has commented that 'The central issue in British politics has not been how to curb the elective dictatorship but how to capture it.'

Enthusiasm for a new politics and constitutional change has mostly been equated with support for electoral reform, and on that issue calculations of party advantage have never been far below the surface of high principle. In the 1970s many prominent Conservatives showed interest in schemes of proportional representation when it appeared that a Labour government elected on a minority of the vote could push through policies to which a majority of the public was clearly opposed. But this interest faded as the boot shifted to the other foot and Conservatives established their electoral hegemony in the 1980s. The

Gang of Four when they first publicly broke with Labour made no reference whatsoever to proportional representation in the Limehouse Declaration. However, by the time the Social Democratic Party was launched, eight short weeks later, the necessity of an electoral agreement with the Liberals and the dawning realisation of the perilous position of a fourth party under the present 'first-past-the-post' system had dramatically forced the issue up their list of national priorities.

Until recently, Labour maintained its distance from this whole debate. In the late 1980s shadow home secretary Roy Hattersley dismissed constitutional reformers as 'another outbreak of radical chic'. This sentiment can still be heard among some today. When voters complain about the political system, the sceptics say, it is principally because they don't like the decisions emerging from the system. When the public bemoans the state of politics, it's because there is not an effective government. Change the government and the decisions can be changed: politics is about winning power and using it to show people that democracy can make a difference to their lives. The opponents of constitutional reform plead with Labour not to take any notice of theorists whose fancy schemes will first limit Labour's ability to win power on its own and then limit its ability to use that power, once obtained, to effect real change. Constitutional reformers, they argue, are the real enemies of democracy, because they will deter people from ever believing that their vote can make any difference at all.

Understandably, many Labour members remain sceptical or unconcerned about this debate. They half acknowledge a case for reform, but do not see why it should be a legislative priority when there is so much to be done in society.

This attitude is wrong. Tony Blair's ambitious project for national renewal cannot draw the line at Westminster and Whitehall. The case for constitutional change cannot stop with the internal machinery of the Labour Party: Labour politicians need to look at their ways of working in government. They must demonstrate convincingly that they recognise the public's deep-seated disillusionment with politics, and that it will be unacceptable for the same old show to go on with only different-coloured rosettes.

As Blair himself has put it, 'A government of national renewal requires a national renewal of government':

- First, a government setting out to modernise Britain cannot be conservative about Britain's institutions. We cannot credibly face the challenges of the twenty-first century with a hangover of habits, attitudes and privileges that reflect views of parliamentary representation as it was in the nineteenth. We need to institute a modern view of the relationship between the citizen and the state.

- Secondly, a government that believes in decentralised solutions to complex social and economic problems will not release the energies of local communities and businesses through the machinery of a top-down, centralised state.

- Thirdly, a government that wants to see a new style of politics in Britain – less pointlessly polarised, more relevant to ordinary people's lives, and more open and honest in its style – will not achieve this without wide-ranging reform.

- Fourthly, a government committed to a long-term strategy of national renewal needs to discover a new basis for trust between itself and the electorate: it needs to build a broadening consensus in the country that will enable it to make decisions for the long term and secure its re-election. A government that believes in partnership must foster a new politics that enables the country to work as one.

To go down this road may involve some sharing of formal power. New Labour is about building change that enjoys wide consent and so will last, and about demonstrating that a new government can make a real difference in the time-frame that chiefly matters – the longer term. The only way to make people understand the party's new seriousness about political reform is to state this quite openly and explain why it is integral to New Labour's governing approach.

A modern relationship between the citizen and the state

New Labour makes no apology for its belief in the potential of good government to underpin the strong society which it sees as essential to individual self-fulfilment. But, because of that conviction, it is especially incumbent on democratic socialists to offer guarantees that the rights of the individual and of free associations will always be protected. Never must the power of the collective, exercised through the state, be allowed to transgress the fundamental rights of the individual – as in the Marxist heresy. Because individuals have inalienable rights, these should be clearly and unambiguously expressed.

Thinkers on the left have a long record of addressing these issues. Indeed the first great social-democrat revisionist, Eduard Bernstein, wrote about them as long ago as 1899. The agenda he outlined for the German SPD remains astonishingly relevant today: the extension of rights, the need for checks on arbitrary rule and for democratic accountability, the necessity for the constitutional and peaceful change of government, the case for the dispersal and decentralisation of power, the argument for citizen participation, and the insistence on the overriding importance of democracy.

In Britain today, the laws of Parliament have established many different statutory protections of individual rights, but these fall short of the clear positive statement of rights that citizens of most other countries can rely on. That is why Labour now advocates as a first step the incorporation of the European Convention of Human Rights into British law, as the basis for Britain's own Bill of Rights.

Under Attlee's Labour Party, Britain was, in 1950, one of the first countries to ratify this Convention, which emanated from the newly formed Council of Europe. But, in a Europe still in the early stages of recovery from war and fascism, establishment legal opinion in Britain saw the Convention as very much for 'lesser breeds without the law'. According to Anthony Lester, the distinguished human-rights lawyer who has made the cause of constitutional reform his life's work, William Jowett, Labour's lord chancellor, told his colleagues at the time that he was not 'prepared to encourage our European friends to jeopardise our whole system of law, which we have laboriously built over the centuries, in favour of some half-baked scheme to be administered by some unknown court'. The attorney general at the time, Hartley Shawcross, was equally robust on the side of legal conservatism: 'Any student of our legal system must recoil from this document with a feeling of horror.' Infringements of basic rights in Britain now force a rethink.

The Convention, which came into force in September 1953, covers such 'classical' freedoms as protection against torture or inhuman or degrading treatment or punishment (Article 3) and against slavery or forced labour (Article 4); the right to liberty and security of person (Article 5), to a fair trial (Article 6), to freedom of thought, conscience and religion, of expression and information, and of peaceful assembly and association (Articles 9-11); and the right to respect for private and family life (Article 8). Protocols added to the Convention protect property (except in the public interest), ensure the right to education, and provide for free elections and liberty of movement.

The upholding of these rights is a matter for the European Court of Human Rights in Strasbourg, which is nothing to do with the European Union. Shamefully, it is Britain that has kept the Court at its busiest. Since 1979 there have been seventeen judgements against Britain – more than against any other country. Astonishingly, the government is not strictly bound in law by the Court's decisions, but the Court's judgements have acquired great moral authority – even on matters of great political sensitivity, such as the security services' shooting of IRA terrorists in Gibraltar – and the government invariably acts on the Court's rulings.

But such a process is not one to engender respect. In other countries the rights enshrined in the European Convention are part of their own national law, with the means available to pursue disputes in the first instance in domestic courts. Because British citizens do not have those rights under national law, they must appeal straight to Strasbourg. This involves long delays (of up to nine years) and unnecessary costs, and gives the impression that British people's rights can be secured only in a remote, even alien, way. As Britain is already subject to the Convention's requirements, why not incorporate the protection that it gives into British law, making the rights that it confers explicit and clear? As the Australian constitutional expert Professor Leslie Zines has observed, 'Outsiders see Britain in practical terms as having something in the nature of a Bill of Rights that is interpreted and applied by foreigners. It passes my understanding why the British do not see the virtue of having such questions determined by their own courts, at least initially.'

The question of full incorporation was debated at length by the Callaghan cabinet in the late 1970s. Again Labour showed itself divided, and refused to act. The social-democratic radicals who supported change found themselves blocked by an unholy alliance of legal conservatives on the old Labour right and members of the traditional left, who feared that the Convention's provisions would enable the courts to fetter the trade unions' ability to enforce the closed shop and would uphold the rights of parents to send their children to schools of their choice. The short answer to such objections is that they are unacceptable. It is precisely because old Labour was widely perceived as unwilling to place any restraints on the power of the collective against the individual that it lost public confidence and support.

Of course the more sophisticated opponents of incorporation have since argued that they were not against the principle of legally entrenched rights in itself, but feared the power this might hand over to an unrepresentative, right-wing and socially out-of-touch judiciary. However, the strength of senior judges' strictures against the excesses of the Conservative government in recent years should have convinced even the most prejudiced class warrior not to question judges' independence and integrity on the basis of their social background.

Certainly there is a case for reform of our judiciary to make it more representative. At present judges are selected in a secretive way from too narrow a range of people. The standing of the courts suffers every time the tabloid press recounts a tale of a judge seemingly out of touch with society. Judges must of course be free, and be seen to be free, from political interference, but that is no reason not to appoint them in a proper way and provide adequate training – and retraining (even in decoding the *Sun*). All of this should become the province of a truly independent Judicial Appointments and Training Commission and be taken out of the hands of the lord chancellor, who, despite frequent assertions to the contrary, is a party politician.

Yet no effective system of constitutional checks and balances can operate without a strong judiciary. The challenge is to frame the best available framework of rights and to have it upheld by the best available judiciary – not to pretend, ostrich-like, that neither can be achieved.

With a Bill of Rights enforced by a reformed independent judiciary, the modern age of citizenship will have begun, and no one will ever be able to accuse Labour of being prepared to sacrifice individual rights on the altar of collectivist ideology.

Decentralisation and the revival of civic pride and regional identity

It is hard to believe, but sobering for Labour to recollect, that the Tories came to power on a firm pledge of freeing local government from constraints. Michael Heseltine promised, 'We will sweep away tiresome and excessive control over local governments. Local councils are directly elected. They do not need, they do not want, the fussy supervision of detail that now exists.' However, far from rolling back the central state, over 150 acts of parliament since 1979 have reduced local-government powers. Jack Straw MP has calculated that direct control over £6 billion and partial control over £26 billion of public expenditure has been transferred from local councils to central government and quangos.

The Thatcher government took away Londoners' rights to elect a voice for their city, abolished metropolitan authorities, and introduced ratecapping. The nearest Britain's capital city has to a government is an ad-hoc committee of largely Tory-supporting businessmen. The Major government took powers to limit every local-council budget. It also made chief constables accountable to police authorities that for the first time contained nominated representatives of the home secretary, and would have gone far further in imposing central political control over the police had not the Tory grandees in the Lords broken into open revolt – including a former home secretary, Lord Whitelaw.

The Tories have presided over the explosion of the unelected quango state that now controls over a fifth of public spending – a total of £55 billion. These quangos cover health, schools, training and housing. On a whole range of bodies the Conservatives have introduced rafts of central-government appointees.

According to a recent Democratic Audit report, there are now 5,621 quangos and 70,000 quangocrats. That is nearly triple the number of democratically elected councillors. This gives huge powers of patronage to ministers, and it is no surprise that on these quangos, among those genuinely motivated by public service in all parties, there are Tory MPs' relatives and associates. It's a wonder there are enough boys (and girls) for all the jobs there are to dish out. The Tories' actions have created a democracy deficit where democracy should be strongest – where local services are provided.

There are, of course, a number of relatively easy changes that could be made to reverse the centralising trend. The more obviously political appointments could be rescinded – though Labour would want to be cautious about substituting too many placemen of its own, as this could quickly dissipate public goodwill towards an incoming administration. Legislation could give democratically elected local authorities the right to make appointments to bodies such as NHS trusts and training and enterprise councils. But this would be to tinker round the edges of the problem, not get to grips with its fundamentals.

Reviving local government

Labour must act to reinvigorate local government – and in Frank Dobson Labour has a Shadow Environment Secretary committed to doing so. The task is not simply to reverse quangoisation: it is to promote local democracy and the civil values and civic pride that go along with the best of it. Labour understands that the best thing about local government is that it *is* local. It is localities, rather than regions, with which most people identify. It is no accident that a recent survey found that many people had contact with their local councillor.

The closer politics – and power – is to people, the more chance there is of interaction between them. And that is what democracy is about – not just a vote in a general election, once every five years. Bringing such closeness about has to be a top priority of a government that genuinely believes in a bottom-up, not top-down, approach; that sees the role of national government as that of facilitator and framework-setter, rather than of central planner and state provider; that celebrates diversity and local initiative and believes that uniform solutions won't work.

However, in order to devise a credible strategy to reverse centralisation, the reformer must understand why it has occurred. The main motivation has been the Conservatives' desire to tighten the Treasury's grip on public spending. Of course one can argue that this has been ineffective – centrally imposed limits on council budgets, for example, have had the perverse effect of giving even the most fiscally conservative authorities an incentive to spend up to their budget cap – but it is less easy to devise a workable means of undoing this process of centralisation without at the same time making the disastrous error of risking loss of control of public expenditure.

The problem is exactly the same one that led Margaret Thatcher foolishly to introduce the poll tax. National government is caught on the horns of a double dilemma: how to devolve to locally elected bodies the freedom to spend – and, with it, the power to tax – while ensuring that local voters can hold councillors to account for their decisions; and how to guarantee acceptable standards of service across the whole country and ensure that national policy objectives are met within the necessary limits on total public expenditure.

Twenty years ago the Layfield Committee exhaustively analysed these dilemmas of local-authority finance and concluded that a strategic political choice had to be made between what it termed the 'localist' and 'centralist' options. There are, of course, possible halfway houses, with some services totally decentralised while for others the taxpayer assumes complete responsibility. Schools funding is the largest single item of local-authority current spending, but with Labour's new emphasis on school self-management and independence the case has become much stronger for direct taxpayer funding of schools.

The more complicated one makes the national/local split of responsibilities, the less clarity and accountability local voters will see – but, if decentralisation is to work, clarity and accountability are vital. At present only a fifth of local-government spending is financed by the locally determined council tax. Freedom for local authorities to spend more could therefore imply big increases in local council-tax bills – on average, five times any increase in local-council spending. This would inevitably lead to political pressure on central government to raise its grant to local councils in order to relieve the extra burden on the council-tax payer. Control of public expenditure would be lost.

The only way round this problem is to increase the proportion of council spending that is financed locally (which a switch of schools funding would help bring about) and ensure that accountability to voters for local tax-and-spend decisions is improved. Labour has put forward proposals for all-out annual council elections to achieve that necessary accountability. Other possibilities could include local referenda on local projects. For example, a local vote could be held on whether new public-transport investment should be financed by a local levy on private cars and lorries using city centres at peak times. Alternatively, a tax might be levied on local businesses that would benefit directly from transport investment, as the Corporation of London proposed in a recent discussion paper. These are practical cases of hypothecated, or pledged, taxation.

But local democracy needs to work better as well. The biggest authorities are now complex organisations spending hundreds of millions of pounds of public money, yet they still have a system of governance which was devised in the nineteenth century. Unpaid elected members carry out their functions in their spare time and take decisions in large committees that are often ineffective in either an executive or a strategic policy role. In the biggest authorities the burden of elected office can be so great that people with busy careers or normal family responsibilities find it difficult to cope. It is not a happy situation.

Britain needs to experiment with other arrangements – smaller elected executive boards who might be paid a proper salary, and the US system of elected mayors. Such changes would bring a new dynamism and commitment to democracy in our big cities and, by opening the doors to better-quality civic leadership, would foster the creative partnerships with local business that have done so much to revive American cities.

These issues are intensely political. A Blair government would come to power with the Tories in as weak a state in local government as they have ever been. But such weakness may not always be the case. Would a Labour government be keen to devolve power to newly installed and possibly rampant right-wing Tory councils? Would Labour then attempt to compromise, and legislate for national minimum standards at the same time as devolving greater tax-and-spend freedom? Or would this scenario prove a further incentive for electoral reformers to argue that devolution of power to local authorities must be combined with proportional representation, in order to strengthen local political consensus and guard against extreme swings of the political pendulum? At some stage – probably sooner than it thinks – a Labour cabinet will need to make these choices. If it opts for localism – as we believe it ought – the consequences in terms of devolution of power away from Westminster politicians and Whitehall civil servants could be radical indeed.

Devolution

It is also proper that, as well reflecting local identities, government should reflect regional – and national – ones. That is why Labour is right to pledge devolution for Wales and Scotland.

The reality is that the civil service already runs unified outposts in every region, and millions of pounds of expenditure and many key decisions are taken in regional centres. This is a positive development, but it ought to have some democratic counterpart. In the first instance, local authorities should be encouraged to get together, as happens in the Northern Assembly in the North of England, so that elected representatives are able to have an input to regional decision-making. At a later stage, if there is public backing, this can lead to fuller regional devolution – though imposition of this policy from the centre would be unwise. The strength of regional identities varies in different parts of England. In the English regions the process of devolution should be people-led.

As for the Scottish Parliament, there is overwhelming popular support for this in Scotland, and a large measure of political consensus has been built around the cross-party Constitutional Convention's detailed blueprint for bringing it about. Labour's George Robertson has played a leading part in this.

Sceptics argue that the only reason Labour supports Scottish devolution is to prevent a resurgence of the Scottish National Party. But the demand for home rule goes back deep in the Scottish socialist tradition. It had the passionate support of the first

Red Clydesiders elected to parliament in 1922, and a Scottish Home Rule Bill was introduced in the period of the first-ever Labour government, in 1924. Scottish Labour may no longer wish to match the rhetoric of Jimmy Maxton, the Clydesiders' legendary socialist leader, when he declared that there was 'no greater job in life than to make English-ridden, capitalist-ridden, landowner-ridden Scotland into the Scottish Socialist Common-wealth', but an inescapable commitment to devolution for Scotland must be one of the top legislative priorities for Labour's first term.

It is, however, a mistake to believe that the Scottish question can be settled in isolation from constitutional reform in the rest of the United Kingdom. For one thing, the agreement to elect Scotland's Parliament on a modified version of the German system of proportional representation – which the Scottish Labour Party has endorsed – is bound to have some impact on the wider debate on electoral reform. For another, Scotland's Parliament will be much more than a local authority writ large. It will gain responsibility for the Scottish legal system, which is of course unique. But it will also possess wide-ranging economic-development and industrial powers, with considerable resources to back them up – both through its decisions on the allocation of the Treasury block grant which it would receive on a fixed-formula share-out of UK revenues and through the powers it would be granted to levy taxes by varying income tax by up to three pence in the pound. These new freedoms for Scotland would have considerable implications for all other regions of Britain and are eventually likely to result in demands for matching, if not precisely parallel, treatment throughout England. Jack Straw's plans for an evolutionary two-stage approach to English regional government are designed to accommodate this inevitable pressure.

The Scottish Parliament will have responsibilities for all aspects of the welfare state, other than social security. Indeed the political argument often presented for devolution within Scotland itself is that, with a Parliament of their own, the Scots would never have had to put up with measures such as the NHS internal market, or school opt-outs, which Tory-dominated Westminster has imposed on them. This, of course, raises in stark form the 'West Lothian question' (so called because first posed by West Lothian's MP, Tam Dalyell, during the passage of the 1970s devolution bill): If Scotland can decide such matters for itself, why should Scotland's MPs at Westminster be allowed to participate in votes to decide policy on these matters south of the border? One cynic rightly remarked that the West Lothian question is mostly asked by those not interested in an answer. However, there are issues here which require careful consideration. One option is to exclude Scottish MPs from voting on certain issues at Westminster – but the potential for jurisdictional dispute and political manoeuvring which such an arrangement would create is obvious. As for representation at Westminster, it should be remembered that the government is proposing a separate legislative assembly for Northern Ireland with no mention of any changes in either the voting rights of Northern Ireland MPs or their number. In fact give and take has always been integral to the principles of territorial representation underpinning the British constitution, and this approach should endure.

A new style of politics: open government and reform of Parliament

No single reform will change the culture of British politics, but a number of changes taken in combination should have a powerful impact.

MPs' remuneration and party funding
The first need is to restore belief in the integrity of MPs and political parties.

MPs deserve a salary which is commensurate with their position in society and the necessary expenses of their peripatetic lifestyle, but there should be a ban on MPs' earning money from commercial interests that result from their position as an MP – with the exception of modest fees from journalism, speaking and writing. MPs with legitimate outside professional and business interests should be free to pursue them, as long as they are open and declared. MPs who accept important Commons responsibilities such as chairing select committees might also be paid a higher salary.

As for political parties, many argue that Britain should move to a system of more formalised state funding, as in many continental countries. This should reduce political parties' reliance on dubious corporate sources of income, trade-union largesse, or rich 'sugar daddies'. However, state funding should not simply be allocated on the basis of votes received in the previous general election. That makes it too easy for political parties to rest on their laurels and risk their voluntary effort weakening. If it is introduced it should be incentive-based and related to independently audited figures for membership income. It is vital that political parties build the widest possible membership base and the organisation to support this.

However parties are funded, limits should be introduced on national as well as local campaign budgets.

Parliamentary procedure

Parliament itself needs to be dragged (probably kicking and screaming) into modern times. Some changes have already been introduced, with reformers from both sides of the Commons – like Ann Taylor, the Shadow Leader of the House – leading the way. The hours that Parliament works, the effectiveness of its committees, the way MPs are resourced: all need futher attention. In particular:

- In order to secure continuity of membership and the commitment of MPs of high quality, departmental select committees need to establish greater independence of the party whips, who dominate the Committee of Selection. Back-bench MPs could elect members of select committees by single transferable vote (in order to secure a proper balance of representation). Special provisions to secure fair minority-party representation might need to be retained. (We must accept, however, that we live in a party system, and that there is a limit to the extent that back-benchers will be willing to be critical of their own front bench.)
- Select committees should as a matter of course hold pre-legislative hearings before bills are presented to the House. In other cases, special standing committees should be established. These would help identify the real policy issues and options, and would enable more intelligent and informed debate on legisla-

tion when it is considered in standing committee.

- Prime Minister's Questions should be reformed so that members can no longer table an open-ended question long in advance just to be able to ask a cheap point-scoring supplementary. The leader of the opposition should be allowed to raise issues of great current concern, and other members to raise similar issues after notification to Downing Street that morning.

- The party leaders should make it clear that they will support the Speaker in disciplining members who indulge in persistent barracking and jeering, which has done so much to devalue the standing of the Commons in the eyes of the public.

Public appointments

The Commons should be given an 'advise and consent' role on major public appointments. 'Not, perhaps, since the eighteenth century', John Grigg, the historian and commentator, has observed, 'has government maintained itself so shamelessly by the exercise of patronage.' The Labour government should place all major public appointments before the relevant select committee for scrutiny. The committees should be charged with the task of ensuring that such appointments are made on merit and fully reflect the diversity of our society.

Open government

Greater openness in government should help raise the quality of public and political debate. A cure must be found for what Richard Crossman called 'the British disease of secrecy'.

The fact that the Conservatives, particularly under Margaret Thatcher, seemed at times to be caught up in a farce should not distract us from the seriousness of what was happening. GCHQ, Clive Ponting, the *Spycatcher* affair: these were just the more public aspects of a culture of secrecy that stretches across Whitehall.

New Labour's policy is simple: there should be a public right to know, underwritten by legislation, unless there is a clear stated reason why something cannot be disclosed on grounds of national security, personal confidentiality or strict commercial confidence.

Certain civil-service submissions to ministers on policy

options could be made public. These should not, however, include private office working papers and advice to ministers from senior officials. Disclosure of such documents would fatally prejudice the political independence of the senior civil service and its ability to serve ministers of different political persuasions – within as well as between political parties.

The House of Lords

The Upper House requires reform. The idea that the circumstances of someone's birth should enable him to influence the laws passed in a democracy is a blatant absurdity. Labour should abolish the voting rights of hereditary peers as soon as practically possible.

Whether Labour should go further, and how fast, is a difficult judgement. In the long run it may be that the second chamber needs to be made more representative – perhaps there could be a directly elected element with an avowedly regional flavour. Another possibility is give MEPs the right to sit in the Lords in order to strengthen links between the UK and the European Parliament and facilitate more effective scrutiny of European legislation. A reformed House of Lords would be more powerful *vis--à-vis* the Commons because it would have more democratic legitimacy. That means it would have more power to block what the government of the day wants to do – and this area will inevitably generate a lot of opposition to change.

There are other radical ideas too. Graham Allen MP has proposed that the present chamber become a museum and that a new, electronic, semicircular chamber be built. The mere thought of this would be enough to finish off a few old bewhiskered parliamentarians, but such ideas should be discussed on their merits. Anything should be considered which offers the prospect of changing and tempering the yah-boo politics which is so universally despised by the public.

A new basis for trust and partnership

New Labour has set itself the task of national renewal. That task will not be completed in a single term of office.

A government with its sights on the long term needs to have the broadest possible political base from which to obtain consent for change that will last, to overcome short-run unpopularity, and to govern in the national interest. For those who are stuck in the traditional confines of narrow party politics, this requires a lot of hard thought, inevitably including consideration of Labour's relations with the Liberal Democrats.

The Liberal Democrats will never form a government but they cannot be written off. The SDP failed, but the Alliance bequeathed to the Liberal Democrats a decent legacy: a respectable opinion-poll rating, a sound membership base and constitution, a powerful position in local government, and a strong presence in the South West of England outside the big urban centres. Having survived the amazing upheaval of the SDP-Liberal merger after the 1987 election, it is difficult to conceive of circumstances in which that legacy will totally melt away.

There is, of course, common ground between the parties. There is no doubt at all that, had the outcome of the 1992 election been different, Labour and the Liberal Democrats would have been natural partners in government had the electoral arithmetic demanded it, as both Neil Kinnock and John Smith privately recognised. The parties shared economic priorities for investment and employment, and were strongly committed, within responsible financial constraints, to reducing social inequalities and restoring pride in public services, to putting Britain genuinely at the heart of Europe, and to pushing through a legislative programme of radical constitutional change.

Since Paddy Ashdown ended the Liberal Democrats' formal position of equidistance from Labour and the Conservatives, the overlap between the two parties has become more obvious. The members of both parties want to right the same wrongs, to end the same injustices. Any objective observer who has sat through a Labour or Liberal Democrat conference must admit that truth.

There are, of course, significant differences of tone and substance. Labour is still a national party in every sense. The Liberal Democrats, by contrast, are predominantly a councillors' party, for which the acid test of commitment is 'pavement' politics as expressed through the vehicle of the 'Focus' leaflet. The

Labour Party is more strongly committed to the public sector. But these differences are becoming increasingly blurred.

There is no barrier to cooperation in terms of principle or policy. However, potential cooperation between Labour and the Liberal Democrats need not follow any predetermined pattern. At local government level there are joint administrations in some shire counties and London boroughs; elsewhere there are looser arrangements; and in some places the parties remain bitter rivals. At national level cooperation in specific policy areas does not imply or require a pre-election pact or post-election coalition.

Electoral reform

Would this involve full Labour acceptance of proportional representation at Westminster? Labour's Plant Commission undertook one of the most exhaustive studies of proportional representation ever, and still opinion remained split. Few leading Labour politicians engage in the issue, though notable exceptions include Robin Cook and Jack Cunningham in favour of change and Margaret Beckett and Jack Straw against. Undoubtedly it is possible to devise a system that gives a more accurate arithmetical correlation of seats and votes, but will it lead to stronger or weaker government? And would such a system give too much power to third or fringe parties?

Proportional representation should be considered as an issue of principle, not the subject of horse-trading for narrow party advantage. But it should be remembered that different arguments apply according to the system proposed. Few in Britain would argue for the system of pure proportionality that exists in Israel and permits fringe extremists and every separate ethnic minority and religious group to have representation in Parliament.

The principles that should determine one's view of electoral reform are clear. If it is implemented, it should be as fair as possible, while providing strong government and an effective way for the electorate to change the government. In-built stalemate is not democracy. The link between MP and constituents is also a crucial one, and nothing should be done which would remove it.

Ultimately the decision to change should depend on the number of voters who, over a sustained period, are dissatisfied by the choice on offer between the two major parties in a first-past-the-post system.

Throughout the 1950s and 1960s the case for change was very weak, as over 90 per cent of the electorate voted either Labour or Conservative. Only as Labour threw away its broad electoral appeal did this figure fall, until in 1983 less than three-quarters of the electorate voted Labour or Conservative. If that tendency were to continue, the democratic case for electoral reform would become irresistible. But it is most unlikely this position will be maintained, and the case for wholesale reform is now weak. Indeed the latest British Social Survey suggests that 60 per cent of the electorate would vote against a change in the voting system in a referendum (although other surveys have suggested more widespread public dissatisfaction with first-past-the-post). Labour has recovered the position that it held in the 1960s and earlier, and the collapse of the Conservatives in the current Parliament has not seen a surge in third-party support in opinion polls.

However, it remains clear from by-elections and local elections that voters are still prepared to vote for a Liberal Democrat candidate where he or she is unequivocally best-placed to defeat the Conservatives. As a result the Liberal Democrats retain patches of quite considerable local strength, with the paradoxical consequence that in a general election in those areas members of Parliament can be elected on a clear minority of votes cast. If change is desired, the electoral reform best suited to tackle the remaining unfairness in the British voting system is therefore the alternative vote – the retention of single-member constituencies, but with first-, second-, third-choice voting in order to ensure that MPs are elected with the majority support of their constituents. This is the system that Labour now uses in its parliamentary selection procedures.

What has been outlined here is a far-reaching programme of constitutional reform – probably the most ambitious put forward by a political party in fifty years. It should not, however, be the limit of our imaginations.

Many experiments are taking place in the USA to use the

much-vaunted communications revolution to extend the ability of citizens to influence the political process. Vice-President Al Gore has been involved in 'virtual' town meetings, and some Democratic governors have used the high penetration of cable into US homes to hold instant advisory referenda. A lot of this activity is gimmicky, but only a Luddite would ignore the possibilities that technological change offers for an extension of the democratic process.

Local authorities should be encouraged to conduct their own experiments along US lines. J. A. Hobson, one of the early twentieth-century New Liberals, once remarked that we have only a threadbare doctrine of representation that merely involves the electorate 'plunging into a sensational sporting contest once in six years and registering a single vote upon a medley of personalities and party cries'. New technologies give us the opportunity to extend our thinking about the form that democracy takes. We should grasp it. The crucial point is the acceptance that our constitution should be constantly in evolution, not stuck in a time warp.

Constitutional change cannot be the preserve of one political party. For change to occur, a consensus must be built both between and outside of political parties. That is why the work of groups such as Charter 88 is so important. However, such groups must appreciate that political reform is not Labour's sole concern. Labour's economic and social reforms will require parliamentary time, and to expect constitutional changes to take their place in the queue of priorities is not to renege on commitments but to be practical about making progress.

A reinvigorated democracy will help deliver New Labour's progressive agenda, but we do not believe that constitutional reform offers the panacea that is sometimes claimed. The changes outlined above are right in principle and of themselves. They will play their part in national renewal, but alongside plans for our economy and society, not as a substitute for such plans.

When setting priorities for constitutional change, it is vital to avoid the legislative deadlock that may occur if too much is attempted too quickly. The first priority should be to reflect the public's anxieties about the way we are governed. The reform agenda must spring from the voters' concerns and not follow the master plan of constitutional theorists or be dictated by the interests of the chattering classes.

Renewing a constitution as old and complex as the British one will not be easy. It will require enormous political will-power and energy. It will also require the building of a consensus that reaches far beyond the Labour Party and the signatories of Charter 88. Lasting change will need the full approval and engagement of the people.

Some argue for the big-bang approach, wishing away the difficulties and obstacles. That is not our way. Steady, piecemeal reform is the way forward. That approach, with luck, will give us devolved power in the nations of Scotland and Wales, a Bill of Rights, real freedom of information, and reinvigorated local government – all within the first term of a Labour government. At that stage the debate will move on, and consideration might be given to whether it is time to codify the British constitution.

The French political historian Alexis de Tocqueville made the essential point as long ago as 1835: 'In England the Parliament has an acknowledged right to modify the constitution; as, therefore, the constitution may undergo perpetual change, it does not in reality exist.' According to the political scientist S. E. Finer, only two countries in the civilised world – Israel and the United Kingdom – lack a written constitution.

In the long run the pressure will build for Britain to follow New Zealand, which, after years of debate, and a full referendum, adopted a formal, written constitution with its 1986 Constitution Act. The first step, however, is to make explicit the rights that citizens have and to clean up the system and practice of our government. On those firm foundations, as citizens rather than subjects, we could then seek to build.

9

A New Party

Not long ago, in a South London theatre, a host of politicians and Labour-supporting celebrities assembled at a Young Labour gala evening. Neil Kinnock, the host for the evening, received a rapturous reception from the two thousand young activists in the audience, as did Mo Mowlam, MP, who is now Labour's Youth Co-ordinator. But the biggest applause of the night went to someone else: James Callaghan, a man who represented something few in the hall could even remember – Labour in power.

The applause for the former premier is deeply ironic. Parts of the Labour Party spent the early 1980s attacking the record of Callaghan's government, accusing it of having betrayed socialism. In the years after Margaret Thatcher's election victory in 1979, speakers at the Labour Party conference trying to defend the former government's actions were routinely booed, with the hard-left-controlled Labour Party Young Socialists in the vanguard. It is a very far cry from that to the reception Lord Callaghan received from today's burgeoning youth membership.

The difference in attitude goes to the heart of Tony Blair's claim that a 'literally new Labour Party' is being created. Instead of a party which believed its role was to attack its leaders, the new party's instinct is to be their ally.

This transformation has not occurred by accident. First Neil Kinnock then his successor, John Smith, and now Tony Blair have devoted enormous energy to reforming the Labour Party. Some people, both inside and outside the party, cannot understand why so much effort has been put into this task, arguing that it is a distraction from fighting the Tories. They have not understood what each of these three leaders has realised: that creating a healthy, vibrant and confident Labour Party is essential both to defeating the Tories and to building a new relationship of trust with the British people. A reformed, stronger Labour Party is the necessary foundation-stone of a successful

Labour government. The process of reform is not yet complete, but the momentum for change is unstoppable.

The present condition of the Conservatives demonstrates the importance of a party's grass roots. The Tories' internal difficulties over Europe and, more deeply, over the whole direction of their post-Thatcherite agenda have gravely damaged their credibility as a governing party. And these frictions are much more than the surface manoeuvrings of ambitious politicians and their various cheer-leaders in different sections of the Tory-supporting press. They reflect deeper stresses within the Conservative Party – a narrowing of the party's membership base, a sharp decline in the influence of One Nation 'paternalist' Tories, and the rise of militant 'Essex' men and women and their hard-line cousins, the 'young fogey' British nationalists among the Conservatives' lay membership.

Like its earlier counterparts in the Labour Party, with their intolerance and shouts of betrayal, the Tories' militant tendency is succeeding in its appeal to local activists but is driving away middle-of-the-road voters. These voters are not opposed to radicalism as such. They can be persuaded of the case for new ideas and strong policies, as Tony Blair is demonstrating at the moment, but not for policies born from dogma and extremism. Voters have turned away from the Conservatives since it became clear that the fundamentalist right wing is holding sway in the party. In Labour's case, a remarkably similar lurch to extremism in the 1970s and early 1980s caused a deep rift between the party and all sections of the electorate. The resulting fear of Labour among voters has taken a generation to repair.

What went wrong in Labour was not the fault of the party's grass-roots members but was a product of outdated power structures and organisation. Only since the structures have been changed and decision-making power has been put into the hands of the individual members has the party's health been restored. Instead of an unrepresentative, activist-driven structure which generated policies and attitudes at odds with what Labour has traditionally stood for, Labour's introduction of one-member-one-vote democracy for all members has unleashed new energy and support for sensible thinking which was hidden ten years ago.

Labour's wilderness years

The reasons why Labour was 'captured' by the far left in the first place are important to understand, because their permanent removal is the key to Tony Blair's confidence that a Labour government will not be derailed in the future.

The old Labour Party never sought to modernise its structures in the light of changes in society. In the 1950s and 1960s it was kept together by a combination of monthly meetings of delegates drawn from the branch members and affiliated trade unions and of evening socials and activities organised around the co-op and the women's guilds. As social and generational habits changed, and as industrial change started to disrupt patterns of working and association, popular participation in the party started to decline and the party structure weakened, leaving by the 1970s an empty shell in many constituencies. Far too often this suited the small cliques of party loyalists who remained to run things as they wanted. Some councillors even wanted as few local members as possible, so they weren't challenged for their jobs.

There will always be an extremist fringe hovering on the edges of any political party, but in Labour's case strong organisational efforts had previously succeeded in keeping the undemocratic left at bay. But this discipline relaxed just as the party structures were starting to decay, and many local constituencies became easily dominated by individuals who were unrepresentative of the wider membership. Some constituencies in London and the big cities became playgrounds for the manoeuvrings of different Trotskyist factions. A wider group of first-generation graduates also joined the party, many of whom had been radicalised by their experience at university in the 1960s. Often they identified with a strong state through their membership of public-sector unions.

The only senior party figure who succeeded in reaching out to these new activists was Tony Benn, a very independent-minded minister when Labour returned to power in 1974, who from his privileged seat in the Labour cabinet fostered the belief that the main obstacle to the achievement of radical socialism was the feebleness of will among his leadership colleagues. He systematically fed suspicions of leadership betrayal among party activists, distorting the motives and misrepresenting the actions of the Labour government so as to increase support for his brand of centralised state socialism.

As Benn and the gallery of activists to whom he played promulgated a programme of reform designed to 'democratise' the party (that is, make themselves more powerful within the existing party structure) and make the leadership and MPs more 'accountable' (to small groups of party activists), the mainstream leadership of the party failed to fight back. Its members had no coherent ideas to advance in opposition to the Bennite reforms, preferring instead to put their faith (and their positions) in the hands of those wielding the trade-union block votes against the radicalised constituency delegates at the party's annual conference, where all the big decisions were taken.

The Bennites easily broke through the resistance of the old guard, gathering support among the 'soft' left and others who thought they knew which way the wind was blowing and so winning major policy victories at the party conferences of the early 1980s. In 1981 they attempted to replace the then deputy leader, Denis Healey, with Tony Benn himself; they failed by only a hair's breadth. Interestingly, this was as a result of surprise backing for Healey by the then left-dominated public employees' union, which had balloted its branch members and came out strongly for Healey. Over a decade later Tony Blair received nearly 60 per cent of the votes of constituency members in his election as leader – a massive swing back from the extremism of those days when Tony Benn received 80 per cent of the constituency party general committee votes under the old system.

Neil Kinnock's election as party leader in 1983 started the long, slow climb back to electoral credibility. Kinnock created a new coalition of the centre-right and the 'soft' left which started to marginalise the hard left, though their strong presence in certain cities' local government sustained them for several years. From 1983 onwards, though, three factors combined to undermine the left's power. The first was the scale of the 1983 defeat itself, which could not be blamed on Jim Callaghan, even by Tony Benn. Later the romanticism of the class struggle was dealt a fatal blow by the tragic tactical incompetence and subsequent humiliation of Arthur Scargill in the 1984/85 miners' strike. Lastly, the defeat over ratecapping and the excesses of the Lambeth and Liverpool councils showed the futility – and extremist danger – of far-left vanguardism.

Gradually, under Kinnock's determined leadership, the various power bases of the hard left were taken on and defeated – from constituency parties and local councils through the youth and women's sections and up to the party's National Executive Committee (NEC) itself. The hard-left Militant Tendency was driven out and a substantial realignment started towards the centre ground – a process which newly elected MPs like Tony Blair actively promoted, as has been described in Chapter 2.

There are important conclusions to be drawn from this experience for the present day:

• Having experienced the consequences of a big gap opening up between Labour activists and Labour voters, the party constantly has to identify ways of reconnecting itself with ordinary voters, speaking their language and voicing their concerns and aspirations. To do this, the party needs to continue to recruit a mass of new members, so as to become ever more representative of ordinary voters, growing strong roots in local neighbourhoods and communities.

• By moving increasingly from a system of delegate democracy to direct democracy, structures must ensure that the party's mass, grass-roots membership, rather than unrepresentative groups of activists, has the greatest say in the agreement of policies and the election of its leaders.

• The changes in the party's local culture must continue, so that instead of activity dominated by meetings, minutes and agendas, constituencies undertake campaigning, education and socialising, which are more interesting and stimulating for old and new members alike. Thorough debate and political education should be the priorities of the party's policy-making structures, not the resolution-based politics of the past.

• Finally, the leadership must lead – explaining the New Labour government's strategy and persuading the party along every step of the way.

A substantial start has been made in implementing these changes, and, as a result, the difference between the party that at its mildest was a thorn in Callaghan's side to the one that cheered him to the rafters fifteen years later is enormous. Yet the full extent of this transformation has not been appreciated outside the party. People see Labour as more united and purposeful. They know that the leadership is more in control of the party. But they fear that the old influences and attitudes they vaguely remember from the early 1980s are lurking below the surface, waiting to reemerge. To those who still say that they like Blair but are not sure of his party, the full picture of New Labour needs to be explored.

A members' party

The most fundamental evidence for the existence of a 'literally new Labour Party' is that the party is running itself in radically different ways now, and even if the activists of the past wanted to reassert themselves the new structure of the party would not permit them to take back control. This is because of the introduction of one-member-one-vote for all the party's main decision-making.

Before, a relatively small number of individuals could control constituency parties by becoming delegates from local branches and affiliated trade unions to the constituency general management committee, which had the power to pass resolutions on policy, to select (and threaten to deselect) the local Labour MP, and to mandate delegates to the annual conference which decided policy, elected the NEC, and had a large share in electing the party leader after 1980. These general committees still exist, and they play an important role in organising the party locally, but in all crucial respects it is now the mass membership, not the committees, that calls the shots on the big decisions.

When the Labour candidate is chosen in Swindon, Pontypridd or Chorley, the six or seven hundred party members there get a vote, not just the forty general-committee members of yesteryear. In a recent selection for a by-election candidacy, over 100 members had asked for postal votes and another 250 turned up on the night to hear the potential candidates speak and to ask questions. The hall was full to capacity – young and old, men and women, company managers and the unemployed, all with one thing in common: a belief in Labour's cause and, because they had joined Labour, the right to have their say.

All individual members also get a vote when it comes to choosing Labour's leader and electing the party's ruling NEC. In the recent past both elections were the preserve of the activist élite. The NEC in Callaghan's day was full of people who made a virtue out of their opposition to what the party leadership was doing. Now it is those who impress party members by attacking the Tories, not their own party, who get support. It was no accident that, as the use of ballots expanded, Tony Benn and Ken Livingstone were voted off and the likes of Gordon Brown and Harriet Harman were voted on to the NEC.

Last year over 123,000 party members voted. This expanded democracy is guaranteed to keep the party more in touch with ordinary people. After all, in the average town, every other street and every large workplace boasts a Labour Party member. As one young moderniser quipped at a conference fringe meeting recently, when there is a Labour government 'every member will be a party spokesperson and there will be a "source close to the prime minister" on every street'.

There is no going back. Like any group of people who are given democratic rights, Labour Party members aren't going to allow them to be taken away. There are some who say that changes in the Labour Party are superficial, that Tony Blair may represent a new Labour Party but the grass roots are acquiescent only because an election draws near. But all the evidence suggests the opposite.

Local parties were not required to ballot when the party came to make a decision on Clause IV of its constitution last year, but when the leader and the NEC recommended it a full three-quarters of them did ballot their individual members. There could have been a central diktat issued insisting on ballots, but instead the leadership hoped that the culture of the party had changed sufficiently that the local constituency parties would opt of their own accord to pass power downwards to the members. They were proved right, and it is a precedent that is likely to become permanent practice in important party decision-making in the years to come. Of the 470 constituency Labour Parties that held ballots, 467 voted for change and only 3 voted against – a result that surprised even Tony Blair.

Tony Blair is sometimes compared to the great revisionist leader Hugh Gaitskell. He, of course, tried but failed to change Clause IV in 1960. At the time Gaitskell told the party, 'We have long ago come to accept a mixed economy, in which case, if this is our view – as I believe it to be at 90 per cent of the Labour Party – had we better not say so instead of going out of our way to court misrepresentation?' It is a great irony that the constituency vote at the Clause IV conference in Westminster Central Hall in April 1995 was nine to one in favour of change: Gaitskell had been absolutely right about the party's true opinion all those decades earlier. Having completed the necessary changes to the party's decision-making structure, Tony Blair can now lead a party with the internal democracy to make that clear at long last.

A mass party

Building the party's membership to bolster this system of one-member-one-vote is the key to ensuring that democratic momentum is maintained. After all, Labour now has a leader who literally owes his own position to the one-member-one-vote system, having been elected on to the NEC when postal ballots of the membership were initially being introduced. His own constituency boasts over 2,000 members

While shadow home secretary, Blair found time to sit on the party's youth committee, overseeing the transformation of the party's youth wing from the Militant Tendency shell of the Young Socialists to its vibrant, campaigning successor. Young Labour now boasts 25,000 members – three times more than the Young Conservatives and Young Liberals combined. So Labour has a leader who takes the party seriously and who has been instrumental in its changes. Blair believes that a strong, representative party is a necessary foundation of a radical Labour government. Since being elected to Parliament he has put his time, and his energy, where his mouth is.

Recruiting new members has been the biggest organisational priority of the party. In the last eighteen months, since Blair became leader, the British Labour Party has become the fastest-growing political party in Europe. At over 363,000, the party has its highest level of membership since 1979 and the early 1980s, when people were turned off Labour in droves and the Social Democratic Party was formed. Indeed, before Labour's unique national members database was set up, local membership figures were often exaggerated, so the true improvement is even greater.

Many of Labour's new members are returners from the SDP, including quite a number of the Labour MPs who transferred at the time. Those who have come back include Dick Mabon, George Brown's brother Ronald, James Wellbeloved, John Grant, Edward Lyons and Jack Diamond – and also Michael Young, the drafter of the 1945 manifesto. The former Labour MP and influential academic David Marquand, who joined the Liberal Democrats, has also returned to Labour, as have a great many of his talented generation, who despaired of Labour's ability to modernise itself at the time but now believe that New Labour rather than the Liberal Democrats is the best vehicle to achieve what they want to see changed in Britain. More recently the twenty-somethings have been moving over to Labour. And Councillor John Dickie, the former English treasurer of the Lib Dems, has joined rather than 'come back' – he had never been in the Labour Party before.

The biggest influxes of members occur when Labour is prominently in the news. This suggests that, when the party is being extensively reported in the media, people now like what they hear and see – unlike a generation ago. During last year's party-conference season, for example, 7,000 new members joined Labour. In total, 130,000 people have signed up to the party since Tony Blair became leader. That is more than the entire membership of the Liberal Democrats.

In general, the new members tend to be younger: their average age is thirty-nine, compared to around forty-three for existing members, which is significantly younger than both the Tories' average age of sixty-two and the Liberal Democrats' fifty-five. Over 62 per cent of the new members are under forty-five, and just under half are women. The largest single age group to have joined are those under the age of twenty-seven, swelling the ranks of Young Labour – perhaps the most hopeful sign yet both for the party and for democratic politics as a whole. Of these new young recruits, most are university-educated and professionally employed, as much in the private as in the public sector. Labour is now appealing to young people in ways that are radically different from the Young Socialists of old.

In previous eras Labour Party recruits tended to come from those contacted locally, often through trade-union organisations or activist groups of one sort or another. Indeed, it was formerly only possible to join Labour locally, through a laborious process of written application, scrutiny by the branches and, finally, endorsement by the general management committee. It was usually insisted that the applicant be a trade-union member, even if he or she did not work or had employment where unions did not organise. The system seemed designed to keep people out rather than recruit them. Now a national membership scheme has been introduced which allows people to join directly and immediately.

The 'recruit a friend' programme, pioneered by John Prescott, has been most successful in bringing in new members (responsible for 28 per cent of new joiners). However, the number of people recruited through the party's union-affiliated organisations has been disappointing, despite the emphasis that has been placed by the party nationally on recruiting individual members from among trade-unionists. On the other hand it is encouraging that, according to membership surveys, individual recruits see themselves as making a positive decision to join Labour in order to be active, not just to be paper members, and there is strong participation in political education and discussion and campaigning activity. In a party survey of new members as a whole, 47 per cent described themselves as professional, 25 per cent as retired, 10 per cent as manual workers, 9 per cent as students, and 9 per cent as unemployed. It is particularly helpful that 60 per cent of the new members have joined in the electorally crucial areas of the Midlands and the South.

Modern policy-making

People join political parties for a variety of reasons, but the one most frequently mentioned is their desire to improve the country and to influence the policies they believe will achieve this.

The annual party conference is where policy is formally debated and agreed. Resolutions are submitted by constituencies and trade unions; amendments are tabled and finally grouped together in 'composites'. These are put before the conference delegates, and after short debates – sometimes not more than an hour long – votes are taken and the resolutions are accepted or rejected. It is not a satisfactory way to make policy, and it was in this way that many of the unrealistic positions adopted by the party in the 1970s and 1980s were put into Labour's programme. The 1980 decision to withdraw from Europe was taken after a debate of only thirty minutes.

The votes cast for and against resolutions run into millions, because the unions' block votes supposedly represent vast numbers of trade-union members. In practice, these huge block votes represent little more than the views of the union general secretaries, their executives or their delegations to the party conference (a few dozen people), though they usually broadly reflect the policies of their respective union conferences. Some unions are now choosing to ballot their members beforehand, and this is to be welcomed.

Wisely, Labour is moving away from these methods of making policy. Neil Kinnock and the current general secretary of the party, Tom Sawyer, started to implement reforms by creating a broadly based National Policy Forum, and also regional forums, to enable more of the party's membership to discuss policy in a more considered way. Longer, better argued policy statements are now discussed during the course of a whole day's debate, making the National Policy Forum a platform for more open and constructive discussion than is possible on the conference floor. Unlike in the past, when the party head office, supervised by the National Executive, would drive policy-formation, the policy statements presented to the membership forums are drawn up chiefly by the shadow cabinet and its staff, assisted by relevant officials and others in the party. Only after full discussion in forum meetings are the full statements then put to the annual conference, where they are voted upon without further amendment.

The other big difference in policy-making is that the shadow cabinet consults extensively with outside interests in the development of policy – often helped by commissions established by sympathetic think-tanks. In recent years a Commission on Social Justice drew up policies for reform of the welfare system. Another commission, with strong representation from industry and the private sector, is considering policies to promote economic competitiveness. Yet another has made proposals for developing the information superhighway, involving all relevant parts of the private and public sectors.

All this activity means that the policies that emerge are better thought-through and more relevant to the real needs of society and industry, as well as commanding substantial consensus in their support. The old days of the party deciding by a quick show of hands to set off on a completely different – and often totally impractical – road from the parliamentary leadership are, thankfully, over. Labour now prepares for government as a cohesive party should: testing ideas, forging new policies, and trying them out on those who will be involved in implementing them.

It is hard for some observers of New Labour to appreciate just how far the policy-making culture of the party has changed since the days of splits and dissension in the 1970s and 1980s. Many journalists attending the annual conference still wait in eager anticipation for the delegates to fall out with the platform, for the leader to be rebuffed, and for policy to be overturned as it used to be. Instead they see a unity of purpose and a determination to agree. This is not because dissidents are being muzzled or debates suppressed. The same opportunities exist for people to speak and act as they used to; but very many of the people attending are new, and those who remain from the past have different attitudes.

Will the change last?

This is all a vast improvement on what has gone before, during the party's long years in opposition. But what will be the practice in government? Will the party conference once again try to impose policies on reluctant ministers? When this occurred previously it was organised by determined groups of people in the party who had a coherent alternative set of policies to those of the leadership and some articulate leaders of their own to advance them. Such an internal opposition within the party no longer exists, although individual MPs will express different views from time to time. This positive change will only be lasting, however, if a future Labour government does two things: if it fully engages the party membership in all that it is doing and if it talks frankly with the trade unions who are affiliated to the party about the sort of relationship the government needs to have with them.

Relationship between the government and the party

For all these reasons, good communication is vital, and the party has to think very seriously about how this is going to be organised when it is in government.

Ministers will need to make conscious efforts to keep in touch with what is happening around the country, rather then simply pronouncing to the regions from ivory towers in Whitehall. They could attend regional policy consultations and ensure that briefings on government policy go out to members from party headquarters. Astonishing though this may seem, that did not happen in the 1960s and 1970s.

This raises the question of whether a cabinet minister (with a salary paid for out of party funds), like the Tory party chairman, should be responsible for liaison between the government and the party and for presenting the party's policies professionally. The Tories have always given themselves this advantage, while in Labour's case the government and the party head office were allowed to grow more and more distant from each other as administrations wore on.

In preparation for government, the party has already established an unprecedented programme of political education that should make possible a constructive two-way dialogue between the party membership and the Labour government. Also, an independent organisation has been created to supplement the party's educational programme. Called 'Progress', this organisation aims to promote political discussion, sensible debate and skills training among party members, ensuring, alongside party HQ, that the parliamentary leaders remain in close touch with the grass roots at all times. If such initiatives had existed at the time of the last Labour government, the distance and disenchantment that then grew up within the party could have been greatly reduced.

Union links

An equally high priority is for the Labour government to get its relations with the trades unions right, so that confrontations do not develop as they did before.

Labour's relations with the union leaders will always be controversial, because the Conservatives will go out of their way to make them so. The Tories believe they can whip up anti-union sentiment as successfully as they had done when they first came to power in 1979. For this reason Conservative propaganda is forever recalling the 'Winter of Discontent' which plunged Labour-union relations into chaos and disfigured the end of the Callaghan administration.

The maliciousness of Conservative propaganda is not, however, an excuse for refusing to make necessary change. Together with the unions, the party has to recognise that, before they broke down, relations between the unions and the last Labour government did become too close and incestuous, leading to the common perception that the unions were taking power that did not belong to them – or at least demanding special treatment – and ministers were sharing government responsibilities that should not have been given away. By making it clear that Labour will govern for the whole nation, and that the unions will be offered fairness not favours, Tony Blair and his shadow cabinet are making it as clear as they can that they do not intend to return to previous practices.

At the core of these practices was the 'social contract' by which the unions operated an incomes policy for their members, to combat inflation, in return for policy concessions from the government. As has been argued in Chapter 1, this was an initially attractive – and successful – but unsustainable economic strategy. In addition, the problems it created in party-union relations were great. Every month at the National Executive, and every year at the party conference, government ministers found themselves haggling with union leaders over resolutions about this policy or that action which should have been determined solely on the basis of the national interest. Not surprisingly, the public disliked the process and the Conservatives exploited it.

In a more general sense, the quite legitimate role of trade unions as interest groups – protecting the interests of their current members – means that they are bound to be conservative about change. While that can be appropriate for a trade union it is dangerous for a government, and in the late 1970s various ideas – like selling council houses and raising standards in schools – foundered on the rock of Labour's unwillingness to offend entrenched interests in the party, particularly the unions. That cannot be allowed to happen again.

Today trade unions play a much more progressive role, and some of the work done by the Communication Workers on the information superhighway or the GMB on utilities is deserving of full consideration. Those unions know, however, that they can advise and make recommendations but it is the government that will take the decisions.

Of course the trade unions have always had a wider role than simply representing and protecting their members at the workplace, and this should be respected. For many decades not just Labour governments but Conservative ones too recognised that the unions have a legitimate role within civic society to speak up for millions of men and women on economic and social issues. There is a whole range of matters where it is as wrong for the Conservatives to listen only to businessmen as it would be for a Labour government to listen only to the trade unions. The key to getting relations right in the future is for a Labour government to recognise the unions' legitimate wider public role while the unions accept that to use their relationship with Labour to put improper pressure on ministers is the wrong path to take. This is not a matter of being anti-union, as some will claim. It is about changing the relationship between the unions and a Labour government to make it healthy, and to ensure that neither side is damaged by a repeat of what went wrong before.

The decision already taken to reduce the influence of the unions at the party's conference is a necessary first step in modernising the party-union link. In the last three years the voting strength of the unions has been virtually halved. Further changes are bound to evolve, because the structure of the unions is changing. Recent years have witnessed the amalgamation of many of the big unions and the absorption of others. If, as seems likely, we move to the age of the 'super-union', there might then be only five or fewer separate union institutions. Imagine if the old block vote still existed and the whole of the Labour conference was looking over to a huddle of half a dozen men (it does still tend to be men who have 90 per cent of the votes) to see them determining policy for the rest of the party. It would be ludicrous. The Clause IV debate led to strong calls from grass-roots trade-unionists for members' ballots to determine the unions' views, as happens in local Labour Parties. This pressure is bound to continue.

The best way for the concerns of trade-unionists to be addressed is by more and more of them becoming individual members of the party. Far from this being the breaking of a link, it is actually the establishment of thousands of individual, unbreakable links. In branch meetings, on campaign committees, in council chambers and in Parliament, trade-unionists will be able to participate fully in Labour's affairs, for themselves.

The unions reinvigorated

The unions themselves must then devote more energy to modernising their own ways of working and organising. They have to address the explosion in part-time and female working, the growth of small businesses, the shrinking of factory working, and the shift of focus from collective bargaining to individual contracts. To arrest their decline in membership, the unions have no alternative but to change.

Most trade unions now offer legal services, insurance and other services to their members as well as help and advice when negotiating contracts of employment. TUC-affiliated unions dealt with over 125,000 personal-injury cases in 1994 alone, and over £300 million in settlements was recovered. Whether at a coalface or at a VDU, terrible debilitating work-related injuries can occur, and the trade unions' traditional role in health and safety has as much relevance today as ever.

Unions need to concentrate on what they are best at, where

they can maximise their influence and provide the best service for their members. This will require taking account of the many different sorts of workplace that are emerging as the pattern of employment changes, and the overwhelming bulk of unions are acting on this. Most union leaders also see the argument for an arm's-length relationship with political parties, as in the rest of Europe. The success of the unions on the Continent is based on winning policy debates with the public rather than simply trying to get their own way by dominating the party structures to which they are linked.

Changes in local government

In local government, where Labour representation is stronger now than ever before, the picture has changed too. It is no longer possible to pick out 'loony left' councils and tar all of Labour-controlled local government with the same brush.

In London (for example in Lambeth), and in Liverpool, Manchester, Sheffield and many other cities where problems previously existed, there has been a sea change in attitudes among Labour councillors. Where once they were out of touch with the aspirations of the people they claimed to represent, they are now pragmatic and innovative in their approach – involving the local communities in their work, advocating close partnership with the private sector, and prepared to take tough decisions even where these bring them into conflict with the public-sector unions. When this is not the case, Labour – unlike the Tories – takes firm action, as happened over problems in Walsall in autumn 1995. The result of all of this is praise for Labour councils from the government-backed Audit Commission, and growing support from the electorate.

The revolution goes on

So Labour has changed, and is still changing. A vibrant Labour party, rooted in the communities it serves, is taking shape. But the improvements of recent years should not breed complacency.

Some have complained of feeling that the party is engaged in a 'permanent revolution'. But what is wrong with that? Shouldn't any organisation committed to changing society be constantly seeking ways to improve itself? The simple truth is that it is an absence of change that should be alarming to the true radical, otherwise atrophy will surely follow.

The leadership's view is clear. Tony Blair told the GMB trade-union conference last year, 'People ask me when I will draw the line under reform. When can we say it is done with? The answer is never.'

Reaching out

Anyone who has been involved in political activity – or even just church or charity work – knows that it is all too easy to get sucked into a world of resolutions, minutes etc. divorced from the people who one is supposed to be helping in the first place. Political activity often becomes absorbing to those engaged in it. There is a clutch of political obsessives in every party branch – Labour and Tory – in the country. But to be effective our parties have to involve more than the politically obsessed. They must reach out to others, for whom politics is an interest but not the ruling passion of their lives.

The Labour MP for Southampton Itchen, John Denham, makes the point whenever he speaks at gatherings of Labour Party members. 'Let's see just how active you are,' he asks. 'How many meetings have you been to in the last fortnight?' Most people have usually been to three or four – some more. There is always a welling-up of pride in the room until he then asks, 'And how many voters did you speak to in the last fortnight?' Usually most people in the room haven't spoken to any.

For too long Labour's view of activism has been inward and exclusive. The crucial first step in rectifying this must be to continue to recruit more members, and give them and existing members more rights and opportunities to involve themselves in local activities.

Giving members more say

One-member-one-vote should be extended to include other elections in the party, such as that for the constituency delegate to the annual conference. Where decision-making needs to be by representative means, the representatives must represent the ordinary membership.

It is also right to move away from delegate democracy to direct democracy. There should be ballots on major policy issues, accompanied by all-member education meetings and debates. Already some local parties are holding such ballots of their own accord. In Mitcham and Morden, a recent ballot on the minimum wage supported Tony Blair's view that the exact level of the wage should be introduced at a sensible rate once Labour is in government, not set beforehand. The vote was 73 per cent in favour of this, supporting the view that the party membership and the leadership have similar attitudes to these big policy questions.

Chapter 7 of this book argues strongly for increased democracy for the country in an age where individuals are now better educated and more informed. The days of deference and 'doffing your cap' are over, and if we insist on giving people a direct say over decisions that affect them when it comes to the British political system we should accept the same logic when it comes to the Labour Party.

Introductory sessions and training should be expanded so that less active members can find a way to become more active. In a mass party, many will want to contribute financially and perhaps help out on election day. We should welcome their contributions. Not everyone will want to become more active, but the party should create a participatory and welcoming culture for those that do.

Community involvement

Local parties must turn outwards, involving themselves in their local communities. If there is a need for a new pelican crossing, or the youth club needs new equipment, local Labour Party members should be ready to help. In short, where community activity is taking place Labour members should be getting involved and expressing their activism – as party members out in the community, not shut away from it.

It is just as desirable for party members to show their commitment by their involvement in community groups or local campaigns, or by serving as school governors, as by attending

Labour Party meetings twice a week. A local Labour Party should revolve around what is happening to the people in its local community as well as what is coming up on an agenda at some conference. The way the party works should be changed to reflect these priorities. Campaigning and activity are the aim, not endless meetings.

Better management

Those involved in the party will see the sense in slimming down the general committee to a management committee, with people on it elected to do specific jobs. Every local party should reorganise itself to be task-based. Why doesn't every party have an electoral-registration officer and a postal-vote officer? Working properly, they'd bring in the votes. There should be quarterly all-member meetings, based around the party's political plans, to organise campaigns, discuss issues, and feed ideas and views into policy-making.

A bigger party, run along these lines would have a direct impact on Labour's election results. Studies have shown that a more active constituency can add 4 per cent on to the party's vote – a margin that can make all the difference. It would also make party activity more enjoyable and fulfilling. A Labour Party fully reorientated to the local community would be better able to foster the idea of public service and civic responsibility, and help increase the talent of those involved in local government – and even those standing for Parliament.

Nationally, the party headquarters needs to support local parties in this new approach. Less bureaucracy and more help with training and campaigning are needed.

Gone are the days when Harold Wilson could claim that Labour was still 'at the penny-farthing stage in a jet-propelled era'. John Smith House is improving all the time, and the party boasts many high-calibre, committed staff. But, again, we must constantly review our activity and look for ways to improve. Decentralisation to regions and localities is wise, and perhaps some services could be contracted out, or moved away from London. Whatever happens, the party machine must be focused outward, on its members, who are the party's greatest asset.

The National Executive Committee needs reform too. At present, for example, there is no space for representatives from local government or the regions. That should change.

Whatever happens in the future, however, there is no doubt that the tide of change is flowing in one direction: towards a representative, responsible Labour Party, in touch with the communities it serves. Today's Labour Party reaches out to the electorate, respecting voters' views, and is ready to work with others outside the party. It has a realistic view of the world, and sees itself in partnership with the parliamentary leadership, not engaged in hostilities with it.

Voters are right to trust this new Labour Party, because, as has been shown, it is fundamentally different in character and instincts from the one they turned away from in the early 1980s. Its new MPs are more representative. They are chosen as candidates by, and report back to, a party of hundreds of local people, not an unrepresentative clique of hardened activists.

The constituency section of Labour's ruling body, the National Executive Committee, is now democratically elected by ballot. It will be not 'in opposition' to the cabinet but a sounding-board for it. Troublemakers and extremist groups will get short shrift: the party takes discipline seriously. Most importantly, Labour's new members and its new democratic ways of working ensure a party in touch with ordinary people.

All this is here to stay, there will be no changing back. With its new instincts and new culture, improving all the time, this new party will not, as in the past, be a source of trouble for the Labour government but will instead be Prime Minister Blair's strongest ally.

10

A New Government

When, voters willing, Tony Blair forms his government on the morning after polling day, he will end the longest period Labour has spent in opposition since the party first tasted power in 1924. He will also be the youngest prime minister to assume the office since Lord Liverpool in 1812.

Blair may be inexperienced, but he does not lack advice. He has already started talking at length to former prime ministers, cabinet ministers, senior civil servants and diplomats about what to expect. But, in addition to these contacts, he has another invaluable resource – an equally amusing but far more accurate account of Whitehall life than that offered by *Yes, Minister*. This is the Labour MP Gerald Kaufman's book entitled *How to be a Minister*.

The book contains a mountain of helpful hints on subjects including the relationship to establish with the Whitehall machine. 'Some officials', cautions Kaufman, anticipating the myriad submissions and minutes that will flow through Blair's red boxes, 'will just suggest one course of action. Others, more cunning, will attempt to confuse you with a choice, while carefully steering you in the direction they want you to go. The key, of course, is not necessarily to accept any of the courses of action they recommend – but to come up with some others yourself.'

There is no better advice for New Labour's incoming crop of eager young ministers. The civil service exists to serve – and will do so, in the main, willingly and competently. But to govern is to lead, to inspire, and to pull together a united team. Ministers have to do this themselves; nobody can do it for them. They have to know where they are going and what they want to achieve before anyone else can follow.

After Tony Blair walks through the door of No. 10, having kissed hands with the queen, the prime minister's work will never cease. By convention he will be greeted by all the No. 10

staff, who will line up and clap him through the entrance hall of his new home-cum-office. This welcome has more than a little constitutional significance: it demonstrates the uninterrupted transition of government.

As he surveys the elegant ground-floor rooms, he will see where his private secretaries work (his principal private secretary and those who deal with economic policy, Parliament, home affairs, foreign policy and the diary). Nearby are the offices of his press and political secretaries. In the basement are the 'garden-room girls' and clerks who mind the flow of paper. Upstairs are the honours and appointments staff. On the second floor is the policy unit, and at the top of the building is the family flat.

It will be some time before he sees much of this, however, for he will be shown, without delay, into the Cabinet Room to start his administration. Sitting beside him will be the cabinet secretary (Sir Robin Butler, until he retires in 1998), who will automatically become his adviser and administrative mainstay. Never mind that Sir Robin has already served Blair's two Conservative predecessors – he has also successfully served Labour administrations and, like the members of the private office whom the new prime minister will also inherit, his whole professional training requires him to transfer his loyalty and dedication to the new incumbent without pause.

Blair will be presented with his first day briefs, telling him what he has to decide that day, and following these he will receive the briefs for the weekend, the next week and so on, day and night, until he finally departs office. Probably the greatest shock awaiting all incoming ministers is the sheer volume of work and paper they will have to plough through. Some will see the never-ending stream of red boxes as typical civil-service obstruction, preventing ministers from getting on with the real job of running the country. But this paperwork is the real job.

Despite the widespread public disillusionment with government (and the near contempt for politicians), expectations of the new administration will be huge. There will be intense pressure from multifarious interest groups, who will immediately look to a new government to offer them a better deal than they had received from the out-going administration. While giving people real hope of change, Labour must take care not to promise more than can realistically be delivered.

If public support is to be sustained, Labour must not only have a clear idea of what it wants to do, it must also have the best possible idea of how it is going to do it. This is not always easy for an opposition party, with its lack of access to hard information and to the wealth of experience that civil servants can offer. But preparation for government is as much as anything about not making commitments that are impractical and cannot be kept, whatever the temptation to say yes. Prospective ministers should ask some key questions of every suggested manifesto commitment: Does it reflect the world realities? Is it affordable? Can it be implemented in practice? Once in government, manifesto commitments also need to take account of changing circumstances. Economic conditions, in particular, may change between the time when election pledges are firmed up and the time when they are to be implemented in government. Unfortunately, supporters' expectations rarely adjust in tandem.

Once Labour is in office, pressures will start to build up in every Whitehall department for this or that decision or item of legislation to implement the party's programme. Many changes can be made by an administrative change or by statutory order, but this will not discourage eager new ministers from putting their particular ingredients into the legislative pie until Parliament is faced with the prospect of sitting round the clock for the ensuing five years. The crucial task is to agree the right priorities.

Every policy is a priority for the minister whose baby it is, but the cabinet (when its members are choosing to think of the government's collective interests as opposed to their own departmental concerns and careers) has to be concerned with wider questions when judging priorities. Is the policy central to laying the foundations for later economic or social success? Will it mire the government in such early controversy that it will make the rest of the government's programme difficult to pursue? Will it take so much legislative time that other urgent measures will be squeezed out? Will it cost so much that it should wait until the economy is stronger? Fundamentally, New Labour's priorities must be shaped by Britain's needs. Anything that is essential to the programme of national renewal must come first; other measures must wait.

Labour needs to prepare for another fact of life: that the economic inheritance from the Conservatives will not be as rosy as present ministers like to imply. The public finances are in a bad state, because of the continued high levels of expenditure on unemployment and social collapse. This is another reason why Labour will have to choose its manifesto commitments with care. Once in office, as the legislative demands pour in, so the public-spending bids will pile up. The new chancellor's hands may be tied even more than he realises now.

New Labour believes that the country's problems cannot be tackled simply by increasing spending. Government by unlimited expenditure and subsidy belongs to the past. But this will not stop requests to spend more being routinely submitted by Whitehall departments. Watching how these spending pressures are dealt with will be a suspicious City and jittery financial markets, waiting to assess the nerve of the incoming government and the mettle of its fresh, untested ministers. No doubt just as eager to test ministers' resistance will be the public-sector trade unions, representing millions of employees who feel badly done by after years of Tory government. Having to say no to many of these pressures and demands for action will be a painful necessity.

Standing behind the new ministers will be their fellow Labour MPs, disappointed in many cases that they do not have their own ministerial desks, impatient for action, and unaware of the scale of the avalanche of demands and difficult choices that is clogging up the government machine. Blair's job is to make this machine work so as to to ensure that the government's programme is delivered, avoiding the pitfalls that Harold Wilson and James Callaghan encountered when they came into office, as well as the mistakes that Bill Clinton made in the White House. Above all, his task is to satisfy the electorate with the performance of his government, so that it will want to re-elect Labour to a second term and see Britain's renewal through.

To succeed in this, Blair needs to achieve three things:
• He has to get personal control of the central-government

machine and drive it hard, in the knowledge that if the government does not run the machine the machine will run the government.

- At the same time, he needs to use all his ministers – and their civil servants and advisers – to the maximum effect in their departments, because the government's overall programme will depend on the successful implementation of each of its component parts.
- He must sustain a vision of what the government is aiming for, so that when times get difficult and rough – as they assuredly will – confidence in the government's purpose and direction is maintained.

Leading from the front

The most difficult task of government is to construct a long-term political strategy and a set of agreed goals and priorities, and to adhere to these in the face of the many problems and distractions experienced by every administration.

Labour governments have always coped with adversity, although none responded better than the 1945 administration, which displayed extraordinary unity and coherence for most of its existence.

Margaret Thatcher's success lay in her ability to focus on a set of clear goals and make everything (and everyone) conform to these priorities, whether in her monetarist economic policies, her love-affair with market forces, her determination to privatise, her dismantling of trade-union power, the rolling-back of local government, or her fight with Britain's EU partners. Mrs Thatcher by and large kept to her programme – albeit with more zigzags than appeared at the time – but she lost a lot of blood (most of it other people's) on the way. Tony Blair's aim must be to achieve a similar level of policy fulfilment without the accompanying costs and damage to relations inside and outside government.

Of course, Mrs Thatcher only got her own way after she had succeeded in forging her government in her own image, two years after entering No. 10. Up to then she had a divided cabinet, travelling in different policy directions. She did not have full control of the centre of government. Prime Minister Blair needs to have an equally clear and bold personal agenda, but he will want to harness the strengths of his cabinet colleagues from the outset rather than suppress them, and he will not be interested in needless conflicts. How much should he learn, though, from Mrs Thatcher's experience in getting control of the centre of government?

There is a story about Margaret Thatcher which, whether true in every detail or not, says a lot about leadership in government. Early on in her reign, she wanted to privatise the British National Oil Corporation (BNOC) and asked Whitehall officials to draw up a plan. After a prolonged delay, a voluminous document arrived which described all the problems of privatisation and concluded that it could not be done. Mrs Thatcher would not accept no for an answer and demanded a rethink, sacking in the meantime the head of the civil service, the highly respected Sir Ian Bancroft. Not long after, a further submission duly arrived describing briefly how BNOC could be brought safely into private ownership. By this early demonstration of her strength of will she won the full attention of the civil service.

Nobody is suggesting that Tony Blair should make similar symbolic sacrifices, but strong leadership at the centre is the making of any government. The machinery will happily function in neutral when left to itself, but will not move forward without strong prime-ministerial direction.

In Mrs Thatcher's case, her statecraft (that is, her methods of conducting government) derived a great deal from her personality – strong, decisive, uncompromising and hectoring – and it was this personality, rather than her values or ideology, which was responsible for her popular appeal. The public may not have liked her, but did think she was good at getting things done. Her approach, and the public's support for it, was a reaction to what she perceived to be the dominant statecraft of the 1960s and 1970s: consensual, drifting, corporatist and operating at a lowest common denominator of agreement.

Blair's approach contains a tension that relates to the Thatcher style. On the one hand, unlike her, he listens to others carefully, taking advice and relying on those who have superior practical knowledge. He builds up consensus, and, whereas Mrs

Thatcher tended to rely upon emotion and outbursts in order to get her own way, he relies on reason. On the other hand, like Mrs Thatcher, Blair always has a clear idea of what he wants, he is impatient when others do not have the courage or imagination to go along with him, and he does not let up once he has resolved on a way forward. Muddling through is anathema to him.

Despite their different temperaments, Blair shares Margaret Thatcher's resolve – more so than does John Major. Major's statecraft, so it is said by some of those who have worked with him, can consist of gathering officials in a room and getting them to list on two sides of paper the pros and cons of a course of action, then plumping for whichever list is longer. Not surprisingly, by behaving as if he is one among equals in his cabinet, Major shows a lack of authority and drive that has contributed substantially to the government's unpopularity – a lesson for Tony Blair.

But if one important aspect of Mrs Thatcher's ability to lead from the front flowed from her dominant personality, another aspect was her use of fear. She terrified her ministers by her detailed knowledge of what they were doing (or not doing) and her interference in their detailed departmental affairs. They knew that if she could not get her way by bullying she would do so, ultimately, by sacking them. This is not the only way for government to operate, still less the ideal, but the prime minister's writ must run in order to get results, and the whole government machine is, rightly, very responsive to the prime minister's will.

Individual ministers will always become preoccupied by their own departments or special interest groups, and this will hinder them in seeing the government's position and direction in the round. The prime minister has no such difficulty, and is further strengthened in relation to his or her colleagues by having a much better public platform than anyone else, in Parliament and the media, to articulate the government's view. Tony Blair takes a great deal of care in projecting himself and his case in the media. As Gerald Kaufman remarks in his ministerial manual, 'If you turn out to be a good minister, make sure everyone knows about it. Only the press, television and radio can tell them: there is no message without the media.'

Mrs Thatcher had Bernard Ingham, her press secretary at No. 10, to implement this doctrine, and he did so with fierce, personal loyalty – which is why he was so controversial and so disliked by her enemies. Sometimes, if you have a difficult and uncompromising job to do, as Ingham did, it is difficult to avoid being hated as well as feared by those around you. But seeing things through in government – that is, getting your own way – requires more than exercising fear or having the last word in the media: it requires taking people on in argument. To do so, a prime minister needs support in taking the initiative and imposing a clear strategy on the government, and this support has to be found among the prime minister's personal advisers in No. 10.

The team that Mrs Thatcher gathered around her was centred, as with all her predecessors, on her official civil servants. Within her small, driven team at No. 10 she had a highly competent private secretary from the Foreign Office, Charles Powell, who, in addition to his formal duties, took on an informal role of immense influence which extended beyond foreign affairs and, indeed, well beyond his routine civil-service tasks. He provided an effective link to an extensive network of contacts who regularly kept her in touch with what was going on in the government, the country and, in many cases, the world. As such he was both controversial and indispensable to the prime minister, keeping her informed, knowing her mind, helping her to get her own way, and giving her encouragement (and the occasional stiff whisky) when she flagged.

Not surprisingly, her other officials and many of her ministers resented this role. Indeed, attempts were made to transfer him back to the Foreign and Commonwealth Office. Successive foreign secretaries particularly disliked being bypassed by the ubiquitous civil servant. The problem with such prominent personal staff as Charles Powell and Bernard Ingham is that elected politicians become jealous of what they see as the officials' unaccountable power and feel threatened by their 'black arts', which then causes dissension in the cabinet.

In a celebrated incident in Mrs Thatcher's time, another of her cronies, as they were seen, her economic adviser at No. 10, Alan Walters, became so opinionated and influential on the subject of exchange-rate policy that her chancellor, Nigel Lawson, felt humiliated and unable to continue in office. He resigned.

This was a classic case of an adviser widening a damaging rift between political colleagues rather than building a bridge between them, disrupting the single most important relationship in any government – that between the prime minister and the chancellor of the Exchequer. How is the prime minister to be properly supported and advised without creating such problems?

The answer lies in a more formalised strengthening of the centre of government, which should not only give much-needed personal support to the prime minister (without isolating him from his colleagues) but provide the means of formulating and driving forward strategy for the government as a whole. There are three engines at the centre of government, each capable of helping to drive the machinery forward – No. 10, the Cabinet Office and the Treasury – and they need to be used together in a Blair-led government.

No. 10

In No. 10, there is a need to make more specialist advice available to the prime minister. However, the great virtue of the place is its intimacy, flexibility and speed, and there is a very short chain of command – the PM works with only around two dozen principal staff. If No. 10 were to grow too much, some of this close working would be lost. There are, in any case, physical limits to its expansion, with only limited space for additional people, because No. 10 is a town house, not a stately home.

Within the existing staff, the principal private secretary plays the most important role, as an accurate and faithful conveyor of the prime minister's wishes. There is need, however, for a stronger political presence in No. 10, providing political advice and contacts which neither the private office nor the Cabinet Office can do because they are not supposed to get involved in politics and cannot meet the prime minister's central need: to focus on and manage the government's political strategy and programme.

The political office at No. 10, the policy unit and the press office all have political roles to play, and, in the case of the political and policy functions at least, there is need for a strong figure to bind them and their work together and to act as the prime minister's principal political adviser. Under Margaret Thatcher, Lord Young wanted to play this role – he saw himself as a chief executive or minister for No. 10 – and David Hunt, also a minister, saw himself playing a similar role for John Major. However, he lacked clout and was not trusted in the role. There is certainly an advantage in having a safe pair of political hands to field the media for the prime minister (a minister for the *Today* programme), although for such a figure to become a fixture in No. 10 might raise questions of authority and accountability (not to mention an enormous amount of political jealousy). In Young and Hunt's case, the idea was not implemented.

It is better for the prime minister to be helped by two different sorts of individual: a senior colleague who can help smooth over frictions and disagreements in the cabinet (a role that Willie Whitelaw fulfilled for Mrs Thatcher, acting as deputy premier, though not formally designated as such) and, in addition, a lower-profile, non-ministerial political manager inside No. 10 – a 'straight' player who is trusted by all, especially by the official machine, whose job is to bring together the political and non-political sources of prime-ministerial advice and ensure that the prime minister's political strategy is kept on track. The effectiveness of both such individuals depends on their personal skills as much as on their status.

A beefed-up No. 10 policy unit should play a key role in this process, producing crisp papers on key policy areas to articulate the prime minister's political agenda. Such a lean and focused unit is probably preferable to the reintroduction of a piece of Whitehall machinery such as the Central Policy Review Staff created by Edward Heath. This body did some important work serving the government as a whole, but did not meet the prime minister's personal need for support. The longer-term perspective that the CPRS offered needs to be incorporated both in the strengthened No. 10 policy unit and in the Cabinet Office in its role as official support to the government's strategy-making.

The Cabinet Office

The Cabinet Office needs to work closely alongside No. 10. Gerald Kaufman remarks in his book that 'If the Whitehall machine as a whole is a Daimler, stately and effective, the Cabinet Office is a Ferrari, built for speed and action.' This is, perhaps, a better description of what it ought to be than of what it is. Others have described it as an Aston Martin – powerful but old-fashioned.

The Cabinet Office certainly attracts high-fliers, but some believe it needs a refit to provide the thrust that's needed at the centre of government. Although it has taken on additional functions since the deputy prime minister, Michael Heseltine, became located in it, the Cabinet Office presently sees its job chiefly as knocking heads together in Whitehall – getting agreement between departments on behalf of the prime minister – and the cabinet secretary acts as the principal manager of this process of government. This is essential, but it is a reactive role – brokering policies and initiatives from the departments and welding them together, lopping off extraneous proposals which do not fit the Whitehall consensus, and thereby establishing a lowest common denominator of agreement among Whitehall's outposts – rather than itself providing policy innovation and actively promoting ideas to the various departments.

A more proactive approach will be particularly important if a Blair-led government wants to create areas of cross-departmental administration which are not covered by existing Whitehall structures – for example, in the fight against drugs or crime, and in creating opportunities for young people who have fallen out or been excluded from the education system. This is an important aspect which is addressed in relation to ministers later in this chapter. The Cabinet Office should be more akin to a Department of the Prime Minister and Cabinet, charged with actively carrying forward the cross-departmental policies agreed by the cabinet, with the cabinet secretary acting more in future like a policy-making permanent secretary than as a business manager and minute-taker.

The Treasury

While the Cabinet Office holds the key to the Whitehall process, the Treasury holds the purse-strings.

In a government system like Whitehall, which has many spokes leading from the centre but a weak hub joining them all together, the tendency is for the prime minister, the chancellor of the Exchequer and the chief secretary to the Treasury to hold the ring by imposing a division of public-spending spoils on each department. The formation of a new cabinet committee (EDX) to apportion public finances more collectively has opened the way to a more considered and sensible allocation of resources which reflects the government's longer-term priorities, and a Blair-led government will want to strengthen this collective approach.

But there is, or should be, more to the Treasury's role than carving up public expenditure. New Labour aims to modernise Britain's economy, and the Treasury should play a central role in this. In the last year, however, the Treasury has undergone a radical transformation, and under plans at present being implemented as many as one-third of its senior posts are being removed. In time, a quarter of the entire staff may be taken out as responsibility for civil-service pensions, pay and industrial relations is delegated to departments. The Treasury's own internal management structure is being 'delayered', needless supervisors are being removed from the hierarchy, and the old 'command and control' style of management is being replaced by more devolved methods.

Undoubtedly it is a good idea to shake up departments periodically, to stop their bureaucracy spreading and ossifying, but it is arguable that the Treasury cuts have gone too far. Some fear that the Treasury's policy-making capability has been seriously undermined, although it can be argued that the reorganisation will help to ensure that the official machine is structured round ministers' key objectives. Inevitably, under the Conservatives, this means that the Treasury's current structure is geared to the narrow objectives of deregulation, low inflation and affordable public expenditure. These are all laudable, but they are insufficient to bring about the changes in the real economy – among firms and companies and in the country's infrastructure – which New Labour seeks and which a different, reshaped Treasury is required to help bring about.

So the first task, in the run-up to government, is to establish a more comprehensive and relevant set of objectives for the Treasury, so that the incoming Labour government can organise the Treasury to deliver them from the outset. Gordon Brown will need a properly staffed, managed and equipped Treasury which understands the key economic objectives of the new administration, and an immediate priority will be to put this in place to work together with No. 10 and the Cabinet Office to implement the prime minister's and the government's strategy.

Meetings

If these are the three engines at the centre of government for delivering New Labour's policies and goals, they require politicians with verve and determination to drive their vehicle forward. Ministers do this through the cabinet and the web of cabinet committees which agree the government's policies. But the prime minister provides the main political leadership. As recent experience has revealed, if this is lacking in vision or substance the government will become rudderless and will drift.

Tony Blair is not an ego-driven politician. He is not especially presidential in style, and he will lead a team of ministers who will all be expected to pull their weight, in charge of their respective functions. But he will also want to counter ministers' natural tendency to identify with their own departments and their own political worlds, to the exclusion of the government's corporate vision and approach. To get ministers to act as an integral part of the government and not simply as heads of sections within it, Blair should emulate some of Mrs Thatcher's practices – while behaving differently in other respects.

Mrs Thatcher conducted a lot of government business through bilateral meetings with ministers and through ad-hoc, relatively informal, ministerial groups meeting under her leadership to agree policies and resolve differences. Indeed, when she first became prime minister she proposed dispensing with any formal committees of ministers at all.

Bilateral and ad-hoc meetings, serviced by No. 10 staff, are a good idea because they are small and manageable and bring together those with real interest and weight, who can reach decisions more rapidly. They can happily coexist with the more formal cabinet committees. They enable the prime minister to pin ministers down to the hard specifics of what they are doing and why. Blair should devote a lot of time to such meetings (in addition to leaving space in his diary free each week just to reflect on what departments are doing), even if this means spending less time on meeting and greeting foreign visitors, which he will constantly be pressed to do. Blair is very interested in foreign affairs, but he will not want these to crowd out his domestic agenda – especially when, in Robin Cook, he has a prospective foreign secretary in whom he has complete confidence.

Making a reality of cabinet government

Where Tony Blair should differ from Mrs Thatcher is in making much better use of his whole cabinet and the strengths of the ministers available to him. With less need to balance right and left since the days of old Labour, ministers at all levels can be selected strictly on merit – producing a government of talents, rather than of interests, to ensure maximum performance. They will be helped to do their jobs if they remain in their departments for longer than the average ministerial spell on the merry-go-round.

The cabinet is a rather inflexible body: a flat structure of more than twenty roughly equal individuals, all of whom report directly to one person, the prime minister. It is impossible to imagine a commercial organisation operating so inefficiently, through such a large number of executive directors reporting to one chief executive. Besides efficiency, another important consideration, which has been touched on in relation to the Cabinet Office's work, is the way in which the government approaches policy objectives that affect a range of departments and tackles the so-called 'wicked' issues – persistent and intractable, mainly social, problems which reach across departmental boundaries.

There is a case for putting publicly identifiable superministers in charge of key areas of the government's overall strategy while retaining responsibilities in their own departments. These individuals would chair the relevant cabinet committees and report directly to the prime minister on these issues. The sort of issues that might fall into this category could include the creation of a new system of lifelong learning for those in and out of work; providing a framework of new opportunities for young people ranging from their early teens upwards; devolving and decentralising government; ushering in the digital information-technology revolution; recreating communities in crime-ridden neighbourhoods; and combating welfare dependency.

Of course, individual secretaries of state have personal statutory duties vested in them which cannot be overridden by other ministers, and it is not envisaged that one cabinet minister should be subordinate to another or that departmental ministers should be undermined. In government, policy should not normally be divorced from administration, and policies and plans should wherever possible be formulated by those who have executive responsibility for carrying them out. But it is equally important to lead the efforts of the cabinet more effectively to meet specific cross-departmental policy objectives. If it is thought impractical to have one departmental minister taking a lead position in relation to others, an alternative method might be to use nondepartmental ministers in this role – those such as the lord president of the council, the lord privy seal, the chancellor of the duchy of Lancaster or a minister without portfolio. They can, of course, combine these roles with leadership of the Commons or the Lords and with chairing the relevant cabinet committees.

The revamped Cabinet Office should support each superminister and his or her cabinet committee charged with responsibility for specific policy objectives, generating ideas and leading policy innovation rather than simply preparing the chairman's brief and taking the minutes. The Cabinet Office should also consider who and which structures beyond central government need to be tied into the effort to take on the 'wicked' issues. This might involve local government, in particular, but also the voluntary and private sectors. The No. 10 policy unit would also make its input, as well as reporting back to the prime minister on progress along with the cabinet secretary.

These arrangements would strengthen the spirit and practice of cabinet government. They could get under way without wasting time on a wholesale restructuring of government departments, and superministers would not have to spend valuable time negotiating complex job descriptions with the rest of Whitehall, as the prime minister would make clear the terms of each appointment from the outset.

Revitalising the civil service

The bulk of day-to-day government business, meanwhile, will be conducted away from the centre and the cabinet in the individual departments. New ministers will find a very different machine from when Labour was last in power – and very different conditions in the civil service. To get the best out of the service, its members need to be valued, managed well, and motivated to work in a committed way.

Civil servants do not attract much public goodwill (although they are more highly thought of than politicians). Their standards of integrity, independence and political neutrality are undervalued and taken for granted.

In their quest for less government and a smaller public sector, the Conservatives have reduced, fragmented, bullied and demoralised the civil service without a thought for the impact of this on the capacity and performance of the individuals remaining in it. Changing the systems and structures of the public service may have been necessary in some respects, but this will not lead to substantial improvement unless the people who staff them obtain greater motivation, skills and a sense of purpose as well. Although Mrs Thatcher esteemed many individual officials, she was generally disparaging of the profession, perpetuating the popular prejudice that, with their jobs for life, civil servants have it too easy. As a result, their commitment to their jobs has been poorly nurtured.

Despite the manifold reasons for the civil service wanting to see the back of the Conservatives, many in the Labour Party suspect that the civil service has adopted a Tory mind-set and that, while being clobbered by the Conservatives, it has been politicised by them at the same time. In order to instil a political orthodoxy in Whitehall, senior appointments, it is alleged, have been influenced by ministers' political preferences; those out of sympathy with the government's agenda have been quietly squeezed out, and others have been discouraged from seeking promotion.

The truth is more complex. Whitehall officials have been colonised rather than politicised. They have worked in the service of government by a single party for a long time, and this is bound to have had an effect on their policy values and habits of mind. In some cases, where they have not been willing policy collaborators, senior officials have learned to be too quiescent for their own or the government's health.

Civil servants, however, are professionals. They loyally serve the government of the day, and the main issue is not that they have given partisan advice to suit Tory ministers' prejudices but that, very often, they have not been asked for their advice at all. Relearning how to give honest, objective policy advice to Labour ministers and rediscovering their courage to speak up after years of keeping their heads down will be the chief challenge for many of them, and there is no evidence that they will be unenthusiastic servants of a Labour government – quite the contrary.

It would therefore be wrong and unjust for new ministers to come into office with a hit list of senior civil servants they want to remove. Of course, the prime minister must give detailed attention to all the senior appointments. It might also be a good idea to introduce a qualified individual to the senior appointments committee which is responsible for putting forward recommendations, so as to get an independent view of the government's needs. In the case of other staff recruitment, individual ministers will be entitled to appoint their own private-office civil servants to replace the ones inherited from their Conservative predecessors. If they think this is necessary, they should do this within a month or so of taking over, after they have had a chance to test the water and the individuals concerned.

Where good civil servants will be useful to Labour ministers is in asking frank questions about new policies, seeking clear departmental goals, clarifying the precise aims of a policy, identifying its costs, and drawing up the criteria for its success. Only by putting questions such as these – and getting reasonably full answers – can policy goals be turned into clear new instructions for the government machine, and prospective ministers should start thinking about the sort of questions that need to be asked before going into office.

When officials speak up to raise difficulties about policy proposals, this should not be dismissed as troublemaking or obstruction. Officials should be encouraged to do this and not be dismissed as 'unsound' when they do, because successful policy implementation depends on robust scrutiny and discussion.

In government, ministers will also benefit from specialist advisers drawn from outside their departments, but these should work with, not against, the permanent staff. In making similar appointments, Tory ministers have tended to surround themselves with political advisers whose only job, it seems, is to agree with their masters, run political errands, fix the press, and flatter their bosses' egos while they try to get Westminster seats for themselves. There is a benefit in having one person (or two in large departments) who is a political pair of hands, preparing political speeches, taking informal soundings, and obtaining advice on matters outside the department's responsibility. Such an individual needs to be fully integrated into the minister's private office. But Labour ministers need people with them who are not simply political sidekicks but who can make a serious contribution to the issues in hand and are able to work closely with departmental officials in developing policy.

It has been suggested that cabinet ministers should go further and introduce around half a dozen or more personal aides who would effectively take over the minister's private office and act as the channel for policy advice from the department. This is the European model – called *cabinets*. However, while a minister should gather around him people whom he trusts and feels comfortable with, it would be a mistake to introduce this model to Britain. Ministers who are new to their jobs and their departments need to be guided by people who know the ropes, not those who are as inexperienced as they are, and in the case of ministers' private offices there is great advantage in having individuals who provide continuity, who are trained in the ways and standards of the civil service and, through their contacts in the system, can plug their minister fully into the Whitehall network.

On the other hand, it may be necessary to appoint some special advisers at a senior level, carrying sufficient weight to match those at under-secretary levels in key departments, to work on the implementation of policies which are central to the New Labour strategy. Labour should identify individuals who can be brought into the government machine in such roles, either directly or in government-related organisations, and also develop links with universities and other representative or professional organisations which have contributions to make to the formulation of policy and its evaluation. This is quite compatible with the practice of non-political outside recruitment, which should also be continued. It enriches the civil service, especially where individuals can bring experience of business or different walks of life, and it enables a government to use individuals who have strong management qualities and drive which it would normally be unable to tap.

The quicker ministers settle down and establish a rapport and confidence with their staff the better. A checklist for incoming ministers should include, first, take the time to meet as many of the department's staff as possible. Second, identify meetings of key personnel and attend them to set out the department's new style and priorities. Third, hold the first of regular 'awaydays' in which senior officials and ministers can think out loud. Fourth, visit the department's front-line posts to get a good idea of the pressures and the issues. And fifth, above all, have a clear view of the half-dozen or so goals to be achieved in the first year, and do not lose sight of them until it is time to move on to the next six.

The restructuring of the civil service by the Conservatives may not have been carried out with the best of motives, but, ironically, because of the flexibility introduced by the changes, it will make it potentially easier for an incoming Labour administration to remould and shape the government machine to its needs. The creation of the plethora of executive agencies (the so-called Next Steps agencies) is a good case in point. There are 108 of these, with another five in the pipeline, and some 80 per cent of all civil servants work in them, the object being to take large executive operations out of day-to-day ministerial supervision. Examples are the Benefits Agency, with 68,000 staff, and the Employment Service, with nearly 50,000.

In many cases these agencies are bits of government that, until their status was changed, nobody was particularly interested in. They have benefited from the attention, breaking down walls which separate division from division and the whole service from the public they are meant to serve. For too long good people had been trapped in bad systems doing this work.

Nevertheless, the Next Steps agencies have attracted criticism because they reduce ministerial accountability for government actions. This is very serious in the case of the prison service, where, in the view of many involved, the home secretary has been guilty both of undue interference in the running of the service, despite its separate-agency status, and of evasion of his responsibilities and buck-passing when things have gone wrong.

Ministerial accountability has also diminished with respect to individual complaints from members of the public, as those who have suffered at the hands of the Child Support Agency have discovered. Instead of receiving replies from ministers about their constituents' complaints, MPs get responses from chief executives (unless, that is, you are the estimable Mr Kaufman, who, having been a minister himself, went to war on the new system and now does receive his replies from ministers).

These agencies can be abolished or transformed without legislation if a new government wishes, but in most cases they have improved the delivery of government services through better management and delegation.

How to couple managerial freedom with political control, however, is a serious matter. Agencies exist to deliver what ministers expect of them, and Sir Robin Butler has made it clear that 'the minister remains accountable to Parliament for everything they do, down to – to quote a phrase once used by Herbert Morrison – the last stamp licked on to an envelope'. It does not follow that the minister is personally to blame for everything an agency does – for example, if the stamp is stuck on the envelope upside down.

There is no reason, in principle, why the operational arms of Whitehall should not continue to be separated from the policy arms, leaving ministers more free to concentrate on politics and strategy. Indeed, in many cases the new agencies are sharper instruments with which to achieve the government's aims than the machinery they have replaced. With clear expressions of policy and instruction issued by ministers in their framework documents – and where the relationship is working well these documents could be made into more explicit contracts between departments and the agencies – the agencies should respond promptly to the government's wishes. But in many cases more ministerial supervision, as oppsoed to day-to-day interference, may be required – on the principle that ministers direct and officials administer – and ministers should ensure that those dealing with issues such as prisons and child support do so with greater public and political sensitivity. In these circumstances, the separation between ministerial and operational responsibility may become bogus, in which case it might be preferable to end the separation altogether. Either way, parliament also has a pivotal role to play in ensuring the accountability of government agencies, and parliamentary committees should not hold back in exposing them to the maximum scrutiny.

A different principle is raised by the wave of market testing of public services, contracting-out to the private sector, and straightforward privatisation introduced under the present government's Competing for Quality programme. There is nothing wrong with the quest for efficiency, and there will be a continuing need for the Prime Minister's Efficiency Unit, for example, to remain in existence to challenge Whitehall practices and get value for money. The net outcome of the introduction of the private sector, however, has not been a uniformly leaner and fitter civil service but a more costly and less efficient operation in many areas.

A lot of the savings have simply been made by slashing the terms and conditions of employment of already poorly paid workers. Moreover, vast sums have been spent on the use of outside management consultants to introduce the private sector to Whitehall. The biggest price for the Conservatives' anti-public-service dogma has therefore been paid by the public. A crude emphasis on 'efficiency', which is at the heart of Competing for Quality, and on the cost of inputs, has replaced concern for the outputs – that is, effectiveness of policy and service delivery and responsiveness to the public.

Incoming ministers, therefore, need to be careful of market testing and contracting-out. It is claimed that, in efficiency terms, market testing has resulted in savings of 25 per cent for each function tested, even when the winners in competition have been the staff already doing the job. But there has been no full evaluation of the initiative across the civil service. Searching questions need to be asked about private companies' compliance with their government contracts, and full audits should be made of the costs of new procedures. The civil service is not a paragon of administrative virtue, and it should not have a monopoly over the delivery of public service. There is room for private-sector involvement. But a 'private = good, public = bad' mentality is a totally unsatisfactory criterion by which to take decisions.

The government needs a permanent, professional core of officials, and ministers will not get the best out of the civil service by denigrating it. As prime minister, Tony Blair should be mean with, not to, the machine.

The civil service needs to be maintained as a proper, professional career with high standards of recruitment, training and reskilling. It is entitled to a code of ethics which protects it against poor standards of behaviour by ministers and allows the whistle to be blown when anyone transgresses. It needs a head of the service (at the moment this is the cabinet secretary) who has enough weight and a power base from which to stand up for it, and who will maintain the right balance of modern managerial practice and traditional ethical content within the profession.

Sustaining the government's vision

Upon coming into office after the election, the first thing cabinet ministers will be asked for will be their proposals for the Queen's Speech, which sets out the government's programme.

In fact this will be something of a technical request, as a draft will already have been drawn up by the Cabinet Office based on the party's manifesto (indeed, the civil service will have been studying all policy utterances made by the Labour Party for months beforehand, scrutinising them nearly as carefully as Conservative Central Office). But it is important for ministers to jump into the driving-seat and set their own political priorities, as they will be the ones who have to justify the speech's contents, first during five days of non-stop debate and then for however long the session lasts, as the legislation is steered through Parliament.

At this stage ministers will be glad of the stalwart support of their parliamentary colleagues on the benches behind them. This leads to Gerald Kaufman's important piece of advice for new ministers after they have received the call from No. 10 – which, they should never forget, many of their fellow MPs will feel should have been theirs. 'Do not assume airs of superiority just because you got it [the call] and they did not. Above all, do not disappear from their company. Some MPs, upon being appointed to government, disappear from Parliament as if swallowed up in a huge pit.'

The Kaufman method of avoiding this trap is well worth adopting by incoming Labour ministers. 'Refuse all those invitations to trade association lunches and dinners, where you will eat expensive processed food in the company of political opponents before delivering a speech which will never be reported, and instead eat cheap processed food in the House of Commons Tea Room, Members' Cafeteria or Members' Dining Room in the company of your colleagues.' In this way, ministers will keep their feet on the ground, keep in touch with the real (political) world, and never forget that their good fortune – and privilege – is the opportunity to serve.

The government's back-benchers, like the general public, will see many measures coming from government departments, each of which will be important in itself, each making a significant difference to standards in schools, the provision of healthcare, the fight against crime, or some other of the country's many problems. But these will be many ideas and many solutions, not one big idea and one big solution. Each will need to be explained and sold. Ministers will have to work hard at keeping the big picture on display, so that the government's overall purpose and direction remain strong and confident in people's minds.

The vision and the system of ideas which New Labour brings into office will have to be sustained, and this can be done only by ministers using the communications machinery available to them. This underlines the importance of close relations and constant contact with the party around the country. It also points to the need for ministers to use the government's information service as effectively and professionally as Tory ministers try to do.

Five years or so after entering No. 10, Prime Minister Blair and his party will be facing re-election. They will win if the electorate knows that they have delivered on their promises, if their unity of purpose is still there for all to see, if they have changed the way people think about politics, and if they can demonstrate convincingly that no alternative to New Labour represents a better way forward for the country.

Most Labour supporters would probably be delighted by the thought that a Blair government might get to the point where its only problems are those of success. At that stage, however, it will need to be careful not to become a victim of its own success and to run out of steam. It must always remember that the process of renewal and modernisation in politics needs to be continuous, not a one-off. The Labour government should use every means possible to keep renewing its vision, communicating it, and ensuring its flame is kept alive. One thing is for sure: the Tory opposition and its supporters in the media will not be sitting on their hands waiting for Blair to get back in. There will be no honeymoon for New Labour, so the government needs to get its act together right from the beginning and keep it well polished throughout.

11

A New Britain, AD 2005

Since the Hodgsons have moved out of London they have for-feited their enjoyable metropolitan lifestyle. Now trips to the theatre or their favourite restaurant have to be planned long in advance. The country air is not much of a consolation, as the asthma that their youngest had developed in Kennington is now triggered by pollen rather than petrol fumes, limiting family enjoyment of the countryside.

But at least the new Tollway has made commuting easier. Access to this new private road cost Ben's company a fortune, and alas there is no refund when it is blocked by protesters still angry at the way it cut through the Kent countryside at the turn of the century, but it does mean that he usually gets to work before his PA, who still has to use the crowded, collapsing A4. Still, there is another medium-priced toll road due in a year or two, paid for by withdrawing the old commuter trains – because when the franchise came up for renewal, the government cut the subsidy and no private operator would take it on. The line could never have survived after most businessmen started switching to the Tollway.

Ben and Laura hadn't wanted to move out of London, but the millennium riots gave them no choice. Ben had remembered the 1981 riots, when, even though Brixton was only a short bus ride away, he had felt pretty safe down the road in Kennington. This time it was different. The 'Portillo Crackdown', as it was dubbed, had resulted in turmoil on council estates across the country. This so-called welfare 'big bang' was supposed to kick-start the underclass into enterprise and self-reliance by slashing benefits – but there were no jobs or training for them to take up. So instead it had led to a huge explosion of crime and disorder. Eventually the army had been brought in, but not before houses at the end of the Hodgsons' street had been set alight, their neighbours running screaming along the road.

The response to the crime explosion had been twofold. First there had been a middle-class exodus from London to the Home Counties, into hastily built private estates with perimeter fences and private security. The government decided to allow building in the Green Belt, local opposition was squashed by new planning laws, and huge profits were made on the backs of peoples' panic and fear. The second consequence had been a massive rise in spending on police and prisons. Labour politicians are forever pointing out that this spending is way in excess of what had been saved in the benefits clamp-down, but this point seems to fall on deaf ears.

The lot of the opposition had been made much harder after the boundary changes of a few years back. Learning from their mistakes in the 1994 review, the Tories had mercilessly cut back Labour's representation in the fast depopulating inner cities and in Scotland and Wales. And voter turnout had fallen dramatically as cynicism about politics reached epidemic proportions. Nor could people look to local councils. Most of their functions had been stripped away and given to the business-dominated 'service development corporations' – an extension of the principle, readily accepted in the mid-eighties, of urban development corporations.

As Ben drives along this morning, his thoughts are, as they often are, on his family. The boys are coming out of university soon, and it is still not clear what they will be doing next. Ben remembers the pile of applications that he sent off to firms eagerly recruiting graduates when he left university. It doesn't really work like that anymore. The government had insisted that the only way forward was for a deregulated labour market, and soon not just manual workers but professionals too were hired on a contractual, temporary, basis. This is great for keeping business costs down and profits up, but how on earth a youngster can find the stability to start a family and home is beyond him. It seems that everyone is on their own now, cut off from everyone else. It hadn't always been like this, he thinks. How did we let it happen?

A few years ago he wouldn't have worried too much, because of the financial security his own business gave him. But Britain has continued to slide down the world economic league. Ben's friends in industry are always bemoaning the fact that the 'New

Conservative' government told them they had to 'go it alone'. Other countries, in booming eastern Europe and Asia, have governments which go out of their way to support business, working for top-flight infrastructure and more investment, skills and technology. Britain is also out of step with the European Union. Ben's company has been hit hard by the withdrawal from Europe, which has damaged its business on the Continent. Clients are switching to German companies. 'Look, Ben,' one had explained, 'Britain's government can force a two-speed Europe, but I'm afraid we want our business to be in the fast lane.' And that was a British company! The great leap forward promised hasn't occurred, and Ben's American friends look on aghast. He can hardly believe that the 'British Conservative Faction' has finally vanquished Foreign Secretary Patten to the back benches, but the whole thing had been brewing for decades.

The tumult among Europe's political élites hasn't affected Eileen very much. All she can think about these days is her hip. She's needed a replacement for two and a half years now. Her GP has been doing his best, wrestling with his practice accountant to try to squeeze the money from his 'fund'. Eileen doesn't really understand. Her doctor is retiring in a few months, and she doesn't know how she'll cope with someone new.

Her daughter, Tracy, is still struggling in the grotty council flat where she has had to bring up her child. The service development corporation says there is no money for repairs and posts glossy DIY brochures through every letterbox instead.

Eileen fears for her grandson. She feels he'll go the same way as Peter, her own boy, who has progressed from truancy to drugs to crime. He's been in and out of prison twice by now. He's been written off, he told Eileen last time she visited. She hadn't had the heart to tell him that he had been written off a long time ago – when he was about twelve.

When she does get out and about, Eileen can't help noticing that even the posh parts of her neighbourhood are going downhill. Houses empty. No sign of kids. Clapped-out old motors lining streets where once Saabs and Golfs were parked. As she shuffles along, Eileen assumes that someone, somewhere, has it better. It isn't much consolation to her. She feels so alone, cut *off from everyone else. It hadn't always been this bad. How had it happened? Could it have been different?*

*

'Morning, mum,' smiles Peter as he arrives to take Eileen for her operation. 'It'll soon be done, and then you'll be out and about again.' Thank God Labour got in and saved the NHS, Eileen thinks. She still remembers her friends waiting years for basic surgery, even though they'd paid taxes all their lives.

Eileen is proud of Peter. He's built a good life for himself, running his own small garage, over the river in Pimlico. He'd been helped by what they'd called his 'mentor' at the school. Ben is still a friend of the family all these years later. He'd helped Peter get on to a proper training scheme, after school, learning mechanics, and had helped him to raise the money to get started in business.

Peter has worked hard, and has even helped his sister, Tracy, get one of the new housing-association houses the council has helped build. They'd been surprised to see them go up, but apparently the council had the money in the bank all the time – they just hadn't been allowed to spend it before. Eileen will never understand how these things worked. Tracy's place even has a small garden. The grandchild is doing well at school. What a difference to how it used to be! The new teachers and especially the smaller class sizes have really done the trick.

Eileen's estate has changed too. Labour had started what they called a task force, which didn't mean much to Eileen until a smart young women turned up to see what decorating she needed doing. There is also a great youth club in one of the blocks. Apparently kids take a year off before university and help out. All the activity has brightened the place up – and made it a safer place to be.

Ben's family are doing well too, and so is the business. There's no doubt that things are more challenging than they were – you can't stop the world and get off, as he is fond of saying – but the big expansion of education and skills training has helped people cope better. His own firm has taken on a few people, older workers, and one guy who'd been unemployed for a long time, helped by some government grant or another, and it has worked out well.

The Conservative opposition still bleats on year after year about the great tax cuts they want to deliver, but people fell for that from the Tories once before, a while back, and they aren't going to fall for it again. No thanks, thinks Ben.

There was a time when he had wondered whether every man for himself perhaps was the way forward. But, as Laura, his wife, said, the problem with 'Let the devil take the hindmost' is that then the hindmost take you. He'd been a bit sceptical of all this Labour talk of community, but now he's seen what it means in practice he is pretty impressed.

The great 'modernisation' of the welfare state has given people a chance to look after themselves and get on. The NHS has been rebuilt – one day he might even not bother with private health insurance. Even the little things, like the streets being clean, vandalism being tackled and the parks being well lit and looked after, make quite a difference. Some great public-private deal has been done for the Underground. Revamped and on time, the Northern Line isn't a bad way to get about now.

All of this seems to be making Britain altogether a rather nicer place to live. There seems to be a sense of solidarity, even pride, among people. Ben hadn't been able to quite put his finger on it, but Laura had said it felt as if we had become a young country again.

J. B. Priestley's play *An Inspector Calls* shows how the apparently minor, unrelated actions of a family can have enormous consequences for an individual the family comes into contact with. Yet we let ourselves think that politics can affect little in our modern world. In fact the government is still a hugely powerful force, spending 42 per cent of our national income, employing over 5 million people, and present at our birth and in sickness and in health throughout our lives.

This book has made the case for the New Labour alternative, explaining the policy ideas the party has and the values underpinning them. Conscious of the scepticism that exists about politics generally, and about Labour in particular after its years in the political wilderness, it has set out to show that the party now has a strategy for governing that will ensure success.

However, something more fundamental than all of that lies

behind this book. It is the belief that, as Nye Bevan said, 'Free men can use free institutions to solve the social and economic problems of the day.' Throughout our history, leaders – and the people, through the ballot box – have shown their faith in this ideal. We have, in the past, acted together to shape our destiny – combating disease and squalor, providing healthcare and schooling, ensuring protection at home, and fighting for freedom abroad. Today there are new, different, challenges, but there is no reason why we should not face them with the same confidence.

Politics *can* make a difference. The policy choices of a government help determine our futures and in a very real way touch peoples' lives. Today the Labour Party, led by Tony Blair, stands ready to serve. Having rediscovered its core beliefs and values, and having applied them to the world as it is now, it possesses realistic and relevant policies and a team itching to get on with the job.

Labour is ready. Is Britain?

Bibliography

Peter Ashby, *Labour and Learning Accounts* (1995)

Michael Benzeval, Ken Judge and Margaret Whitehead (ed.), *Tackling Inequalities in Health* (Kings Fund, 1995)

Nick Bosanquet, *Public Spending into the Millennium* (1995)

Leon Brittan, *The Europe We Need* (1984)

Gordon Brown, *James Maxton* (1986)

Gordon Brown and Tony Wright, *Values, Visions and Voices* (1995)

Alan Bullock, *Ernest Bevin* (1960, 1967, 1983)

David Butler and Dennis Kavanagh, *The British General Election of 1992* (1992)

Alec Cairncross, *Years of Recovery: British Economic Policy 1945−51* (1985)

Bernard Casey and David Smith, *Truancy and Youth Transition* (1995)

Jonathan Charkham, *Keeping Good Company* (1994)

Peter Clarke, *Liberals and Social Democrats* (1978)

Paul Cockle (ed.), *Public Expenditure* (1984)

Bernard Crick, *Socialism Now* (1974)

Anthony Crosland, *The Future of Socialism* (1956)

Lord Dahrendorf, 'Can We Be Civil and Prosperous too?' (Churchill Lecture, 1995)

Edmund Dell, *A Hard Pounding* (1991)

Andrew Dilnot et al., *Pensions Policy in the UK* (Institute for Fiscal Studies, 1984)

Bernard Donoghue, Prime Minister (1987)

Evan Durbin, *Politics of Democratic Socialism* (1940)

Walter Eltis and David Higham, 'Closing the UK Competitiveness Gap' (*National Institute Economic Review* 4/95)

Frank Field and Matthew Owen, *Private Pensions for All: Squaring the Circle* (Fabian Society, 1993)

Richard Freeman, 'Limits of Wage Flexibility to Curbing Unemployment' (*Oxford Review of Economic Policy*, Spring 1995)

J. K. Galbraith, *The Culture of Contentment* (1992)

Paul Gregg and Jonathan Wadsworth, 'A Short History of Labour Turnover, Job Tenure and Job Security 1975-95' (OREP, Spring 1995)

Andrew Glyn, 'Unemployment and Inequality' (OREP, Spring 1995)

Charles Grant, *Delors* (1994)

John Grigg, *Lloyd George: The People's Champion* (1978)

Lord Hailsham, *The Dilemma of Democracy* (1988)

Harriet Harman, *The Century Gap* (1991)

Robert Harris, *Good and Faithful Servant: The Unauthorised Biography of Bernard Ingham* (1990)

Roy Hattersley, *Choose Freedom* (1987)

– *Who Goes Home* (1995)

Denis Healey, *The Time of Life* (1991)

Nigel Healey (ed.), *Britain's Economic Miracle: Myth or Reality* (1993)

Anthony Heath, Roger Jowell and John Curtice, *Labour's Last Chance* (1994)

Peter Hennessy, *Never Again* (1992)

– *The Hidden Wiring* (1995)

John Hills, *Joseph Rowntree Inquiry into Income and Wealth*, Vol 2

Lord Howe of Aberavon, *Forum du Future* (1995)

Colin Hughes and Patrick Wintour, *Labour Rebuilt* (1990)

Will Hutton, *The State We're In* (1995)

Institute for Fiscal Studies, *Options for 1996 The Green Budget* (1995)

Institute of Public Policy Research, *The Constitution of the United Kingdom* (1991)

– *The Report of the Commission on Social Justice* (1994)

Roy Jenkins, *The Labour Case* (1959)

– *What Matters Now* (1972)

– *Life at the Centre* (1993)

Simon Jenkins, *Accountable to None* (1995)

George Jones and Bernard Donoghue, *Herbert Morrison* (1973)

Roger Jowell, John Curtice, et al., *British Social Attitudes: 11th and 12th Reports* (1994, 1995)

Gerald Kaufman, *How to Be a Minister* (1980)

John Kay and Mervyn King, *The British Tax System 1978* (5th edition, 1990)

Nigel Lawson, *The View from Number Eleven* (1993)

Local Government Finance: Report of Committee of Inquiry, 1976

Robert McNamara, *In Retrospect* (1995)

David Marsh, *Bundesbank* (1992)

– *Economy and Europe* (1994)

David Marquand, *Ramsay Macdonald* (1977)

– *The Unprincipled Society* (1988)

Andrew Marr, *Ruling Britannia* (1995)

Geoffrey Maynard, *The Economy under Mrs Thatcher* (1988)

Lewis Minkin, *The Contentious Alliance* (1992)

D. E. N. Moggeridge, *Maynard Keynes* (1992)

Kenneth Morgan, *Consensus and Disunity* (1979)

– *Labour in Power* (1984)

Ferdinand Mount, *The British Constitution* (1992)

Jim Northcott, *Britain in 2010* (The PSI Report, 1991)

Stephen Nickell and Brian Bell, 'The Collapse in Demand for the Unskilled and Unemployment across the OECD' (OREP, Spring 1995)

David Owen, *A United Kingdom* (1986)

Nicholas Oulton, 'Supply Side Reform and UK Economic Growth' (*National Institute Economic Review*, 4/95)

Jeremy Paxman, *Friends in High Places* (1990)

Ben Pimlott, *Hugh Dalton* (1985)

– *Harold Wilson* (1993)

Leo Pliatzky, *Getting and Spending* (1982)

Giles Radice, *Labour's Path to Power* (1989)

John Rentoul, *Tony Blair* (1995)

Peter Riddell, *The Thatcher Era* (1991)

Eric Roll, *Where Did We Go Wrong?* (1995)

Robert Rowthorn, 'Capital Formation and Unemployment' (OREP, Spring 1995)

Patrick Seyd and Paul Whiteley, *Labour's Grass Roots* (1992)

Social Trends (1995)

Jon Sopel, *Tony Blair* (1995)

Robert Taylor, *The Future of the Trade Unions* (1994)

Anthony Teasdale, *The Politics of Majority Voting in Europe* (1986)

Paul Temperton (ed.), *The European Currency Crisis* (1993)

James Tobin, *Policies for Prosperity* (1987)

Lord Tugendhat, 'President's Valedictory Address to Royal Institute of International Affairs' (1995)

John Turner, *British Politics and the Great War* (1992)

Utting, David, et al., *Crime and the Family* (1993)

Helen Wilkinson and Geoff Mulgan, *Freedom's Children* (1995)

Philip Williams, *Hugh Gaitskell* (1979)

Tony Wright, *Socialisms* (1986)

– *Citizens and Subjects* (1994)

Index

Acheson, Dean 9
Adonis, Andrew 119
Asian economies 4–6, 67, 170–71;
  assisted-places scheme 95
Attlee, Clement, compared with Blair
  18, 58. *See also* Labour governments

Bank of England 80
Barber, Michael 92
Benn, Tony, and 'Bennism' 3, 21, 34,
  40, 213–14
Bernstein, Eduard 193
Bevan, Aneurin 23, 140, 261
Bill of Rights 193–6
Blair, Cherie (née Booth) 46, 48
Blair, Hazel and Leo 32, 46
Blair, Tony: Australian lecture
  (1982) 33–5; biography 31–59;
  children's schooling issue 46; and
  crime 47–8, 133; economic policies 37–9; as employment
  spokesman 41–4; as energy
  spokesman 41; and Europe 35, 57,
  157–8; on front bench 36–50;
  Guardian article (1987) 39; influences on 32–3, 38, 57; as leader
  and PM 50–59, 232–55; lifestyle
  46; maiden speech (1983) 32; marriage and children 46, 48–9; and
  the media 53, 55; and nuclear disarmament 35; personality 56–7,
  238; political skills 36–8, 41, 50,
  56–8, 237–8, 244; and religion
  32–3, 49; as shadow home secretary 45–8, 218; and trade unions
  41–4; values 31–6. *See also* New
  Labour; Thatcher, Baroness
Bosanquet, Nicholas 105
Britain: constitution 190; divisions in
  16–21, 100, 110–56; as ex-world

power 9; making it 'young' *see*
  modernisation. *See also* economy,
  British
Brown, Gordon 37–8, 44–5
Bulger, Jamie 47
Business Expansion Scheme 107
businesses: British successes and failures 8–10, 16, 84–5; medium-sized
  87, 106; new 83–4, 87; new obligations on 95–6, 101; small 87, 91,
  106; and training 91, 95–6, 101
Butler, Sir Robin 233, 251

cabinet and cabinet committees
  244–6
Cabinet Office 241–2, 245–6
Callaghan, James 211. *See also*
  Labour governments
Campbell-Bannerman, Henry 57
CAP *see* Common Agricultural Policy
capital gains tax 23, 106
careers and employment services
  138–9
carers 130–31
central Europe 165, 175
Central Policy Review Staff 241
centralisation of government 17, 27,
  187–8, 191–2
CFSP *see* Common Foreign and
  Security Policy
CGT *see* capital gains tax
Chamberlain, Joseph 107
Charter 88 209, 210
childcare 92, 102, 130
children: in care 129; with special
  needs 118
Chirac, Jacques 157, 158–9
Churchill, Winston 107
City of London 12, 23, 38; New
  Labour's policies 88–9. *See also*
  investment

267